Implicit meanings

Implicit meanings

Essays in anthropology

Mary Douglas

Professor of Anthropology
University College, London

Routledge & Kegan Paul
London, Boston and Henley

First published in 1975
by Routledge & Kegan Paul Ltd
39 Store Street
London WC1E 7DD,
Broadway House, Newtown Road,
Henley-on-Thames
Oxon RG9 1EN and
9 Park Street,
Boston, Mass. 02108, USA
Reprinted and first published as a
paperback in 1978
Reprinted in 1979
Printed in Great Britain by
Redwood Burn Limited,
Trowbridge & Esher

ISBN 0 7100 8226 6 (c)
ISBN 0 7100 0047 2 (p)

Contents

Part 3   The *a priori* in Nature

Sources

The chapters in this book first appeared as follows:

chapter 1: Zaïre, 9 April 1955; *chapter 2: Africa*, 27, 1 January 1957; *chapter 3: International Encyclopedia of the Social Sciences*, Macmillan Co. and the Free Press, New York, 1968; *chapter 4: Journal of Psychosomatic Research*, 1968, *12*, *1*; *chapter 5:* 'Heathen Darkness, Modern Piety', *New Society*, 12 March 1970; *chapter 6: Journal of Psychosomatic Research*, *15*, 1971; *chapter 7:* 'The Social Control of Cognition: Some Factors in Joke Perception', *Man*, *3*, 3, 1968; *chapter 8: Cahiers d'Etudes Africaines*, 7, 28, 1967; *chapter 9:* (a review of V. W. Turner's *The Forest of Symbols* and *The Drums of Affliction*): *Man*, *5*, 2, June 1970; *chapter 10:* 'The Meaning of Myth with special reference to "La Geste d'Asdiwal" ', *The Structural Study of Myth and Totemism*, ed. E. Leach, ASA, *5*, 1967; *chapter 11:* (a review of Basil Bernstein's *Class, Codes and Control, Vol. I*): *Listener*, 87, 2241, 9 March 1972; *chapter 12:* Introduction to the Paladin edition of Louis Dumont's *Homo Hierarchius*, 1972; *chapter 13:* 'Torn Between Two Realities', *The Times Higher Education Supplement*, 15 June 1973; *chapter 14:* Inaugural Lecture given at University College, London, 1971; *chapter 15:* Lecture given at ICA, October 1970, published in *Ecology in Theory and Practice*, Viking Press, 1972; *chapter 16: Daedalus*, Winter 1972; *chapter 17:* The Henry Myers Lecture, given for the Royal Anthropological Institute, 4 May 1972.

The author has made occasional slight alterations in the texts. The illustrations on pages 34, 37, 248, 290, have been specially drawn for this book by Pat Novy.

Preface

By piecing together, context to context, the references the Lele
made to animals in their daily life, I reached some understanding
of their main fertility cult, centred on the pangolin. If my fieldwork had been more thorough I would have been able to understand better the meaning this scaly ant-eater had for them. Their
knowledge was not explicit; it was based on shared, unspoken
assumptions. At the grass-roots level of daily behaviour the sense
that emerged from their rituals and beliefs posed the problems
about implicit forms of communication that I have been pondering ever since, as these essays show. Re-reading them, I see how
confused and timid presentation has disguised the unity of
theme. I also realise that with better fieldwork this theme would
certainly have been shelved. For thanks to the work of others in
Central Africa I am even more aware of rich layers of context I
left unexplored. Above all, Luc de Heusch's study of the traditions of Luba royalty has made me see the gap between the
daily-bread, common-sense world that I recorded and the high
tradition of Central African cosmology in which the Lele beliefs
fit so well. Disengaging certain recurring threads and identifying
them as the warp of the different local cosmologies, he has
greatly advanced the analysis of implicit forms of communication. If only the material and the theory had been available
earlier.

The Lele cult of the pangolin was performed by a few initiates
who alone could eat its flesh and were sworn not to reveal its
secrets. It was one of many cults, each vested with its communal
property of esoteric knowledge. I was never made privy to those

secrets. Apart from the aristocratic clan, no women were admitted to knowledge of the cult. If I had stayed longer, and if I had known what theoretical uses the unveiling of their secrets would have served, I could have learnt much from a formidably clever and witty princess from the Eastern Lele. But structural analysis had not at that time redeemed myth and ritual from folklorism. Only now do I glimpse, in the pages of *Le Roi ivre* (de Heusch, 1973), the possible sources of the pangolin's power. For, though I knew that this fish-like tree-dweller was the potent sign for a union of heaven and earth, I did not know that just such a union was celebrated in different ways by other tribes of the region. The pangolin was said to be a chief. The sacral kingship of the Lunda, Luba and Bushong was also instituted in a marriage between celestial and earthly powers and in the rituals and myths about it are many echoes of Lele custom. De Heusch's book makes me see in very different light the brief, mysterious little tales of the origin of the Lele, which I dismissed as truncated and defective. Rather as the synoptic gospels need the structural analyses of John and the Pauline epistles for their exegesis, so the miracles of the pangolin need, for their full meaning to emerge, to be related to the cosmic themes of divine kingship and to the constitution of human nature and the planetary system. All that is too late for me now. Access to that implicit public language (Bernstein, 1972) from which the sacred canopy was woven would have given me enough work for the rest of my days, simply to analyse it. Moreover, the question of why the pangolin had so much power over human destiny would have been satisfactorily answered within the terms of the culture itself. Because my material was poor, I was driven to consider the matter under its more general aspect. In a comparative perspective, the question of implicit knowledge confronts the question of cognitive relativity so that they come to form only one single problem, as I shall try to explain below.

Among the Lele I found that rules of hygiene and etiquette, rules of sex and edibility fed into or were derived from submerged assumptions about how the universe works. It was evident that a very satisfactory fit, between the structure of thought and the structure of nature as they thought it, was given in the way that their thought was rooted in community life. Further, the latter was furnished with an armoury of support by this intellectually impressive fit. If we can understand how the inarticulate, implicit areas of Lele consciousness are constituted, we should be able to apply the lesson to ourselves. If they use appeals to the *a priori* in nature as weapons of coercion or as fences around communal property, it is probable that we do likewise. The anthropologist is inclined to respect the intellectual capacities of the tribe he studies. There is a built-in professional bias to believe that our own implicit knowledge is likely to be of the same order as theirs. Consequently the anthropologist who realises that their idea of nature is the product of their relations with one another finds it of critical importance to know just where and why our own ideas about the world are exempt from sociological analysis.

Around the beginning of this century Durkheim demonstrated the social factors controlling thought. He demonstrated it for one portion of humanity only, those tribes whose members were united by mechanical solidarity. Somehow he managed to be satisfied that his critique did not apply to modern industrial man or to the findings of science. One may ask why his original insights were never fully exploited in philosophical circles. Nowadays they are being joyously rediscovered by phenomenologists on the one hand, and ethnomethodologists on the other. Neither scarcely pauses to ask how their project differs from his, nor why his remained so little used. If Durkheim did not push his thoughts on the social determination of knowledge to their full and radical conclusion, the barrier that inhibited him may well have been the same that has stopped others from carrying his programme through. It seems that he cherished two unquestioned assumptions that blocked him. One was that he really believed that primitives are utterly different from us. A week's fieldwork would have brought correction. For him, primitive groups are organised by similarities; their members are committed to a common symbolic life. We by contrast are diversified individuals, united by exchange of specialised services. The contrast is a very interesting one, full of value (as I suggest in chapters 5 and 14 below), but it does not distinguish between primitives and moderns. It cuts across both categories. However, believing in this sharp difference encouraged him to harbour the idea of another difference between us and primitives. Their knowledge of the world could readily be understood as unanchored to any fixed material points, and secured only by the stability of the social relations which generated it and which it legitimised. For them he evolved a brilliant epistemology which set no limits to the organising power of mind. He could not say the same for ourselves. His other assumption allowed him to reserve part of our knowledge from his own sociological theory. This was his belief in objective scientific truth, itself the product of our own kind of society, with its scope for individual diversity of thought. His concern to protect his own cognitive commitment from his own scrutiny prevented him from developing his sociology of knowledge. His biographer, Steven Lukes (1973:495), says:

> Durkheim was really maintaining two different theses which he failed to separate from one another because he did not distinguish between the truth of a belief and the acceptance of a belief as true. The first was the important philosophical thesis that there is a non-context-dependent or non-culture-dependent sense of truth (as correspondence to reality) such that, for example, primitive magical beliefs could be called 'false', mythological ideas could be characterised as 'false in relation to things', scientific truths could be said to 'express the world as it is' and the Pragmatists' claim that the truth is essentially variable could be denied.

With one arm he was brandishing the sabre of sociological determinism, and with the other he was protecting from any such criticism the intellectual achievements of his own culture. He believed in things, in 'the world as it is', in an unvarying reality and truth. The social construction of reality applied fully to them, the primitives, and only partially to us. And so, for this contradiction, his central thesis deserved to remain obscure and his programme unrealised.

Anyone who takes on the biography of a famous thinker is in a dilemma if he finds he is obliged to toss overboard as useless and wrong his subject's most cherished theory. Normally the would-be historian would have to choose either to look for a worthier subject or to spend the next ten years of research explaining how the thinker acquired an undeserved reputation. Steven Lukes's massive biography of Durkheim makes him a great expert on the man. He must have felt this dilemma when he decided that the contrast of sacred-profane was an empirically inadequate

dichotomy which vitiates Durkheim's analysis in important ways
(1973: 24-8). This judgment attaints also the distinguished group
of Durkheim's colleagues who made central use of the contrast in
their work. Durkheim himself thought the dichotomy was
central to his theoretical position. Even if he was mistaken here
as well, it is cavalier to dismiss an idea which closely parallels
Marx's important remarks on fetishism. I shall argue below that
the latter become a more powerful instrument of social criticism
if added to Durkheim's analysis, once that is purged of the
reserves he made on behalf of modern science.

Durkheim's work was all focused upon the relation of the individual to the group. The excitement he aroused among his close
associates came from his claim to have discovered how the individual internalises the prescriptions of the group. The discovery
is about the process of categorisation. He claimed to reveal the
social factors which bound the categories and relate them to one
another. When the process has worked through, the so-called
individual is shown using a set of conceptual tools generated
from outside himself and exerting over him the authority of an
external, objective power. For Durkheim, sacred and profane are
the two poles of the religious life on which the relation between
individual and society is worked out. The sacred is that which the
individual recognises as having ultimate authority, as being
other than himself and greater than himself. The dichotomy
profane and sacred is not isomorphic with that between individual and society. It is not correct to interpret the individual as
profane and society as sacred, for each individual recognises in
himself something of the sacred. Sacredness inheres in the moral
law erected by consensus to which each individual himself sub-
scribes. The sacred is constructed by the efforts of individuals to
live together in society and to bind themselves to their agreed
rules. It is characterised by the dangers alleged to follow upon
breach of the rules. Belief in these dangers acts as a deterrent. It
defends society in its work of self-creation and self-maintenance.
Because of the dangers attributed to breach of the rules, the
sacred is treated as if it were contagious and can be recognised by
the insulating behaviour of its devotees. This is roughly fair to
what Durkheim says of the sacred in his *Elementary Forms of
Religious Life* and how it is used by Hertz and Mauss.

To reject the concept of sacred contagion is to reject everything Durkheim contributed to comparative religion. From a present day perspective, after fifty years of social anthropology (Kuper, 1973), it is hard to see how such a fruitful approach to religion should cause so much difficulty. One might reject it indeed if one were unable to separate the insight itself from the moral and political conclusions Durkheim and others drew. But this is the elementary exercise of scholarly judgment. Let us address the matter afresh, since so many streams of thought are now ready to converge just here.

Durkheim's theory of the sacred is a theory about how knowledge of the universe is socially constructed. The known universe is the product of human conventions and so is the idea of God, as its ultimate point of appeal. Durkheim saw that all religious beliefs are pulled this way and that in men's haggling and justifying of ways to live together. He could see that in all small, isolated tribal societies men create their entire knowledge of their universe in this manner. They covenant implicitly to breed a host of imaginary powers, all dangerous, to watch over their agreed morality and to punish defectors. But having tacitly colluded to set up their awesome cosmos, the initial convention is buried. Delusion is necessary. For unless the sacred beings are credited with autonomous existence, their coercive power is weakened and with it the fragile social agreement which gave them being. A good part of the human predicament is always to be unaware of the mind's own generative powers and to be limited by concepts of the mind's own fashioning.

For any fundamentalist who would not wish to allow that men's ideas of God have to be refracted through a social dimension, the theory of sacred contagion is straight impiety. One can fully sympathise with the sense of threat and blasphemy. The religious believer normally uses a theory of cognitive precariousness within the framework of his doctrine; his theology provides areas of illusion and scepticism which are clearly bounded so that his own faith is secure while everything else is vanity and flux. But here is an attack on all religious cognition and therefore one to be resisted. One can well understand the initial religious hostility to Durkheim's rationalism. But hostility breeds the wrong atmosphere for philosophising. A little more calm and open reflection on this theme could have shown the devout that what Durkheim claimed for the social construction of reality in primitive society was no more destructive of fundamentalist Christianity than it was of secular theories of knowledge. It is no more easy to defend non-context-dependent, non-culture-dependent beliefs in things or objective scientific truth than beliefs in gods and demons. Clearly Durkheim intended to challenge existing theories of knowledge, for he meant to offer his account of social determinants to qualify or supplement Kant's subjective determinants of perception. Surely Steven Lukes is right to insist that the 1914 war broke the developing thread of that idea. The challenge remained incomplete and few have taken it seriously.

When an important thinker presents two intellectual positions which contradict one another, a sensible procedure is to choose the most original and push it to its logical conclusion. If it is a good theory it will end by transforming the more established one. Durkheim used the sacred-profane dichotomy to develop a completely sociological theory of knowledge. The theory comes to a halt in his thinking when it reaches objective scientific truth. It peters out when it seems about to conflict with the most widely held beliefs of his own day. Therefore we should take the sacred-profane dichotomy and see if in its most extreme application it does not engulf fundamentalist theories of knowledge as well as fundamentalist religious doctrines.

The first essential character by which the sacred is recognisable is its dangerousness. Because of the contagion it emanates the sacred is hedged by protective rules. The universe is so constituted that all its energies are transformed into dangers and powers which are diverted from or tapped by humans in their dealings with the sacred. The sacred is the universe in its dynamic aspect. The second essential character of the sacred is that its boundaries are inexplicable, since the reasons for any particular way of defining the sacred are embedded in the social consensus which it protects. The ultimate explanation of the sacred is that this is how the universe is constituted; it is dangerous because this is what reality is like. The only person who holds nothing sacred is the one who has not internalised the norms of any community. With this definition in hand one should divest oneself of any preconceived ideas of what is going to be discovered to be sacred in any given cognitive scheme. If there are sprites and goblins which do not protect their sanctuaries with sanctions unleashing mysterious dangers, then they have nothing to do with the sacredness we are investigating. The definition quickly identifies the sacred which in Durkheim's universe is not to be profaned: it is scientific truth. In Steven Lukes's universe it would seem to be commitment to a non-context-dependent sense of truth (as correspondence to reality). Each of them risks a big sacrifice to his deity: both risk professional success and the acclaim of posterity by protecting their sacred thing from profanation. Both demonstrate in their work itself the validity of the sacred-profane dichotomy. It is entirely understandable that Durkheim should have internalised unquestioningly the categories of nineteenth-century scientific debate since he strove to have an honourable place in that very community from which the standards of conduct emanated. His blind spot, for all the theoretical weakness it brought him, at least vindicates once and for all the value of his central theory of the sacred. At that time science itself was unselfconscious about how its edicts were formulated and followed. But science has now diversified. It has moved from the primitive mythological state of a small isolated community to an international body of highly specialised individuals among whom consensus is hard to achieve. According to his theory, such a new kind of scientific community would be hard put to identify anything we could have recognised as sacred fifty years ago. So he is vindicated again by the passage of time which has made 'correspondence-to-reality' a fuzzier concept than it used to be.

In his Inaugural Lecture to the Collège de France, Michel Foucault focuses on the procedural rules which control discourse, including those which separate true from false (1971). He observes that humanity's long drive to establish truth in discourse has gone through many historical transformations. First, starting with the Greek poets of the sixth century, true discourse was the prophecy which announced what would happen, helped to bring it about and commanded men's assent to its justice. True discourse then was ritual action in which destiny was seen and justified. A century later, by a shift from action to speech, the truth of discourse was to be found in the correspondence between the form of the statement and the object to which it referred. Since then, while correspondence between word and reality has remained important, a new concern for a new kind of truth developed from the sixteenth century, with the scientific revolution. Its peculiar characteristic is its vast investment in specialised techniques of measurement and testing and in authoritative institutions for proclaiming its truths. Each of these phases he treats as systems of exclusion which impose on discourse their prohibitions and privileges. Foucault speaks of discourse as a continuing social process setting up controls and boundaries and shrines of worship in a way that recalls Durkheim. But whereas Durkheim venerates the system of controls, Foucault savagely denounces it. His work celebrates a current phase in the evolution of the ways in which discourse requires a division between truth and falsehood. The present concern is focused on subjective truth; this is the day of consciousness. A sophisticated doubt dogs other forms of truth when they are presented as god-given objective facts with the right to exclude from and to control the discourse. This is a generation deeply interested in the liberation of consciousness from control. It is normal radical criticism to enjoy unveiling the fetishes of past generations. But a philosophy intending to be radical could well sift Durkheim more thoroughly and make use of his theory of sacredness as a tool for relativising the sacred shibboleths of others who would limit and transform the current discourse.

This is why it is timely to inquire again about the philosopher's bogy of relativism. Bracket aside Durkheim's wish to protect from defilement the values of his own community as a distracting illustration of the value of his theory – then follow his thought through to the bitter end: we seem to have a thoroughly relativised theory of knowledge. The boundaries which philosophers rally instinctively to protect from the threat of relativism would seem to hedge something very sacred. The volumes which are written to defend that thing testify to its obscurity and difficulty of access. Relativity would seem to sum up all the threats to our cognitive security. Were truth and reality to be made context-dependent and culture-dependent by relativising philosophy, then the truth status of that philosophy is itself automatically destroyed. Therefore, anyone who would follow Durkheim must give up the comfort of stable anchorage for his cognitive efforts. His only security lies in the evolution of the cognitive scheme, unashamedly and openly culture-bound, and accepting all the challenges of that culture. It is part of our culture to recognise at last our cognitive precariousness. It is part of our culture to be sophisticated about fundamentalist claims to secure knowledge. It is part of our culture to be forced to take aboard the idea that other cultures are rational in the same way as ours. Their organisation of experience is different, their objectives different, their successes and weak points different too. The refusal to privilege one bit of reality as more absolutely real, one kind of truth more true, one intellectual process more valid, allows the original comparative project dear to Durkheim to go forward at last. In the last essay in this collection I try to show how, when relativism is less feared, new questions can be asked about cognition. This project has waited very long to be launched. I venture a Durkheimian speculation on its tardiness.

Relativism is the common enemy of philosophers who are otherwise very much at odds with one another. To avoid its threat of cognitive precariousness, they shore up their theory of knowledge by investing some part of it with certain authority. For some there is fundamental reality in the propositions of logic or in mathematics. For others, the physical world is real and thought is a process of coming to know that real external reality – as if there could be any way of talking about it without preconceiving its constitutive boundaries. Whatever position is taken, the philosopher can be charged by his opponents with committing his theory to an arbitrarily selected and impossible-to-defend fundamental reality. The disestablishing anthropologist finds in W.V.O. Quine a sympathetic philosopher. Quine's whole 'ontic commitment' is to the evolving cognitive scheme itself (1960). This implies a theory of knowledge in which the mind is admitted to be actively creating its universe. An active theory of knowledge fits the needs of a radicalised Durkheimian theory. But active theories of knowledge seem to be especially vulnerable to seduction. Either the thinker in his old age endows a bit of his scheme with privileged concreteness or his followers do. Instead of being seen as a process of active organisation, knowledge is then taken to be a matter of stubbing a toe on or being bombarded by solid reality or being passively processed by the power of real ideas, a matter of discovering what is there rather than of inventing it.

An active theory of knowledge allows full weight to historical and sociological factors. Herein, I suggest, lies the reason for its fragility. It eschews a solid anchorage; it is committed to movement and revision. By definition it runs counter to all the common-sense theories of knowledge which support separate intellectual disciplines using lower orders of abstraction. In these, the bit of the cosmos under specialised scrutiny is being busily furnished with indisputable hardware. Each discipline turns its fundamental knowledge into a piece of professional property. The click between its concepts and the real nature they discover validates the practitioner's status. There are some examples below of how contemporary anthropology tends to endow bits of its data arbitrarily with extra reality. Consequently at every lower level of theorising, fundamentalist theories of knowledge are continually winning the day, until a new theoretical revolution grades their discovered realities as so much junk. No wonder, on such a contrary base, an unanchored, unpropertied theory of knowledge is vulnerable. But it suffers a worse disability. It has no hard core to use as weapon in arguments of a political or moral kind. It can only patiently expound the whole of its coherent scheme. Bludgeonless, such a theory of mind seems doomed to be remote and trivial in relation to human affairs. For, as Durkheim saw for the world of the primitive, and as Wittgenstein for all worlds, the known cosmos is constructed for helping arguments of a practical kind.

Jean-Jacques Rousseau has described an evening he spent with David Hume (Guébenno, 1966: 169). At first he had been suspicious of the latter's good will. Hume's contribution to their conversation seems to have consisted mostly of long silences, interspersed with 'Tut, tut!' or 'My dear Sir!' But such was the reassurance conveyed along these restricted verbal channels, that Rousseau's heart overflowed with affection and Hume recalled a 'tender scene'. If Durkheim and Wittgenstein could have spent such an inspired evening, how few words would they have needed to reach agreement. With a few tut, tuts Wittgenstein could soon have shattered Durkheim's faith in objective scientific truth. He would have put it to him that even the truths of mathematics are established by social process and protected by convention (Bloor, 1973, Wittgenstein, 1956). He would have shown him how much more elegant and forceful his theory of the sacred would be,

stripped of exceptions made in honour of science. Thus encouraged, for his part Durkheim would have guaranteed to
cognitive relativism the vigorous, questioning framework that
would redeem it from triviality. A new epistemology would have
been launched, anchored to ongoing social reality and dedicated
to developing a unified theory of consciousness.

Marx and Freud were not sanguine when they unveiled the
secret places of the mind. Marx, when he showed ideology for a
flimsy justification of control, shook the great chancelleries. The
scene of anguished hate and fear which Freud exposed to view
was just as alarming at a more intimate level. The first looked to
a long-span historical determination of political forms and the
second to a short-span determination of the emotions in family
life. Between these two, another intermediate span is necessary
that Durkheim's insights were ready to supply: the social
determination of culture. It should have become the central
critical task of philosophy in this century to integrate these three
approaches. If Durkheim's contribution was accepted only in a
narrow circle, his friends have to admit frankly that it was his
own fault. When he entered that great debate, he muffed his cue.
He could have thrown upon the screen x-ray pictures just as
disturbing as either of the others. He could have been telling us
that our colonisation of each other's minds is the price we pay for
thought. He could have been warning us that our home is
bugged; that though we try to build our Jerusalem, others must
tear up our bridges and run roads through our temple, the paths
we use will lead in directions we have not chosen. Woe! he
should have cried, to those who never read the small print, who
listen only to the spoken word and naïvely believe its promises.
Bane to those who claim that their sacred mysteries are true and
that other people's sacred is false; bane to those who claim that it
is within the nature of humans to be free of each other. Begging
us to turn round and listen urgently to ourselves, his speech
would have disturbed the complacency of Europe as deeply as
the other two. But instead of showing us the social structuring of
our minds, he showed us the minds of feathered Indians and
painted aborigines. With unforgivable optimism he declared that
his discoveries applied to them only. He taught that we have a
more genial destiny. For this mistake our knowledge of ourselves
has been delayed by half a century. Time has passed. Marx and

Freud have been heard. Wittgenstein has had his say. Surely now it is an anachronism to believe that our world is more securely founded in knowledge than one that is driven by pangolin power.

Bibliography

BERNSTEIN, BASIL (1972), *Class, Codes and Control, Vol. I*, London, Routledge & Kegan Paul.

BLOOR, DAVID (1973), 'Wittgenstein and Mannheim on the sociology of mathematics', *Studies in History and Philosophy of Science.*

DE HEUSCH, LUC (1973), *Le Roi ivre: ou l'origine de l'état*, Paris, Gallimard.

DURKHEIM, É. (1912), *The Elementary Forms of the Religious Life*, London, Allen & Unwin.

FOUCAULT, MICHEL (1971), *L'Ordre du discours*, Paris, Gallimard.

GUÉBENNO, JEAN (1966), *Jean-Jacques Rousseau, 1758–78*, vol. II, London, Routledge & Kegan Paul (trans. J. and D. Weightman).

HERTZ, R. (1960), *Death and the Right Hand*, London, Routledge & Kegan Paul.

KUPER, ADAM (1973), *British Anthropology, 1922–72*, Harmondsworth, Penguin.

LUKES, STEVEN (1973), *Émile Durkheim, his Life and Work*, Harmondsworth, Penguin.

QUINE, W. V. O. (1960), *Word and Object*, Cambridge, Mass., MIT.

WITTGENSTEIN, L. (1956), *Remarks on the Foundations of Mathematics*, Oxford, Blackwell.

Part 1

The Implicit

Introduction

It seems hardly worth noting that some matters are deemed more worthy of scholarship than others. If there is any one idea on which the present currents of thought are agreed it is that at any given moment of time the state of received knowledge is backgrounded by a clutter of suppressed information. It is also agreed that the information is not suppressed by reason of its inherent worthlessness, nor by any passive process of forgetting: it is actively thrust out of the way because of difficulties in making it fit whatever happens to be in hand. The process of 'fore-grounding' or 'relevating' now receives attention from many different quarters. But for obvious reasons the process of 'back-grounding' is less accessible. The papers in this section focus on 'backgrounding'. They identify a number of different situations in which information is pushed out of sight. At one extreme it is automatically destroyed by reason of its conflict with other information. For example, the continuity of human with animal life is a piece of information which is consistently relegated to oblivion by all the social criteria which allow humans to use a discontinuity between nature and culture for judging good behaviour. The history of the behavioural sciences has been to reclaim bit by bit and make significant to us our common animal nature.

By a less extreme process of relegation, some information is treated as self-evident. The logical steps by which other knowledge has to be justified are not required. This kind of information, never being made explicit, furnishes the stable background on which more coherent meanings are based. It is referred to obliquely as a set of known truths about the earth, the weight and powers of objects, the physiology of humans, and so on. This is a completely different pigeonhole of oblivion from the first. Whereas the former knowledge is destroyed by being labelled untrue, the latter is regarded as too true to warrant discussion. It provides the necessary unexamined assumptions upon which ordinary discourse takes place. Its stability is an illusion, for a large part of discourse is dedicated to creating, revising and obliquely affirming this implicit background, without ever directing explicit attention upon it. When the background of assumptions upholds what is verbally explicit, meanings come across loud and clear. Through these implicit channels of meaning, human society itself is achieved, clarity and speed of clue-reading ensured. In the elusive exchange between explicit and implicit meanings a perceived-to-be-regular universe establishes itself precariously, shifts, topples and sets itself up again. Of all the essays here, the four in the last section deal most directly with this aspect of the implicit.

The seven essays here deal with a third kind of backgrounding which stems from the first two. This is the creation of dirt, rubbish and defilement. The first two essays show how the topic is raised in fieldwork. Humble rules of hygiene turn out to be rationally connected with the way that the Lele cosmos is constructed. Rejection of body dirt and rejection of inedible animals is an indivisible part of the foregrounding processes by which the universe is classified and known. For example, there cannot be any possibility of truth, in a cognitive system such as that of the Lele, for the notion that menstrual blood is harmless or that its contagion is not conveyed through food cooked on a fire tended by a menstruating woman. The whole cosmos would topple if such a piece of tendentious and obviously false information were accepted.

The essay on 'Pollution' (p. 47) opens the topic in a strictly anthropological vein. Defilement and magic were not thought to be worthy of a nineteenth-century scholar's attention and to poke into the processes of thought which attached the label of impurity was suspect in the same way as the investigation of sex or death in our day. In consequence, a lot of unexplained assumptions have lumbered the study of primitive religion. This paper was being editorially processed before *Purity and Danger* was drafted, though it was published two years later – producing an encyclopedia is necessarily a stately business. The central theme of *Purity and Danger* is stated here: each tribe actively construes its particular universe in the course of an internal dialogue about law and order. The currently accepted tribal wisdom invests the physical world it knows with a powerful backlash on moral disorder. Peter Berger and Thomas Luckmann say much that is valuable about the social construction of reality (1961). But, like other followers of Alfred Schutz, they make an unnecessary and misleading distinction between two kinds of reality, one social and one not social. This prevents them from being able to appreciate the social uses of the environment as a weapon of mutual coercion. If they could be more radical in their thought, if they could admit that the environment is for enlisting support, and therefore that all reality is social reality, then they could embark on the comparative project. How many kinds of appeals to the objective environment can be used to drum up support? What sort of typology of morality-sustaining universes could be made that would embrace ours and those of primitive societies? It is easier to see that tribesmen project the moral order upon their universe than to recognise the same process working among ourselves. Therefore the two essays, one on 'Environments at Risk' (p. 230) and one on 'Couvade and Menstruation' (p. 60), take the argument of *Purity and Danger* out of its secluded anthropological context. They challenge us to discover how we ourselves have constructed in collusion the constraints which we find in our universe. Our fears about the perils of global over-population or destruction of resources or the evil effects of thoughtless procreation, pornography, and a failure of parental love match those of a tribal society worrying about epidemics unleashed by incest or game animals disappearing from the forest because of human quarrelling. Our consciousness has so internalised these fears that we are fascinated by the symptoms and unable to look dispassionately at the social relations that generate them.

But the alternative of true consciousness scarcely bears contemplation. The implicit is the necessary foundation of social intercourse. For men to speak with one another with perfect explicitness, uttering no threats of a backlash from nature – science fiction would be hard put to make such a society convincing. Ethnomethodologists, who disparage the assumed environment for its political inertia, cannot tell us what society would be like with all communication fully verbalised and none oblique. But if that is unimaginable, there are many problems about the implicit that can be discussed. Once we agree that the idea of nature is put to social uses, the challenge is to examine the social relations it masks.

The next two essays (chapters 4 and 5) consider how and why some information has to be discounted. Information that forms an intelligible pattern in that very process destroys competing information. How the notion of primitive man is presented at any one time is a case in point. 'Heathen Darkness' (chapter 5) shows the idea of primitive man being chopped to this or that shape to fit the dialectical needs of parties to a political debate. It was modern man they were talking about when they hotly argued that primitives were deeply religious or deeply super-stitious. Realising that primitive man includes the whole gamut of human possibility, and realising that how he worships is part of how he lives and has little comfort one way or another for theology, we can remove the filters that showed him in any pre-ordained light. Suddenly masses of suppressed information sur-face about thoroughly secular, pragmatic primitives. The screen-ing out process is switched off, but not before we have caught it at work.

'Do Dogs Laugh?' considers the screening of information from another angle. It asks the reader to take a standpoint from within any verbal debate and note how much information is given and received though it uses non-verbal channels. It is an attempt to reverse the usual organic analogy by which society is seen as a body. Instead the body is seen as an information coding and transmitting machine, a communication system which can be wired to carry a number of different loads. The heavier the load of messages, the more economical the use of available space and time. The total load and the total pressure of control are determined by the expected density of significant interactions, by something, that is to say, in the social system as it affects the communicating individuals. In a heavily loaded system each signal has to register its effect with less use of the resources of the bodily system as a whole. Vice versa, with light loading, each signal can use more of the communication resources. The underlying assumption reverses a common one in the social sciences, that loss of control is the exception needing to be explained. Here it is assumed that more control is more improbable and needs more explaining than less control. The narrower upshot is to suggest that the screening out of irrelevant bodily information is one of the distinctively human capacities. Animals are presumed to take account of involuntary smells and eructations: we select according to a screening and assessing principle which submits free bodily expression to the demand to be informed about the social situation. By means of such a systemic approach, problems can be solved which cannot even be formulated by a piecemeal interpretation of discrete signals and responses.

It is all very well to repeat that foregrounding and backgrounding are necessary for creating form. When the whole social process is taken integrally as the production of meaning, the next sets of questions to be tackled have to do with the relation between different channels of expression.

In 'Jokes' (chapter 7) we suppose that in communication the conveyor of information seeks to achieve some harmony between all possible sources of information. It is not exactly a daring assumption. We have seen that the cognitive drive to demand coherence and regularity in experience requires the destruction of some information for the sake of a more regular processing of the rest. At the same time, for the same reasons, it musters agreement from the different channels of communication. Senders of information seek to convince their would-be receivers. Under the threat of refusing to ratify the credibility of information given in contradictory styles, the very situation of communication forces the different channels to strive to match their separate performances. This article uses joke-perception as an example of concordances between different channels. In its structure the verbal joke replicates the situation in which it is uttered and so it can be perceived to be a joke. The laugh is a bodily response which mimes both the verbal and social structures. Freud's analysis of wit suggests further miming at a psychological level. By such mimesis, when one area of experience figured upon another is rendered intelligible, all domains, the social, the physical, the emotional, snap into alignment. This set of correspondences, which results from the subject's organising effort, is the subjective recognition of truth.

Intelligibility organises the subject as well as the object of knowledge. If this description holds good for jokes, it ought to be demonstrable from other formally patterned experience.

Where does the energy for foregrounding some information and destroying or backgrounding some other information derive? In case the point is missed, I emphasise again that this vast energy is not an undirected, random intellectual force. It can only be generated directly in and as part of social interaction. Most forms of social life call somewhere for coherence and clear definition. The same energy that constrains disruptive passions and creates a certain pattern of society also organises knowledge in a compatible, workable, usable form.

Since the whole social process is too large and unwieldy for dissection, there are great problems of method in trying to study how related channels of communication agree so well that they tend to deliver the same message each in its different way. One solution is to study units of behaviour whose limits are formally recognised within the flow of communications. Like an illness, a rite or a meal, a joke's beginning and end are established. This is because the social roles which sickness, ritual, meals and jokes permit are also bounded. As a delimited enactment the joke lends itself to our study. By noting the multi-layered repetition of formal patterns that deliver the joke we can see that it is anchored in a social situation. Particular meanings are parts of larger ones and these refer ultimately to a whole in which all the available knowledge is related. But the largest whole into which all minor meanings fit can only be a metaphysical scheme. This itself has to be traced to the particular way of life which is realised within it and which generates the meanings. In the end, all meanings are social meanings.

Though all the essays in this section deal with rituals and symbolic systems, they all transcend the distinction between sacred and secular, mystical and real, expressive and instrumental. They approach the so-called expressive order full of wariness against the misleading implications of the verb 'to express'. That word establishes a distinction between the expression and that which is expressed. The object of our study discloses no such cleavage. Knowledge is a continuous process of realisation involving both the implicit and the explicit.

1

Social and Religious Symbolism of the Lele[1]

Like many other primitive peoples the Lele have no systematic theology, nor even any half-systematised body of doctrines through which their religion can be studied. As practised by them, it appears to be no more than a bewildering variety of prohibitions, falling on certain people all the time, or on everybody at certain times. For the people who obey them, there is presumably some context in which these prohibitions make sense. But what is intelligible in them is not extracted from the rituals and presented in the form of myths or doctrines. Like all ritual, they are symbolic, but their meaning must remain obscure to the student who confines his interest to the rites themselves. The clues lie in everyday situations in which the same sets of symbols are used. It is like a religion whose liturgical language, by metaphor and poetic allusion stirs a profound response, but never defines its terms, because it draws on a vocabulary which is well-understood in nonliturgical writings.

By learning the symbols in their secular context we can find a kind of back-door approach to Lele religion. We need to appreciate their idea of propriety, their ideals of womanhood and manhood, and of personal cleanliness, in order to interpret their rites.

The Lele inhabit the southern margin of the tropical forest of the Kasai District. They grow maize, hunt, weave raffia, and draw palm wine. Of all their activities, hunting is the highest in their own esteem. It is not suprising that the richest vein of symbolism is derived from reflections on the animal world, on its relation to the human sphere, and on the relations between the different breeds of birds and beasts. They are keenly interested in the natural history of their region and their attitude to animals is fraught with ambivalence. They are hunters, and yet at the same time they feel a certain sympathy with the other living inhabitants of their land. Animal symbolism in their religion is a whole subject in itself. The point I wish to emphasise here is the constant reiteration in daily social intercourse of the basic distinction, the opposition between mankind and animal kind.

This idea, central to Lele culture, is expressed most usually by relating it to one dominant value, the virtue of *buhonyi*, which is shame, shyness, or modesty. Animals are thought of essentially as being without *buhonyi*. They urinate publicly, snatch without asking, are not embarrassed by refusal, they eat filth, and mate incestuously. Some animals intrigue the Lele because they seem to act with a measure of *buhonyi*. Animals which show a dislike of dirt, and frequent water to wash, are in a class of their own in Lele religious practice. Animals which shyly hide in holes or curl up into little balls at the approach of the hunter, instead of rudely making off (such as porcupines and pangolins), are also in a special class of animals associated with spirits for this reason. The most shameless animal is the dog. Dogs share their masters' domestic life, but never acquire the human virtue of *buhonyi*.

Buhonyi is the sense of propriety. It is nothing less than the reaction of the nicely cultivated person to any improper behaviour. It provides the standard for all social relations. Every kind of claim that a man or woman can make against another is backed by an appeal to their feelings of *buhonyi*. It is the product of culture not natural virtue. Infants are not expected to feel it, but the informal training of childhood is directed to awakening a lively sense of *buhonyi*. If a whole moral code can be summed up in one word, such as honour, or charity, for the Lele it would be *buhonyi*.

All recognition of status is expressed in terms of this concept. Respect for elders is a matter for embarrassment, shyness. To see an old man insulted should fill bystanders with shame. A father feels constrained in the presence of his son, and the son stands silent and respectful before his father or elder brother. Only between equals (age-mates) is there no embarrassment. Any loss of face causes *buhonyi*.

Relative status is capable of being worked out in terms of this attitude. As all bodily dirt is *hama*, disgusting, it is a matter of *buhonyi* shame, to have contact with the hair-shavings or nail-clippings of a man of different status. A man will dress the hair of his social equal, age-mate or classificatory grandfather or grandson, but *buhonyi* would be too great for him to perform this service for his father, mother's brother, or father-in-law. Anal injections, the commonest method of administering purges, are given subject to similar rules, by age-mates and equals to each other, but never by persons between whom social distance is recognised.

As the relations of women to each other are less governed by considerations of status than are those of men, it is consistent that women are at times less sensitive to *buhonyi* of this kind. Adult men should avoid seeing the loins of their fathers, mother's brothers and fathers-in-law. When they go to the stream to wash, they shout to warn any of these relatives to clothe themselves. But mother and daughter go together to the stream, and standing naked, scrub each other's backs without the least embarrassment. Nor do they hesitate to administer anal injections to each other. Men express disgust at such insensibility on the part of women and remark that they are no better than animals.

The idea that other people's dirt is more disgusting than one's own is so well recognised that a piece of magical therapy is based on this principle. Hens normally roost in their owner's hut, and the latter sweeps out their droppings in the morning. Sometimes a hen will decide to nest and lay in another hut. Then it is the custom to leave her to hatch her brood there, the bird's owner giving one of the hatched chickens to the owner of the hut which sheltered them. This gift is sanctioned by the belief that a man who sweeps up the droppings of another man's bird is exposed to the risk of developing a water-filled cyst unless one of the chickens can be called his own. Sweeping the droppings of one's own hen is not supposed to have any ill effects.

At its strongest *buhonyi* is sexual shame. All sexual intercourse is embarrassing and should be hidden. The strict avoidance by a man of his mother-in-law, by a woman of her father-in-law, is an expression of *buhonyi*. All natural functions are embarrassing and should be performed in private. Eating is embarrassing, so men and women eat apart. If an infant defecates in the presence of its elders, its father will call a child to remove the dirt, commenting on his own confusion and *buhonyi*.

Revulsion from dirt is of course an important part of the general sensibility of the man, of *buhonyi*. The word *hama* refers to rotten, smelly things: corpses, excreta, suppurating wounds, clotted blood, and maggots. In use the word is extended to apply to anything which produces a feeling of disgust. Vermin, frogs, toads, snakes, bodily dirt and used clothing are *hama*. So are foods, the thought of eating which would be revolting. For example, the European habit of drinking milk of cows, and of eating the eggs of birds is revolting to the Lele and these things are called *hama*. The flesh of cats and dogs, and even of goats and pigs is abhorred, and called *hama*, on the grounds that it would be disgusting to eat tame or domesticated animals.

I avoid translating the word as unclean, partly because unclean is the negative of clean, whereas the Lele word *hama* is positive. Also, unclean has a specialised meaning in Semitic and European traditions. The full list of things regarded as *hama*, as inspiring disgust, reveals an arbitrary and conventional application of the concept. The list differs for men, for women, for children. There is no need to consider whether any individual Lele ever does experience revulsion at the thought of eating foods proscribed by his culture. It is enough to know that they say they do, are expected to do so, and gain prestige by exhibiting susceptibility of this kind.

The importance of *hama* as a dominant theme in Lele culture can hardly be exaggerated. The avoidance of dirt is the earliest lesson of childhood and forms the constant preoccupation of women in their work in the home, and in cooking. It is natural that it should provide the culture with vivid intelligible symbols. The emotional power of the contrast between human and animal is largely based on the idea of *hama*, animals, particularly the dog, being unaware of it.

In any culture insulting terms are the most illuminating indication of accepted values. In the heat of a dispute a man has recourse to standardised expressions which are hurtful just because they carry the strongest implications of contempt which the symbolism of the culture is capable of concentrating into a word or phrase. In other societies the deepest insults may be based on obscenities of a sexual kind. By contrast, the Lele when quarrelling does not try to insult his enemy by asserting that he was born of incestuous or extra-marital union. The effective insult is *ipondela hama* or *iponj*, that is, putrid, rotten thing. Or a man may reproach his rival for not washing, or for not paring his nails. This is almost as good as calling him an animal to his face. Proverbially, animals do not wash or manicure.[2] To call him a dog and tell him to go and eat excrement like a dog, that is the deadly insult, for which a man will try to kill his defamer. This is, of course, between men. A man can with impunity, and regularly does, call his wives 'beasts, dogs'.

The word *tebe* (excrement) is constantly flung in quarrels. They say that to insult a man is like rubbing *tebe* in his face. To submit to such treatment would be to admit lack of manliness. Another common taunt is to say 'You are not a man'. Women may literally rub each other's faces in *tebe*. This was the conventional form for expressing disgust and anger with a woman who had been the cause of fighting and loss of life. The female relatives of the dead man, distraught by grief and rage, would tear off their loin cloths and, insulting her with their nakedness, dance up to the offending woman, rub her face in the dirty cloth, forcing her to inhale smells of *tebe*.

Rules of cleanliness largely amount to an attempt to separate food from dirt. Cleaning of food vessels, washing of hands before eating, before cooking, before drawing palmwine, are insisted upon. Personal cleanliness requires the Lele to use the left hand for dirty work, the right for noble work and for taking food. The left is therefore associated with *hama*, and it is an insult to offer anything with the left hand. Lefthandedness in children is punished. The symbolism of male and female is also associated with left and right symbolism by a habit of language which refers to the left side as the woman's, and the right as the man's. In sexual intercourse the man holds the woman in his left arm, and afterwards she is required to clean him with her left hand. The constant dissociation of right from filth, and its association with male, builds up the positive value of the male symbol.

In their general attitude to food the Lele show their awareness of the two cultural themes, man's superiority to animals, and the need to avoid dirt. Essentially they might say that 'man is a culinary animal', or rather that he is a man, not an animal, because he exercises discrimination in eating. A conventional expression of anger or of mourning is to refuse cooked food for a period. The mourner or the angry man will eat groundnuts and pieces of manioc roasted in the embers. This is a recognised gesture of abandoning the arts of civilisation. Ordinarily, food, when possible, should be pounded and cooked, not eaten in its natural state. Vegetables, groundnuts, even mushrooms, are pounded before being cooked and served. Pineapple is not offered 'nature', but in a pepper and salt dressing. Cooked maize or manioc meal should be hard and stodgy, not mushy. Mushy foods suggest to them excreta, *tebe*. Bananas are eaten before they are fully ripe, and if they should chance to soften and blacken on the outside, they are thrown away. One must think of the Lele as hungry, but always discriminating.

Animal foods offer a particularly rich field for discernment. Certain animals are abhorrent to all the Lele, men and women, and not considered as edible: rats, dogs and cats, snakes and smelly animals such as jackals. Other animals are avoided by adults, but children, if they have not reached the age of discernment, may eat them. For example, if little boys can catch bats, they roast and eat them. Hunters, if they should kill a Nile monitor, though they feel revolted at the idea of eating anything so like a snake, will bring it home for their children. A little girl may eat eggs, hard-baked in their shells of course, before she is married, but after marriage will disdain them as food. Discernment in eating is made the basis of status-evaluation, not only between men and women, adults and children within the tribe, but between tribes. The Cokwe are thought of as rat-eaters, the Luba as winged-termite eaters, or goat-eaters, the Nkutshu as snake-eaters, and consequently despised.

There are numerous foods which men relish, but which women avoid. No automatic or other sanctions attach to these observances. Few women can give any explanation of why they avoid certain animals. Some may say, 'We avoid them because our ancestors did.' Others that 'If we eat them we will come out in spots'. Others, 'We don't eat carnivorous animals because they are men's food.' Or, 'If I were to eat a long-nosed rat my next child might have a long nose.' The most usual answer is simply to reiterate blankly: 'Women never eat them.' When I found women voluntarily imposing further restrictions on themselves, and boasting of their susceptibility, I realised that the last was the true explanation: the eating of certain animals conflicts with the Lele ideal of womanhood.

Fastidiousness in feeding is part of the definition of womanhood. As soon as the importance of this theme struck me, I collected what information I could about Lele natural history, and found an interesting classification of fauna.

One whole class of animals is set aside for avoidance by women, as 'spirit animals'. I do not consider them here, as the rules applying to them are part of religious symbolism, whereas at this stage I want to discuss the underlying secular symbolism which provides the raw material for religious symbols.

All the other animals which women avoid are labelled by them as *hama* for one reason or another: carnivorous animals, smelly animals, dirty feeders, and rat-like animals. Women usually eat monkeys; but one, which I have not been able to identify, is avoided by them. It feeds on the secretions of palm trees, and as the Lele word *tebe* is the same for vegetable secretions as for animal excreta, the animal naturally counts as a dirty feeder and so is unfit for women.

There are a number of little animals which are not classed as rats by the Lele, but are admitted to be rat-like, a little tree mouse and a long-nosed rat, for example. These can be eaten by men under the stress of hunger, but never by women. The cane-rat[3] which lives in the grassland outside the village is highly prized as meat by men and women, yet one woman told me that it looked so like a rat that she herself could never stomach it. She told me this with evident pride.

There is an animal, half-bird, half-animal, the flying squirrel or scaly tail,[4] which seems to the Lele uncanny because it defies normal classification, and so this too is avoided by women. Poultry is unsuitable food for women, for the same kind of reason as makes all Lele abhor flesh of dogs and goats. Whereas men confine their discrimination to animals, women carry it on to bird-life, and so a womanly woman is expected to feel disgust at the thought of eating chicken.[5] Feminine tenderness seems to be involved: the wife feeds the hens, and calls them into her hut at night. She should feel too strong a sympathy to be capable of eating them.

The idea of eating that which is *hama*, disgusting, often implies that there would be danger in doing so. The Lele recognise that to eat putrefying matter would cause illness. Anything labelled in their culture as *hama* would produce a feeling of revulsion and nausea if offered as food. So it is that aesthetic rules are also rules of hygiene. A man who felt hopelessly surrounded by enemies, told me that he no longer cared to live: he would eat foul rotten things and die. Another man accounted for his superb health by his care in not eating *hama* things.

Certain animal meats would seem to pose a cultural dilemma for the Lele, in being highly delicious, and yet, on the face of it, liable to be classed as disgusting. It is significant that a cult group exists whose members can enjoy these meats because an initiation rite has made it safe for them.

Cult groups are a central feature of Lele social organisation. Men gain entry to them by payment of heavy fees, and by a painful initiation. To join the outer group, that of Begetters, *Baboci*, a man must first beget a child in wedlock. A special title *Bina Pengu*, is given to members who have gone on to beget a male and a female child by the same wife, and from their ranks are elected the members of the most influential cult group of all, *Bina Luwawa*, or the Pangolin Men. They are men qualified to officiate in important public rites for the village.

Nearly all the male population belongs to the group of Begetters. No man who had begotten a child would fail to join. They enjoy three privileges. Only initiates may eat the chest of game, carnivorous animals, and the young of animals. Non-members who infringe their privileges are held to incur an automatic sanction, pulmonary disease which will be fatal unless the initiates intervene and do magic for them. The Begetters have no function, no responsibilities, no special ceremonies other than the initiation of their members. They seem to exist to enjoy their own privileges, to perform magic to save the lives of penitent transgressors. They are scarcely deserving to be called a cult group. Yet the Lele recognise the Begetters as the foremost of their several cult societies.

Like any important institution in a closely integrated society, the Begetters' group has multiple functions. Its initiation is a typical *rite de passage* which must be understood in relation to the whole society. Full manhood is attained only when proof of sexual potency has been given. The couple who are honoured as *Bina Pengu*, for having male and female offspring, have, demographically speaking, reproduced themselves. By limiting membership to those who have begotten in wedlock, since the age of marriage used to be late, privilege was retained in the hands of the old men, and wealth as well, for the entrance fees were heavy. In addition to these various sociological functions, the society also satisfies other less evident requirements of a culture which is preoccupied with a certain number of contradictory ideas. The opposition of mankind to animal-kind is basic to Lele ways of thinking about humans. Man is defined by contrast with animal. At the same time, they cultivate a sensibility in regard to animals, which causes a man to mourn for his dog as he might mourn a wife, to go away and hide if he has arranged for one of his goats to be slaughtered, and to express horror at the idea of eating 'baby animals' (*bana bahutu*). The cult group enables its initiates to suppress feelings of squeamishness which, in the general context of their attitude to different meats, we can see might be evoked by the foods reserved to them. The creation of a sacred privilege entails at the same time that the eating of the meats by non-initiates should be regarded as dangerous, even fatal . . . a belief which is easy to accept in terms of the usual attitude to foods classed as *hama*. And at the same time, the whole complex of notions regarding food fit for humans is further entrenched in their culture.

The cult group is always called *Baboci*, the Begetters. A fuller designation runs as follows: 'The Begetters are those who can eat the chest of game.' This privilege is connected with Lele theory of physiotherapy and sympathetic magic. Ribs are, according to them, liable to get twisted, or to rub against each other. A bad fit of coughing may displace them, and bronchial wheezing, the noise made by the rubbing together of the rib bones, is taken as proof that the displacement has occurred. If they are not put back into place, the sufferer will die of a pain in his chest. In all dangerous conditions Lele avoid eating animal parts corresponding to the afflicted part. A man with a bad headache would avoid the head of animals, a man with intestine trouble would avoid eating intestines. Since all humans are held to be prone to rib trouble, it is understandable that ribs should be dangerous meat, only eaten safely by initiates. The belief emphasises the basic opposition between men animals, since men, weakened by certain diseases, are held to be endangered by contact with the corresponding animal organ, whereas, in another cultural context, where sympathy with the animal world is emphasised, one might expect to find that such a contact might strengthen. In his preface to *Androcles and the Lion*, Bernard Shaw discusses the English faith in the value of beef-eating as a simple example of sympathetic magic.

The second privilege of the Begetters is to eat the young of animals. The symbolism here would seem to be that only men who have given proof of their own sexual potency, who are complete in their manhood, can make this possibly dangerous contact with the animal world with impunity. Without what I have said about Lele fastidiousness in feeding, the implications of the Begetters' right to eat the young of animals would appear fanciful. We can enter into their feelings if we feel disgust at the sight of grotesque, transparent-skinned nestlings, or at the thought of eating the antelope foetus from the womb of its dam. The Lele never speak of these as *hama*, only as forbidden and fatal to the uninitiated; but significantly, they never speak of the Begetters as those who can eat young animals, only as those entitled to eat ribs, as if there were something embarrassing about eating 'baby animals', which would make this an unflattering description.

Men who have begotten twins are held to have an intimate connection with animals (who also reproduce by multiple births). For this reason they have special hunting magic, and also special avoidances. By reason of their peculiar connection with the animal world twin-begetters, alone of all initiated begetters, are not allowed to eat, or even to see, on pain of illness, the unborn young of animals. When the division of the meat is being made for the begetters, the carver shouts a warning to twin-begetters when he sees that he is going to expose foetus in the womb, and they must turn aside their heads, shielding their eyes with their hands in the conventional expression of *buhonyi*.

The third privilege of the Begetters is to eat carnivorous animals. These are in a special category for two reasons. For one they prey on the human sphere. Unlike other wild animals, which keep to the forest, they enter the village and steal goats and chickens. Carnivorous animals which do not keep to the normal animal sphere are thought to be sorcerers' familiars, or sorcerers in disguise, or the unhappy ghosts of sorcerers' victims. To eat of them is to run the risk of indirect anthropophagy. Secondly, an animal which fights and kills its fellow creatures is obviously a symbol of men as warriors. Their meat is described as unfit for women: 'men's food'. There is evidently something universally repellant about an animal which preys on its fellows. As far as I know the fox does not figure in the diet of any European country. Lele women are prohibited anyway (with all non-initiates) from eating carnivorous animals, but they also abstain from carnivorous birds, which men eat freely. They say simply that they would not eat, say a kite[6] because it kills the chickens of the village.

The first two privileges of the Begetters, ribs and young of animals, are sanctioned by the threat of rib trouble. Pulmonary complaints provide the greatest single cause of mortality among the natives of the Congo. Any uninitiated man who falls ill with coughing wonders whether he can have infringed the privilege of the Begetters, and asks them to do healing magic for him. The third privilege, to eat the meat of carnivores, is not sanctioned by any automatic danger. It is a prerogative which the initiates insist upon, and which they will sanction with sorcery if they hear of a case of breach.

In discussing the food privileges of the cult groups I have had to broach already symbolism which operates in a ritual, not simply in a secular context. I started to show that the opposition of men and animals, which inspires much of their etiquette (the presentation of food, the care of the body, the symbolism of right and left, and the definition of cleanliness and propriety), produces a body of what can be called secular symbolism. Of this, discrimination between various animal foods leads us straight into the domain of religious symbolism. Just as safety for a sick man lies in avoiding certain animal foods, for the ritual specialist ritual power is procured by avoiding the meat of certain animals.

Diviners have to observe prohibitions on numerous meats, and one class of diviner practises near-vegetarian austerity as part of the vocation which gives powerful hunting magic.

Here I want to show how the crude symbolism of everyday life provides a basic vocabulary on which religious symbolism draws. I do not at all mean to imply that religious notions are simply derived from everyday experience. It would be consistent with my theme even to conclude the contrary, that ordinary life is experienced through categories which are essentially religious. Everyday experience provides a welter of words, religion selects from these to produce a number of themes which are regulative in everyday life just because they express religious values. The secular and the religious are two aspects of the same collective representations which give the society its distinctive structure.

The distinction between man and animal is largely based on the reaction to *hama*, the feeling for propriety in humans, its absence in animals. *Hama* and *buhonyi* provide a standard of values against which a certain number of contrasted pairs of ideas are immediately judged. The superiority of human to animal food to excreta, right to left, male to female, is self-evident, because of the stock associations made with *hama* and *buhonyi* in each case.

These sets of contrasted ideas in various combinations provide some of the main ingredients for religious ceremonies. For example, the distinction between forest and grassland is important in religious practice. The fertility of the forest contrasts with the barrenness of the grassland. The forest is seen as the place of God, the haunt of powerful spiritual beings, the source of all the necessities of life, maize, raffia, wine, meat, fish, water and firewood. Various rites emphasise the distinction between the two, and the superiority of the forest to the grassland, by associating the forest with males, the grassland with females.

In the first place, women are prohibited from entering the forest on religious occasions, the Lele day of rest, and after the new moon and as a regular part of numerous rituals. The day of rest is not a day of abstention from work, but of separation of women from the forest. On these days they cannot draw water, go fishing, prepare salt from water-plants, cultivate forest clearings, sow or harvest crops. There is an appropriateness about the association of men with the forest, since men are hunters, go through the forest armed, are not afraid of the dark, and control magic which protects them against malign spiritual forces. Women are nervous, defenceless, and burdened with baskets.

There is a compensatory association of women with the grassland, in the practical and the ritual spheres. Work which can only be pursued there is regarded as proper to women. Groundnuts, which are cultivated in the grassland, are from first to last a woman's crop, and from the first hoeing of the ground until the plants are established, women avoid male contact.

At their times of periodic uncleanness women are excluded from the forest, though they may work in the grassland. Men like to blame their failures in hunting on women whom they suspect of infringing the taboo.

Although the forest is not normally thought to be ritually polluted by sexual intercourse taking place in it, on the day following the new moon such intercourse is forbidden under sanction of 'spoiling the forest' for hunting and for palmwine, two male activities. Other important ritual injunctions separate the forest sphere of spirits and animals from the village sphere of humans. This separation fully allows of human dependence on the forest.[7] It is like the separation of male and female, which is necessary for an orderly social life, and which yet recognises the interdependence of the sexes. Without knowing the secular association of the contrasts which are made in ritual, the numerous ritual prohibitions would be difficult to interpret. Knowing something of the implications in social life of the ideas of propriety, manhood, womanhood, etc., it is possible to recognise the rites as a set of dramatised analogies.[8] They use symbols which are already established in, and rich with the associations of daily life. Without this element the ritual injunctions would have no power over the imagination, no force to compel assent. They are symbolic. They make analogies between the relations of male to female, man to animal, forest to grassland, and through these analogies a further relation between man and God and the spirits is indicated. The analogies are not statements about the nature, only about the relations of things. It would be grotesque to conclude that the forest is thought of as male, or the grassland as female, clean or unclean. Nor are there persons, or actions or spheres that are in themselves either sacred or profane. Only in certain contexts, on certain occasions, do these categories apply in a strictly relative sense.

To illustrate the fruitfulness of these dramatic analogies for religious symbolism, I must introduce another contrast, that between upstream and downstream, *tende* and *angele*. These terms are used for position and direction in various contexts. *Tende*, upstream, has all the prestige. It is also used for the entrance side of the hut, contrasted with the back, interior part, and for the head of the bed, as contrasted with the foot. A bed is supposed to be placed so that its head, *tende*, is in alignment with the *tende* of the hut, that is, with its head near the entrance. *Angele* is the bottom of the mug, as contrasted with the brim. *Angele* is also used as a euphemism for sexual organs, the lower part of the body as contrasted with the head.

Every year at the opening of the dry season, a rite used to be performed to ward off coughs and illness from the village. The official diviner, *ilumbi*, would prepare a magic brew of which every man, woman and child took a little. Some would be drunk, some given as an anal injection. When the purge began to have its effect everyone had to defecate on one of the paths leading from the village. To separate the women from the men it would be arranged that the men should soil the upstream path, *tende*, and the women the downstream path, *angele*. Then these paths would be abandoned, strangers could carry off the dirt of the village on their feet, or the rains would wash it away. The symbolism is obvious.

The coherence and force of the ideas I have discussed, of *buhonyi*, shame, *hama*, filth, and of the contrasted ideas of food and excreta, human and animal, appear when we consider the persons whom the Lele consider to be without shame: chiefs and sorcerers. The idea of the sorcerer, as the epitome of badness, is contrasted with the idea of the good man who is sensitive to *buhonyi*. The sensibilities of the sorcerer are blunted and his ingrained malice drives him to heap grief and shame on his fellow men. The concept is based on the full range of paired contrasts. His lethal charms are supposed to be concocted with faecal matter. Disgusting things arouse no revulsion in him, and are the hallmark of his trade. Given the associations of the contrast of food with excreta, it is intelligible that the faeces used by the sorcerer are considered as potent to destroy life as food is to nourish it. He is, for Lele culture, the type of the complete pervert. He is thought to have turned against his own flesh and blood, human-kind, and to have made an unholy alliance with the animal world. He kills humans and strikes women with barrenness, yet protects animals, runs with the hunted, uses his magic to turn aside arrows, and springs traps. A denatured man, he uses animals as his familiars to carry out his nefarious work. Even his supposed lack of interest in the hunt, incomprehensible to the normal Lele, is explained by the association of sorcery with *hama*, disgusting things. The ordinary healthy-minded man has a craving for meat, and would not wish for the hunt to be anything but successful. But as the sorcerer is supposed to be thoroughly corrupt, it is intelligible to the Lele that he should even abhor fresh animal meats, and should lust for the putrefying flesh of his human victims.

Of course no man would ever admit to being a sorcerer. But there is no doubt that individual Lele try to satisfy their jealousies and get vengeance by recourse to magic, and others exploit the current ideas about sorcery to achieve their private ends. Several times I heard of people who found *tebe*, human excreta, in their huts, at the climax of some quarrel, and had taken it as frightening proof that sorcery was being employed against them.

In one case, an old widow was disputing the right to draw palmwine from a palm which had been planted by her late husband. The latter's sisters' sons ignored her claim, and started to draw the wine for themselves, arguing with her every time they met. One day one of the young men passing her hut on the way to draw the wine, was surprised to find her standing at the doorway, watching him in grim silence. He climbed the palm, and came down quickly in horror and disgust, reporting that he had put his hand into a mess of *tebe*. All the villagers were interested in the case; several climbed the palm to verify for themselves, and all agreed that it was indeed *tebe*, and that the palm would have to be abandoned. The widow was accused of sorcery, and was eventually driven away from the village, a number of cases of recent deaths being laid to her charge. Her own kinsman in her defence asked how anyone supposed that a woman would be physically capable of climbing a tall palm and defecating on the top of it, but her enemies replied that the extraordinary feat was further proof of her mastery of the black arts of sorcery. The problem which mystified the villagers seems to me also to be insoluble, unless the woman or someone else had placed the offending matter on a long pole and so lifted it into the palm.

Other pairs of contrasts are also used to build up the idea of the sorcerer. He is supposed to meet his colleagues at night, in the grassland, to carry out bargaining for the lives of men. A convicted sorcerer is buried, without honours, like a dog, in the grassland, whereas ordinary men are buried near the village, and diviners are buried in a secret place in the forest.

Chiefs are the other class of persons said to be wanting in *buhonyi*. This is regarded as an inevitable aspect of the exercise of authority. Feelings of compassion, respect for age, recognition of the claims of hunger and fatigue, these aspects of *buhonyi* are incompatible with chiefship as the Lele think of it, arbitrary, irregular, and predatory in the enjoyment of its prerogatives. Significantly, the chiefs are supposed to be the arch-sorcerers. They say that sorcery came originally to the Lele from God, who gave it first to a chief who wanted to punish his subjects for associating with his wives. If a chief is without shame, it is because he is not completely in the same category as other human beings. Chiefs are 'with God'; when they speak, God hears. Sometimes they say that chiefs are spirits, *ngehe*. A chief can break the ordinary rules of social life, without being classed with animals. Ritual incest is an essential part of the accession rites. A young chief is supposed to kill a sibling at each of the transition rites of his adolescence. These transgressions against the normal code are, for chiefs, a source of magic power, though for ordinary humans they would bring down divine retribution. The normal symbolism is here inverted, giving sinister power to the idea of chiefship. To kill a fellow clansman, and to commit incest with a clanswoman are the two major crimes against the solidarity of the clan. Both are regarded as bestial behaviour. For chiefs to flout these norms is to assert the gulf that separates them from commoners. They say: '*Biitu Bakumu, kacuapa malunji, bo.*

Ilunji diitu, bukumu'. 'We chiefs, we have no clans. Our clan is chiefship.'

The idea of chiefship thus symbolised for the Lele is hardly warranted by their actual experience of the chiefs, who are ineffectual and weakened by rivalry with each other. Like much else of their culture the idea is probably taken from their neighbours, the Bushongo, whose Nyimi is the most powerful chief west of the Mwatiamvo of the Lunda. However, the symbolism is not without its relevance to the actual Lele political scene. Village organisation is characterised by an absence of authority, or rather by such an elaborate system of checks and balances that there is no seat of influence. There is little scope for personal leadership; pressure is exerted in devious and hidden ways. The Lele obviously have very little experience of authority in any form. It is perhaps understandable that in circumstances such as these the idea of strong government should be a frightening one, and that chiefship should be symbolised by inhuman behaviour.

Notes

1 The fieldwork on which this article is based was undertaken under the auspices of the International African Institute, and with generous assistance from IRSAC. The first draft was read as a paper to the Royal Anthropological Institute, 6 May 1954. I am grateful to Dr Louis Dumont for his criticism and suggestions.

2 Native riddle – *To! ibamba! Teteti? Mbwa, kaha tet biala bo.* Scrape, scrape? A dog, he does not scrape his nails.

3 *Thryonomys swinderianus angola.* I am grateful to M. Jobaerts, for the identification of these animals.

4 *Anomalurus beecrofti citrinus.*

5 This explanation is the only one which holds good for Lele culture but there is little doubt that they are influenced more than they know by their neighbours the Bushongo. There, according to Professor J. Vansina, the chicken is reserved as food of initiated men, as it is a symbol of the sun, and therefore of God. See his article 'Initiation rituals of the Bushong', *Africa*, April 1955.

6 *Miluus aegyptius.*

7 See chapter on the Lele of the Kasai, in *African Worlds*, Oxford University Press, 1954, for greater detail about the contrast of forest and grassland, and its working out in terms of the distinction between male and female.

8 I am indebted to Professor Evans-Pritchard's discussion of the use of analogy in the religious thought of the Nuer. See 'A problem of Nuer religious thought' in *Sociologus*, 1954, *1*, 23–41.

2

Animals in Lele Religious Symbolism

Lele religious life is organised by a number of cult groups. For a long time they seemed to me to be a collection of quite heterogeneous cults, uncoordinated except for a certain overlap in membership. In one of them, the Diviners' Group, entry is by initiation only, though the candidate is supposed to give evidence of a dream summons. In another, the Twin Parents, there is no initiation. Parents of twins have no choice but to pay the fees and become Twin Diviners. In another, the Begetters, candidates must have begotten a child, pay fees and undergo initiation. Members of this group who have begotten children of both sexes are qualified for entrance into another group, which makes a cult of the pangolin (*Manis tricuspis*).[1] Lastly there are Diviners of God (*Bangang banjambi*) who are supposed to acquire their power not by initiation, but by direct communication with supernatural beings, the spirits. The primary objects of all these cults[2] are fertility and good hunting.

The Pangolin cult is the only one in which an animal is the cult object. In the other cults parts of certain animals are reserved to initiates: the head and stomach of the bush pig to Diviners, the chest and young of all animals to the Begetters. Or parts of animals or whole animals may be prohibited to them as a condition of their calling: Twin Parents must not eat the back of any animal; so many animals are prohibited to the Diviners of God that they practise an almost vegetarian austerity.

Regarding these practices the Lele offer very little explanation of the symbolism involved. The different animals are associated traditionally with the different cults. The symbolism of the bush pig is relatively explicit. It is the Diviners' animal, they will say, because it frequents the marshy sources of streams where the spirits abide, and because it produces the largest litters in the animal world. In very few other instances is the symbolism so clearly recognised. In most cases one would be justified in assuming that no symbolism whatever is involved, and that the prohibitions concerning different animals are observed simply as diacritical badges of cult membership.

If this be the correct interpretation of the different observations, one must equally accept the view that there is no single system of thought integrating the various fertility cults. At first I felt obliged to adopt this point of view. Believing the Lele culture to be highly eclectic and capable of assimilating into itself any number of cults of neighbouring tribes, I concluded that the connection between the various cults was probably only an historical one, and that in the absence of historical or ethnographic data from surrounding areas, it was impossible to take the problem any further.

Although I could never get a direct answer that satisfied me as to why the pangolin should be the object of a fertility cult, I kept receiving odd scraps of disconnected information about it and about other animals in different religious and secular contexts. Gradually I was able to relate these ideas within a broad framework of assumptions about animals and humans. These assumptions are so fundamental to Lele thought that one could almost describe them as unformulated categories through which they unconsciously organise their experience. They could never emerge in reply to direct questions because it was impossible for Lele to suppose that the questioner might take his standpoint on another set of assumptions. Only when I was able to appreciate the kind of implicit connections they made between one set of facts and another, did a framework of metaphysical ideas emerge. Within this it was not difficult to understand the central role of the pangolin, and significance of other animals in Lele religion. The different cult groups no longer seemed to be disconnected and overlapping, but appeared rather as complementary developments of the same basic theme.

Animals in the Natural Order

The Lele have a clear concept of order in their universe which is based on a few simple categories. The first is the distinction between humans and animals.[3] Humans are mannerly. They observe polite conventions in their dealings with each other and hide themselves when performing their natural functions. Animals satisfy their natural appetites uncontrolled. They are regarded as the 'brute beasts which have no understanding' of the Anglican marriage service. This governing distinction between men and animals testifies to the superiority of mankind. It gives men a kind of moral licence to hunt and kill wild animals without shame or pity.

A subsidiary characteristic of animals is held to be their immense fecundity. In this, animals have the advantage of humans. They give birth to two, three, six or seven of their young at a time. Barrenness in humans is attributed to sorcery: barrenness in animals is not normally envisaged in Lele ideas about them. The set incantation in fertility rites refers to the fecundity of the animals in the forest, and asks why humans should not be so prolific.

The third defining characteristic of animals is their acceptance of their own sphere in the natural order. Most animals run away from the hunter and shun all human contact. Sometimes there are individual animals which, contrary to the habit of their kind, disregard the boundary between humans and themselves. Such a deviation from characteristically animal behaviour shows them to be not entirely animal, but partly human.[4] Two sets of beliefs account for the fact that some wild animals occasionally attack humans, loiter near villages, even enter them and steal chickens and goats: sorcery and metempsychosis. I do not propose to describe them here.

Apart from these individual deviants, there are whole deviant species. Breeding habits, sleeping, watering, and feeding habits give the Lele categories in which there is consistency among the secondary characteristics, so that different species can be recognised. Carnivorous[5] animals have fur and claws as distinct from vegetarian animals, such as the antelopes with their smooth hides and hoofs. Egg-laying creatures tend to fly with wings. Mammals are four-footed and walk or climb, and so on. But some species defy classification by the usual means. There are four-footed animals which lay eggs, and mammals which fly like birds, land animals which live in the water, aquatic animals which live on the land.

Avoidances in Connection with Animals

These problems in animal taxonomy struck me first when I inquired into the food prohibitions observed by women. Some animals they avoid simply because they are anomalous, no ritual sanction being involved. For example, there is a 'flying squirrel', the scaly tail, which women avoid, because they are not sure what it is, bird or animal.[6] I have described elsewhere[7] their self-imposed prohibitions on foods which they consider disgusting apart from any religious symbolism. Here I am concerned with the provisions made in Lele religion for regulating human contact with animals. Restrictions on the contact of women with one species or another is the most usual ritual rule.

A wide diversity of animals are classed as 'spirit animals' (*hut a ngehe*). I could not clarify in what sense these creatures are spirits. In some contexts they are spoken of as if they were spirits or manifestations of spirits. In others they are animals closely associated with spirits. They can be divided according to the restrictions which are imposed on women's contact with them.

Women may never touch the Nile monitor (*Varanus niloticus*) or the small pangolin (*Manis tricuspis*). Concerning the pangolin I shall say more below. The Nile monitor is a large aquatic lizard. The Lele describe it as a cousin of the crocodile, but without scales; like a snake with little legs; a lizard, but bigger, swifter, and more vicious than any lizard. Like the crocodile, it is a large, potentially dangerous amphibian.

Women may touch, but never eat, the tortoise and the yellow baboon (*Papio cynocephalus kindae*). The tortoise is a curious beast. Its shell distinguishes it from other reptiles but, as a four-footed creature, it is anomalous in that it lays eggs. The baboon is interesting in several ways. Unlike other monkeys it is reputed not to be afraid of men, but will stand up to a hunter, strike him, talk, and throw sticks at him. When the troop of baboons goes off from the grassland to the water, the females pick up their young in their arms, and those which are childless hitch a stone or stick into the crook of their arms, pretending that they too have babies. They go to the water, not merely to drink, but to wash. Moreover, they shelter in deep erosion gullies which are associated by the Lele with spirits who are thought to dig them for their own inscrutable purposes. Some of these gullies are very deep and become rushing torrents in the rains. As one of the ordeals of initiation, Diviners have to climb down into one of these gullies and carry back mud from the bottom. Baboons, then, are unlike other animals in that they will stand up to a man, they experience barrenness, they wash, and they undergo one of the ordeals of initiation.

There is one animal which women never eat unless they are pregnant. It is the giant rat (*Cricetomys dissimilis proparator*) which has a white tail and burrows underground. It is associated with the ghosts of the dead, perhaps because of the holes in the ground. The ghosts of the dead are often referred to as *bina hin*, the people down below. The habit of sleeping in a hole also seems to be associated with the spirits. Several of the spirit animals which women have to avoid are characterised as sleeping in holes, but I am not confident about this category, as there are other burrowing animals which are not classed as spirit animals. The porcupine (*Hystrix galatea*) and the giant pangolin (*Manis gigantea*) are spirit animals which women may not eat if they are pregnant. The ant-bear (*Orycteropus afer*), which digs holes to escape from its pursuers, may be eaten by women except during the four months immediately following a certain fertility rite.

Water creatures are all associated with spirits and pregnant women must avoid them. The wild bush pig (*Potamochaerus koiropotamus*), as I have already said, is a spirit animal because it frequents the streams and breeds prolifically. Pregnant women avoid it. There are two antelopes associated with spirits, which women must avoid during pregnancy. One is the water-chevrotain (*Hyemoschus aquaticus*) which hides itself by sinking down into the water until only its nostrils appear above the surface. The other is *Cephalophus grimmi*, whose idiosyncrasy is to sleep in daylight with its eyes wide open, so soundly asleep that a hunter can grab it by the leg. This habit associates it with the spirits, who are supposed to be active at night and asleep in the day. The little antelope is thought to be a servant of the spirits, resting in the day from its labours of the night.

So far as I know, this is the complete list of the animals whose contact with women is normally restricted. There are local variations. In the north crocodiles may be eaten by pregnant women; in the far south women's postnatal food includes squirrels and birds, i.e. animals of above (*hutadiku*) as opposed to ground animals (*hutahin*). In reply to my queries, Lele would merely reiterate the characteristics of the animal in question, as if its oddity would be instantly appreciated by me and would provide sufficient answer to my question.

No doubt the first essential procedure for understanding one's environment is to introduce order into apparent chaos by classifying. But, under any very simple scheme of classification, certain creatures seem to be anomalous. Their irregular behaviour is not merely puzzling but even offensive to the dignity of human reason. We find this attitude in our own spontaneous reaction to 'monstrosities' of all kinds. Paul Claudel understood it well, in depicting the disgust of a seventeenth-century grammarian confronted with a female whale suckling her young in mid-Atlantic:[8]

> *Vous trouvez ça convenable? C'est simplement révoltant! J'appelle ça de la bouffonnerie! Et pense que la nature est toute remplie de ces choses absurdes, révoltantes, exagérées! Nul bon sens! Nul sentiment de la proportion, de la mesure et de l'honnêteté! On ne sait où mettre les yeux!*

The Lele do not turn away their eyes in disgust, but they react to 'unnatural behaviour' in animals in somewhat the same way as did the author of Deuteronomy – by prescribing avoidance.[9]

> Every beast that divideth the hoof into two parts, and cheweth the cud, you shall eat. But of them that chew the cud, but divide not the hoof, you shall not eat, such as the camel, the hare and the rock-badger . . . these shall you eat of all that abide in the waters, all that have fins and scales you shall eat. Such as are without fins and scales, you shall not eat.

The baboon, the scaly tail, the tortoise, and other animal anomalies are to the Lele as the camel, the hare and the rock-badger to the ancient Hebrews.

The Pangolin

The pangolin is described by the Lele in terms in which there is no mistaking its anomalous character. They say: 'In our forest there is an animal with the body and tail of a fish, covered in scales. It has four little legs and it climbs in the trees.' If I had not by chance identified it at once as the scaly ant-eater, but had thought of it always as a scaly fish-like monster that ought to abide in the waters, but creeps on the land, its symbolic role would not have eluded me for so long.

Anomalous characteristics, like the scaly tail, would set the pangolin apart but would not explain its association with fertility. The fertility of humans is thought to be controlled by the spirits inhabiting the deepest, dampest parts of the forest. The symbolic connection of water with fertility and with the spirits who control human fertility, is fairly explicit for the Lele. All aquatic things – fishes, water animals, and water plants, as well as amphibians – are associated with the spirits and with fertility. Creatures which have the same outward characteristics as aquatics, but live on the land (the pangolin), or which are essentially land animals but frequent the water (the water chevrotain), are also associated with the spirits. In this context the pangolin's association with fertility becomes clear.

According to the Lele, the pangolin is anomalous in other ways. Unlike other animals it does not shun men but offers itself patiently to the hunter. If you see a pangolin in the forest, you come up quietly behind it and smack it sharply on the back. It falls off the branch and, instead of scuttling away as other animals would do, it curls into a tightly armoured ball. You wait quietly until it eventually uncurls and pokes its head out, then you strike it dead. Furthermore, the pangolin reproduces itself after the human rather than the fish or lizard pattern, as one might expect from its appearance. Lele say that, like humans, it gives birth to one child at a time. This in itself is sufficiently unusual to mark the pangolin out from the rest of the animal creation and cause it to be treated as a special kind of link between humans and animals.

In this respect the pangolin would seem to stand towards humans as parents of twins stand towards animals. Parents of

Figure 2.1 Tree pangolins

twins and triplets are, of course, regarded as anomalous humans who produce their young in the manner of animals.

For a human to be classed with animals in any other connection – because, for instance, of unmannerly behaviour – is reprehensible. But to vie with animals in fertility is good. Men do not beget by their own efforts alone, but because the spirits in the forest consent. The parents of twins are considered to have been specially honoured by the spirits. They are treated as diviners and are exempt from the initiation which ordinary men must undergo if they wish to acquire magic powers. Twin children are spoken of as spirits and their parents as Twin Diviners (*Bangang bamayeh*). They pay an entrance fee into their own cult group, and learn 'twin magic' for fertility and good hunting.

The most striking proof of the high ritual status enjoyed by parents of twins is that the usual ritual disabilities of women are disregarded in the case of a woman who has borne twins. She attends the conferences on twin magic on exactly the same footing as the men, performs the rites with them, and at her death is supposed to be buried with all the other diviners. This is quite out of character with the normally subordinate position of women in Lele ritual. Parents of twins are regarded as having been selected by the spirits for a special role, mediating between humans and animals and spirits. Pangolins perform a corresponding role in the animal sphere.

Humans, Animals, and Spirits

Lele religion is based on certain assumptions about the interrelation of humans, animals, and spirits. Each has a defined sphere, but there is interaction between them. The whole is regarded as a single system. A major disorder in the human sphere is presumed to disturb the relations which ought to exist between all the parts. Major disorders in the other spheres are not expected to occur.

Animals live their lives, each behaving according to its kind. Their sphere does not impinge on the human sphere. No animal will molest a human, enter a human habitation, or steal chickens and goats, unless made to do so by sorcery. Nor will an animal become a victim to a hunter unless the spirits are willing. For their part, humans cannot expect to intervene in animal affairs, even to sight or pursue, still less to kill an animal, unless their relations with the spirits are harmonious. The approval of the spirits is assured if human relations with each other are peaceful and if ritual is correctly performed. The goodwill of the spirits notwithstanding, the hunter's success may be spoilt by sorcery.

The hunt is the point at which the three spheres touch. Its significance far surpasses its primary object – the supply of meat. The whole range of human aspirations – for food, fertility, health, and longevity – is controlled by the spirits and may be thwarted by sorcery. If the hunt fails, the Lele fear that their other enterprises also are in danger. Not only do they feel angry at a wasted day and meatless fare, but they feel anxious for the recovery of the sick, for the efficacy of their medicines, for their whole future prosperity.

In the delicate balance between humans, animals, and spirits, certain humans and certain animals occupy key positions of influence. Among humans, the Begetters' Group honours those who have been blessed with a child. At their initiation rites ribald songs mock the sterile. The Pangolin cult honours those who have been blessed with children of both sexes; the Twin cult honours those who have been blessed with multiple births. The qualification for membership of any of these cults is not something which a man can achieve by his own efforts. He must have been chosen by the spirits for his role as mediator between the human and the supernatural. In theory, the candidates for the Diviners' Group are also believed to have been made aware of their vocation in a dream or by spirit-possession, though in practice men are known to fake this qualification. Once initiated these men have access to magical powers which can be used on behalf of their fellows.

In the animal world certain creatures mediate between animals and humans. Among these the pangolin is pre-eminent. It has the character of a denatured fish: a fish-like creature which lives on dry land, which bears its young after the manner of humans, and which does not run away from humans. In order to see the full significance of its fish-like scales, one should know more of the symbolic role of fish for the Lele.

Fishes belong so completely to the watery element that they cannot survive out of it. Bringing fish out of the water and the forest into the village is an act surrounded with precautionary ritual. Women abstain from sexual intercourse before going fishing. Fish and fishing gear, and certain water plants, cannot be brought into the village on the day they are taken from the water unless ritual is performed. The woman who is carrying the fish sends a child ahead to fetch a live firebrand with which she touches the fish. The other things are left for one night in the grassland before being taken into the village (see Figure 2.2).

Figure 2.2

I might interpret this behaviour by saying that they wish to avoid any confusion of the dry and the watery elements, but this would not be a translation of any Lele explanation. If asked why they do it, they reply: 'To prevent an outbreak of coughing and illness', or 'Otherwise the furry animals [*hutapok*] will get in and steal our chickens, and coughing will break out among our children.' But these are merely elliptical references to the communion between spirit, animal, and human spheres. The furry animals which steal chickens and cause illness are not ordinary carnivorous animals, but sorcerers' familiars, whose access to the sphere of living humans is made more difficult if the proper distinctions between human and animal, day and night, water and land,[10] are correctly observed.

In accordance with the symbolism relating fishes with fertility and with spirits, pregnant women and novices for initiation must totally avoid eating fish. Certain fishes are more specially associated with spirits than others, and Diviners are supposed to avoid eating them. Fishes do nothing to bridge the gap between human society and the creatures of the forest. Unprepared contact with them is potentially dangerous and is hedged with ritual. People in a marginal ritual condition avoid them altogether. But pangolins, part fish, part animal, friendly to humans, are apt for a mediatory role. This, I suggest, is the context of the underlying assumptions by means of which the Lele cult of pangolins is intelligible to themselves. This is why killing and eating pangolins, with proper ritual observances, are believed to bring animals in droves to the hunters' arrows and babies to women.

Pangolin Ritual

In a village of forty men and fifty women, all the adult male pagans save one were Begetters, sixteen were initiated Diviners, three men and their wives were Twin Parents, four men were Pangolin initiates. I was present and able to record the results of a number of hunts in the dry season of 1953.

All the villages to the north, and many to the south of my village had adopted a new anti-sorcery cult, Kabengabenga, which was sweeping across the whole Kasai district. It promised hunting success, health, and long life to its initiates by threatening automatic death to anyone who attempted sorcery after initiation. Men and women in Kabengabenga villages brought pressure to bear on their kinsmen in other villages to follow their example and rid themselves of sorcery, and those who hesitated were accused by the initiates of culpable neglect if any of their kinsmen fell ill or died. Deaths in Kabengabenga villages were attributed to the boomerang action of the cult magic, so that anyone who died was held to be convicted of attempted sorcery. The mission and the Administration had taken strong action to stop the spread of the Kabengabenga cult, and in our own village the young Christians threatened to run away if the village were initiated.

Tension was running high in the village. Hunting failures, personal or communal, were attributed to sorcery; so also was sickness. Scarcely a night passed without someone shouting warnings to unnamed sorcerers to desist, to leave the sick to recover, to leave the hunter in peace to kill his quarry. They were begged to consider the reputation of the village in the eyes of other villages. One old man declared: 'The villages to the north and the villages to the south have taken Kabengabenga. They are all watching us. They used to say: "The men of Lubello kill quantities of game, without taking Kabengabenga." Now we go out hunting, and we come back empty-handed. That is a disgrace. They watch us and say we have sorcerers in our midst.'

Alternative explanations for misfortunes were offered. The senior Pangolin man said that after a strange woman had entered the village recently, it was discovered that she had borne twins; no twin rites had been performed to prevent her entry from spoiling the village; the Twin Parents should now perform rites and send the village on a hunt that would make good the breach of the twin ritual.

On 6 August the Twin Parents duly consulted together. A Twin Parent is supposed to be an 'owner' of the village (*muna bola*) in the sense that his or her anger would render hunting fruitless unless a rite of blessing were performed. One of them, therefore, drew attention to her ulcerated leg, and protested that, in spite of the callous disregard of others in the village, she held no grudge against them for their neglect. If she had been heard to complain, it was in pain, not in anger. She performed the ritual of blessing. Instructions were given for a hunt for the next day.

7 August. The hunt was moderately successful; although four duikers escaped, two small 'blue duikers', one water chevrotain, and one young bay duiker were killed. The success was attributed to the performance of the twin ritual.

There was no more communal hunting until 12 August. Individual hunters complained of their lack of success, and considered the village to be 'bad'. The senior official diviner of the village, the *ilumbi,* was informally approached and asked to take up his magic for the next hunt. It required some courage and tact to ask him to do this, as he was widely thought to be the sorcerer responsible for the bad condition of the village. On the eve of the hunt, he ordered those who had quarrelled to pay fines, and announced that he would do magic. Before the hunt one of the Pangolin men spoke a blessing, in case his grief at the obstinate and rude behaviour of the young Christians should spoil the hunt. They drew three covers, saw little game, killed only one adult and one young 'blue duiker' – a quite negligible bag. The *ilumbi* felt discredited. He announced that the animals which he had seen by divination had been escaping behind the hunters; next time he would do different magic.

13 August. In the dawn an old man got up and harangued the sorcerers, asking what they ate if they didn't like animal meat? Dogs? People? What? He warned them that he did not consent to the illness of children in the village.

During the day it transpired that the twin ritual was still outstanding. The village had been tricked into believing that the successful hunt on 7 August had been the result of twin rituals whereas, in fact, the junior *ilumbi,* himself a Twin Parent, had persuaded the others to let him try a 'spirit magic' which had been highly successful a month earlier. Everyone was angry at the deception. The senior Pangolin man, who had originally diagnosed that a breach of twin ritual had 'spoilt the village', declared that if only the Twin Parents had been frank, the Diviners themselves would have stepped in to perform the necessary twin rites. Twins (*mayehe*) and spirits (*mingehe*) are all the same, he said, and initiated Diviners do not need to beget twins in order to do twin rites. Angriest of all was the senior *ilumbi,* hurt in his pride of magic, who now saw the reason for the failure of the hunt he had arranged on 12 August. More serious than being made to look a fool, he had looked like a sorcerer chasing away the game. In the next village the *ilumbi* had been hounded out for failure to produce game, and in the old days he would have been made to take the poison ordeal. He was obliged to dissemble his anger, as the village could be 'spoilt' by the ill will of any of its ritual officers.

In the next week men refused to go on a communal hunt as the village seemed obviously 'bad', i.e. infected with sorcery. Individual hunters had some success: a duiker was caught in a trap, a man chanced on a wild sow just after she had farrowed and easily shot her and killed her young; and a large harnessed bush-buck was shot. In spite of these successes, there was an atmosphere of frustration and acrimony in the village.

On 24 and 27 August the women went on two long fishing expeditions. While they were away there was little food, and work in the village just ticked over till their return. On 28th two pangolins were killed. When the women came back the atmosphere in the village had changed overnight to one of general rejoicing. The village evidently was felt to be vindicated in the eyes of its Kabengabenga critics. A neighbouring village asked to be allowed to send a candidate for initiation into the Pangolin cult. Among the ritual specialists annoyance about the overdue twin rite still rankled, but the Pangolin rites had to take precedence now.

The junior Pangolin man announced on behalf of the initiates that the village was 'tied' (*kanda*), that is, that sexual intercourse was banned until after the eating of the pangolin and the shedding of animal blood in the hunt that should follow the feast. Etiquette appropriate to the presence of a chief in the village was to be observed. He used the words: '*Kum ma wa*: The master is dead. Let no one fight.' *Kum* can be translated as master or chief. Unfortunately a quarrel between children dancing broke out, adults took sides, and blows were struck. A fine had to be paid to the Pangolin group for this breach of ritual peace.

29 August. A meeting was called. The village was in a ferment because a man had been caught seducing the wife of the senior Pangolin man. The latter refused to carry on with the Pangolin initiation and feast.

30 August. There was a spate of early morning speeches. The senior Pangolin man was reproached for turning household affairs into village affairs, and for making the village suffer for his private wrong. Someone pointed out that if the pangolins were left to rot, the people of the next village, who wanted their candidate vested with Pangolin power, would think we had refused to eat the pangolin to spite them. All those who had quarrelled were roundly taken to task in public speeches. All were convinced that to go hunting while the senior Pangolin man was feeling angry would be useless.

31 August. Village opinion, originally sympathetic to the senior Pangolin man, now turned against him. He was insisting that full adultery damages should be paid before he proceeded with the Pangolin rites. There was anxiety lest the pangolins should go bad; they had already been dead five days. If they were to go bad without being eaten with proper ritual, the whole village would go 'hard' and suffer for a long time, until Pangolin magic had been done again. Repeated injunctions were made to keep the peace until the pangolin hunt. Two more cases of fighting occurred.

2 September. Fines for fighting were all paid up, and the major part of the adultery damages had been given. Ritual was performed to make the way clear for hunting the next day. The two *ilumbi*, the four Pangolin men, and the Twin Parents met and agreed to do two rites: twin ritual and Pangolin ritual, for the hunt.

3 September. Before the hunt, two Twin Parents aired their grievances; one on account of her ulcerated leg, which she felt no one took trouble to diagnose and cure; the other complained that her husband had abandoned her for a new young wife. Her husband's colleagues replied for him that it was nonsense to suppose that a man would leave a woman through whom he had attained three of God's callings or vocations (*mapok manjambi*). He was, through her, an initiate of the Begetters, of Twins and of the Pangolin. She was reminded of the danger to the village if a woman who was in these three senses one of its 'owners' were allowed to nurse her anger.

The hunt that followed this concerted ritual effort was a failure. Seven animals in all were seen, but only two small duikers were killed. There was great anger and agreement that the village was bad. However, blood had been shed and the Pangolin feast could proceed. After the Pangolin rites had been performed, people assured each other, we should all see great quantities of game being brought back. The pangolin would draw animals to the village. The next day was fixed for the feast.

That very afternoon a third pangolin was killed. There was great satisfaction. 'Just as we were saying "Tomorrow we shall eat pangolin, and invest new members" . . . behold, another pangolin comes into the village!' They spoke as if the pangolin had died voluntarily, as if it had elected to be the object of Pangolin ritual and to offer itself for the feast of initiates; as if it had honoured this village by choosing it.

At night the junior Pangolin man announced that no one was to fight, above all no one was to fight secretly. 'If you must fight, do it openly and pay up. He who fights tonight, let him be rich. The fine will be twenty raffia cloths.'

5 September. The Pangolin feast and initiation rite were eventually held. I was unfortunately unable to see the rites. I was told that emphasis was laid on the chiefship of the pangolin. We call him *kum*, they said, because he makes women conceive. They expressed shame and embarrassment at having eaten a *kum*. No one is allowed to see the pangolins being roasted over the fire. The tongues, necks, ribs, and stomachs were not eaten, but buried under a palm tree whose wine thenceforth becomes the sole prerogative of the Begetters. Apparently the new initiate was made to eat some of the flesh of the first two pangolins which were in process of decay; the more rotten parts, together with the scales and bones, were given to the dogs. The senior initiates ate the flesh of the more recently killed animal. All were confident that the hunt on the following day would be successful.

6 September. The hunt went off in good heart, twenty men and eight dogs. It was an abject failure. Powerful sorcery was evidently at work, since all ritual had been duly performed. People discussed the possible significance of a leopard that had been heard to bark in the precincts of the village that night, and of leopard tracks that had been seen on the way to the hunt. The leopard is one of the forms which the *ilumbi* is supposed to be able to take, and the *ilumbi* was suspected of having gone ahead of the hunters in leopard's guise, and scared off the game. The *ilumbi* himself, realising that suspicions of sorcery were again directed at him, suggested that he would gladly go with the rest of the village to take Kabengabenga magic, if only the Christians

43

did not hold such strong objections. He evidently saw it as a means of clearing his own name. In his youth he had twice taken the poison ordeal and confounded his accusers. He also suggested to me privately that he might leave the village and live elsewhere, as his enemies had never forgiven him for the disputes over women in which he had been embroiled.

In the meanwhile, the village was still 'tied': the ban on sexual intercourse had not been lifted since 28 August, and could not be until blood had been shed in a hunt following the feast of Pangolin initiates.

9 *September.* A hunt took place in which one small duiker was killed. The ritual requirement was fulfilled, and the ban on sexual intercourse was lifted, but from every other point of view it was felt to have been a failure.

Accuracy of Lele Observation of Animals

Writing strictly from the point of view of religious symbolism it is not relevant to ask how accurate is Lele observation of animal behaviour. A symbol based on mistaken information can be fully effective as a symbol, so long as the fable in question is well known. The dove, it would seem, can be one of the most relentlessly savage of birds.[11] The pelican does not nourish its young from its own living flesh. Yet the one bird has provided a symbol of peace, and the other of maternal devotion, for centuries.

However, it would be interesting to know whether the symbolism described above is based on fables or not. I must confess that I was able only with great difficulty to identify most of the animals. Many of the rarer ones I never saw alive or dead and in any case should not have been able to recognise them at sight. I was fortunate in securing the kind collaboration of Monsieur A. J. Jobaert, Warden of the Muene Ditu Game Reserve, who knew the Kasai and several of the local languages well. By sending him the native names in two local languages, together with a description, I obtained translation into French, Latin, and English, and these names were checked again by Mr R. B. Freeman, the Reader in Taxonomy at University College, London. My remarks are based on identification obtained in this roundabout and unreliable way. The point I thought it most important to check was whether the Lele are right in considering the breeding habits of pangolins anomalous: first, do pangolins give birth to their young one at a time? Second, how unusual is this among the smaller mammals? In pursuing this inquiry I was interested to find how little scientifically tested knowledge there is concerning the manner of reproduction of mammals, common and uncommon. Such information as is available serves to justify the Lele in both these views.[12]

One interesting point that I am still unable to elucidate is the principle on which the Lele discriminate between the small pangolin (*Manis tricuspis*) which they call *luwawa*, and the giant pangolin (*Manis gigantea*) which they call *yolabondu*, making a major cult of the first but not of the second. Zoologists may be able to give information about the distribution and habits of the two species which may throw light on the question. It may require an historical solution, since pangolin cults are found in other parts of the Congo.[13]

Notes

1 The pangolin is a scaly ant-eater.
2 The Begetters are an exception, their initiation being mainly a *rite de passage*. They give indirect support to the other fertility cults by honouring virility and penalising impotence.
3 See my article 'Social and religious symbolism of the Lele of the Kasai', *Zaïre*, ix, 4, 1955, in which I give in detail the various situations of cooking, eating, washing, quarrelling, etc., in which these categories become evident.
4 Domestic animals and vermin are major exceptions. Before the recent introduction of goats, pigs, and ducks, the only domestic animals which the Lele kept were dogs and chickens. There is a fable which describes how the first ancestors of these, a jackal and a partridge, came to throw in their lot with man, and how both dogs and poultry are continually begged by their forest kin to leave the villages of humans. Conventional attitudes to both of these in a number of situations are consistent with the notion that a domestic animal is essentially an anomaly. For rats, which infest the huts of humans, Lele feel nothing but disgust. In conformity with their attitude to other anomalous animals, they never eat dog, domestic rats, or mice, and women extend the avoidance to a number of other rats and to all poultry.
5 For brevity's sake I use here some terms of our own categorisa-

tion. Lele use no one word to render 'carnivorous' exactly, but they indicate carnivorous animals by the term *hutapok* – animals with skins, or 'furry animals'. I do not know any Lele term for 'oviparous' or 'mammalian', but it is clear that the manner of reproduction provides criteria for classification as surely for the Lele as for our zoologists, for their descriptions never fail to mention an animal's breeding habits.

6 Significantly, its zoological name is *Anomalurus beecroftii*.

7 *Zaïre*, op. cit.

8 *Le Soulier de Satin*, Troisième Journée, Scène II.

9 Deuteronomy 14:7; Leviticus 11: 4–5.

10 I have given an outline of the most important of these distinctions as they appear in ritual, in 'The Lele of the Kasai' in *African Worlds*, ed. Daryll Forde, London, Oxford University Press, 1954.

11 K. Lorenz, *King Solomon's Ring*, London, Methuen, 1952.

12 S. A. Asdell, *Patterns of Mammalian Reproduction*, Ithaca, New York, Comstock, 1946, p. 184.

13 D. Biebuyck, 'Répartitions et droits du Pangolin chez les Balega', *Zaïre*, 9 November 1953, vii. Subsequently Professor Vansina pointed out to me that the answer to this question is contained in the text. The small pangolin is the only beast that is a fish-like, bird-like quadruped mammal.

3

Pollution

One of the great puzzles in comparative studies of religion has been the reconciliation of the concept of pollution, or defilement, with that of holiness. In the last half of the nineteenth century, Robertson Smith asserted that the religion of primitive peoples developed out of the relation between a community and its gods, who were seen as just and benevolent. Dependent on a sociological approach to religion, Robertson Smith continued always to draw a line between religious behavior, concerned with ethics and gods, and nonreligious, magical behavior. He used the term *taboo* to describe nonreligious rules of conduct, especially those concerned with pollution, in order to distinguish them from the rules of holiness protecting sanctuaries, priests, and everything pertaining to gods. The latter behavior he held to be intelligible and praiseworthy and the former to be primitive, savage, and irrational—'magical superstition based on mere terror.'

He clearly felt that magic and superstition were not worth a scholar's attention. But Sir James Frazer, who dedicated *The Golden Bough* to Robertson Smith, tried to classify and understand the nature of magical thinking. He formulated the two principles of sympathetic magic: action by contagion and action by likeness. Frazer followed Robertson Smith in assuming that magic was more primitive than religion, and he worked out an evolutionary scheme in which primitive man's earliest thinking was oriented to mechanical ideas of contagion. Magic gradually gave way to another cosmology, the idea of a universe dominated by supernatural beings similar to man but greatly superior to him. Magic thus came to be accepted as a word for ritual which is not enacted within a cult of divine beings. But obviously there is an overlap between nonreligious ideas of contagion and rules of holiness. Robertson Smith accounted for this by making the distinction between holiness and uncleanness a criterion of the advanced religions ([1889] 1927, p. 153):

> The person under taboo is not regarded as holy, for he is separated from approach to the sanctuary as well as from contact with men, but his act or condition is somehow associated with supernatural dangers, arising, according to the common savage explanation, from the presence of formidable spirits which are shunned like an infectious disease. In most savage societies no sharp line seems to be drawn between the two kinds of taboo . . . and even in more advanced nations the notions of holiness and uncleanness often touch . . . [to] distinguish between the holy and the unclean, marks a real advance above savagery.

Frazer echoes the notion that confusion between uncleanness and holiness marks primitive thinking. In a long passage in which he considers the Syrian attitude to pigs, he concludes ([1890] 1955, vol. 2, part 5, p. 23):

> Some said this was because the pigs were unclean; others said it was because the pigs were sacred. This . . . points to a hazy state of religious thought in which the ideas of sanctity and uncleanness are not yet sharply distinguished, both being blent in a sort of vaporous solution to which we give the name taboo.

The work of several modern-day students of comparative religion derives not directly from Frazer but from the earlier work of Durkheim, whose debt to Robertson Smith is obvious in many ways. On the one hand, Durkheim was content to ignore aspects of defilement which are not part of a religious cult. He developed the notion that magical injunctions are the consequence of primitive man's attempt to explain the nature of the universe. Durkheim suggested that experimentation with magical injunctions, having thus arisen, has given way to medical science. But on the other hand, Durkheim tried to show that the contagiousness of the sacred is an inherent, necessary, and peculiar part of its character.

His idea of the sacred as the expression of society's awareness of itself draws heavily on Robertson Smith's thesis that man's relation to the gods, his religious behavior, is an aspect of prescribed social behavior. It followed, for Durkheim, that religious ideas are different from other ideas. They are not referable to any ultimate material reality, since religious shrines and emblems are only themselves representations of abstract ideas. Religious experience is an experience of a coercive moral force. Consequently, religious ideas are volatile and fluid; they float in the mind, unattached, and are always likely to shift, or to merge into other contexts at the risk of losing their essential character: there is always the danger that the sacred will invade the profane and the profane invade the sacred. The sacred must be continually protected from the profane by interdictions. Thus, relations with the sacred are always expressed through rituals of separation and demarcation and are reinforced with beliefs in the danger of crossing forbidden boundaries.

If contemporary thinkers were not already well prepared to accept the idea that 'religious' restrictions were utterly different from primitive superstitions about contagion, this circular distinction between two kinds of contagion could hardly have gone unchallenged. How can it be argued that contagiousness is the peculiar characteristic of ideas about the sacred when another kind of contagiousness has been bracketed away by definition as irrelevant?

This criticism of Durkheim's treatment of sacred contagion is implicit in Lévy-Bruhl's massive work on primitive mentality (1922). Lévy-Bruhl documented a special kind of outlook on the universe, one in which the power to act and to be acted upon regardless of restrictions of space and time is widely attributed to symbolical representations of persons and animals. He himself explained the belief in such remote contagion by the dominance of the idea of the supernatural in the primitive view of the world. And since he would expect 'supernatural' to be equated with Durkheim's 'sacred', he seems to have seen no conflict between his and the master's views.

We cannot accept Durkheim's argument that there are two kinds of contagion, one the origin of primitive hygiene and the other intrinsic to ideas about the sacred, because it is circular. If we approach the problem of contagion in Lévy-Bruhl's terms,

49

then the scope of the answer is broadened: there is not simply a residual area of magical behavior that remains to be explained after primitive religious behavior has been understood but rather a whole mentality, a view of how the universe is constituted. This view of the universe differs essentially from that of civilized man in that sympathetic magic provides the key to its control. Lévy-Bruhl is open to criticism; his statement of the problem is oversimple. He bluntly contrasts primitive mentality with scientific thought, not fully appreciating what a rare and specialized activity scientific thinking is and in what well-defined and isolated conditions it takes place. His use of the word 'prelogical' in his first formulation of primitive thinking was unfortunate, and he later discarded it. But although his work seems to be discredited at present, the general problem still stands. There is a whole class of cultures, call them what you will, in which great attention is paid to symbolic demarcation and separation of the sacred and the profane and in which dangerous consequences are expected to follow from neglect of the rituals of separation. In these cultures lustrations, fumigations, and purifications of various kinds are applied to avert the dangerous effect of breach of the rules, and symbolic actions based on likeness to real causes are used as instruments for creating positive effects.

The Cultural Definition

If we are not to follow Robertson Smith in treating the rules of uncleanness as irrational and beyond analysis, we need to clear away some of the barriers which divide up this whole field of inquiry. While the initial problem is posed by the difference between 'our' kind of thinking and 'theirs', it is a mistake to treat 'us' the moderns and 'them' the ancients as utterly different. We can only approach primitive mentality through introspection and understanding of our own mentality. The distinction between religious behavior and secular behavior also tends to be misleadingly rigid. To solve the puzzle of sacred contagion we can start with more familiar ideas about secular contagion and defilement. In English-speaking cultures, the key word is the ancient, primitive, and still current 'dirt.' Lord Chesterfield defined dirt as matter out of place. This implies only two conditions, a set of ordered relations and a contravention of that order. Thus the idea of dirt implies a structure of idea. For us dirt is a kind of compendium category for all events which blur, smudge, contradict, or otherwise confuse accepted classifications. The underlying feeling is that a system of values which is habitually expressed in a given arrangement of things has been violated.

This definition of defilement avoids some historical peculiarities of Western civilization. For example, it says nothing about the relation between dirt and hygiene. We know that the discovery of pathogenic organisms is recent, but the idea of dirt antedates the idea of pathogenicity. It is therefore more likely to have universal application. If we treat all pollution behavior as the reaction to any event likely to confuse or contradict cherished classifications, we can bring two new approaches to bear on the problem: the work of psychologists on perception and of anthropologists on the structural analysis of culture.

Perception is a process in which the perceiver actively interprets and, in the course of his interpreting, adapts and even supplements his sensory experiences. Hebb has shown that in the process of perception, the perceiver imposes patterns of organization on the masses of sensory stimuli in the environment (1949; 1958). The imposed pattern organizes sequences into units – fills in missing events which would be necessary to justify the recognition of familiar units. The perceiver learns to adjust his response to allow for modification of stimuli according to changes in lighting, angle of regard, distance, and so forth. In this way the learner develops a scheme or structure of assumptions in the light of which new experiences are interpreted. Learning takes place when new experience lends itself to assimilation in the existing structure of assumption or when the scheme of past assumptions is modified in order to accommodate what is unfamiliar. In the normal process of interpretation, the existing scheme of assumptions tends to be protected from challenge, for the learner recognizes and absorbs cues which harmonize with past experience and usually ignores cues which are discordant. Thus, those assumptions which have worked well before are reinforced. Because the selection and treatment of new experiences validates the principles which have been learned, the structure of established assumptions can be applied quickly and automatically to current problems of interpretation. In animals this stabilizing, selective tendency serves the biological function of survival. In men the same tendency appears to govern learning. If every new experience laid all past interpretations open to doubt, no scheme of established assumptions could be developed and no learning could take place.

This approach may be extended to the learning of cultural phenomena. Language, for example, learned and spoken by individuals, is a social phenomenon produced by continuous interaction between individuals. The regular discriminations which constitute linguistic structure are the spontaneous outcome of continual control, exercised on an individual attempting to communicate with others. Expressions which are ambiguous or which deviate from the norm are less effective in communication, and speakers experience a direct feedback encouraging conformity. Language has more loosely and more strictly patterned domains in which ambiguity has either more or less serious repercussions on effective communication. Thus there are certain domains in which ambiguity can be better tolerated than in others (Osgood and Sebeok, 1954: 129).

Similar pressures affect the discrimination of cultural themes. During the process of enculturation the individual is engaged in ordering newly received experiences and bringing them into conformity with those already absorbed. He is also interacting with other members of his community and striving to reduce dissonance between his structure of assumptions and theirs (Festinger, 1957). Frenkel-Brunswik's research among schoolchildren who had been variously exposed to racial prejudice illustrates the effects of ambiguity on learning at this level. The children listened to stories which they were afterwards asked to recall. In the stories the good and bad roles were not consistently allocated to white and Negro characters. When there was dissonance between their established pattern of assumptions about racial values and the actual stories they heard, an ambiguous effect was received. They were unable to recall the stories accurately. There are implications here for the extent to which a culture (in the sense of a consistent structure of themes, postulates, and evaluations) can tolerate ambiguity. It is now common to approach cultural behavior as if it were susceptible to structural analysis on lines similar to those used in linguistics (Lévi-Strauss, 1958; Leach, 1961). For a culture to have any recognizable character, a process of discrimination and evaluation must have taken place very similar to the process of language development – with an important difference. For language the conditions requiring clear verbal communication provide the main control on the pattern which emerges, but for the wider culture in which any language is set, communication with others is not the only or principal function. The culture affords a hierarchy of goals and values which the community can apply as a general guide to action in a wide variety of contexts. Cultural interaction, like linguistic interaction, involves the individual in communication with others. But it also helps the individual to reflect upon and order his own experience.

The general processes by which language structure changes and resists change have their analogues at the higher level of cultural structure. The response to ambiguity is generally to encourage clearer discrimination of differences. As in language, there are different degrees of tolerance of ambiguity. Linguistic intolerance is expressed by avoidance of ambiguous utterances and by pressure to use well-discriminated forms where differences are important to interpretation and appropriate responses. Cultural intolerance of ambiguity is expressed by avoidance, by discrimination, and by pressure to conform.

The Functions of Pollution Beliefs

To return to pollution behavior, we have already seen that the idea of dirt implies system. Dirt avoidance is a process of tidying up, ensuring that the order in external physical events conforms to the structure of ideas. Pollution rules can thus be seen as an extension of the perceptual process: in so far as they impose order on experience, they support clarification of forms and thus reduce dissonance.

Much attention has been paid to the sanctions by which pollution rules are enforced (see Steiner, 1956: 22). Sometimes the breach is punished by political decree, sometimes by attack on the transgressor, and sometimes by grave or trivial sanctions; the sanction used reflects several aspects of the matter. We can assume that the community, in so far as it shares a common culture, is collectively interested in pressing for conformity to its norms. In some areas of organization the community is capable of punishing deviants directly, but in others this is not practicable. This may happen, for example, if political organization is not sufficiently developed or if it is developed in such a way as to make certain offenses inaccessible to police action. Homicide is a type of offense which is variously treated according to the relationship between killer and victim. If the offender is himself a member of the victim's group and if this is the group which is normally entrusted with protection of its members' interests, it may be held contradictory and impossible for the group to inflict punishment. Then the sanction is likely to be couched in terms of a misfortune that falls upon the offender without human intervention. This kind of homicide is treated as a pollution.

We would expect to find that the pollution beliefs of a culture are related to its moral values, since these form part of the structure of ideas for which pollution behavior is a protective device. But we would not expect to find any close correspondence between the gravity with which offenses are judged and the danger of pollution connected with them. Some moral failings are likely to be met with prompt and unpleasant social consequences. These self-punishing offenses are less likely to be sanctioned by pollution beliefs than by other moral rules. Pollution beliefs not only reinforce the cultural and social structure, but they can actively reduce ambiguity in the moral sphere. For example, if two moral standards are applied to adultery, so that it is condemned in women and tolerated in men, there will inevitably be some ambiguity in the moral judgment since adultery involves a man and a woman. A pollution belief can reduce the ambiguity. If the man is treated as dangerously contagious, his adulterous condition, while not in itself condemned, endangers the outraged husband or the children; moral support can be mustered against him. Alternatively, if attention is focused on the pollution aspect of the case, a rite of purification can mitigate the force of the moral condemnation.

This approach to pollution allows further applications of Durkheimian analysis. If we follow him in assuming that symbolism and ritual, whether strictly religious or not, express society's awareness of its own configuration and necessities, and if we assume that pollution rules indicate the areas of greater systematization of ideas, then we have an additional instrument of sociological analysis. Durkheim held that the dangerous powers imputed to the gods are, in actual fact, powers vested in the social structure for defending itself, as a structure, against the deviant behavior of its members. His approach is strengthened by including all pollution rules and not merely those which form part of the religious cult. Indeed, deriving pollution behavior from processes similar to perception comes close to Durkheim's intention of understanding society by developing a social theory of knowledge.

Pollution rules in essence prohibit physical contact. They tend to be applied to products or functions of human physiology; thus they regulate contact with blood, excreta, vomit, hair clippings, nail clippings, cooked food, and so on. But the anthropologist notes that the incidence of beliefs in physiological pollution varies from place to place. In some communities menstrual pollution is gravely feared and in others not at all; in some, pollution by contact with the dead is feared, in others pollution of food or blood. Since our common human condition does not give rise to a common pattern of pollution observances, the differences become interesting as an index of different cultural patterning. It seems that physiological pollutions become important as symbolic expressions of other undesirable contacts which would have repercussions on the structure of social or cosmological ideas. In some societies the social definition of the sexes is more important than in others. In some societies social units are more rigorously defined than in others. Then we find that physical contact between sexes or between social units is restricted even at second or third remove. Not only may social intercourse be restricted, but sitting on the same chair, sharing the same latrine, or using the same cooking utensils, spoons, or combs may be prohibited and negatively sanctioned by pollution beliefs. By such avoidances social definitions are clarified and maintained. Color bars and caste barriers are enforced by these means. As to the ordered relation of social units and the total structure of social life, this must depend on the clear definition of roles and allegiances. We would therefore expect to find pollution concepts guarding threatened disturbances of the social order. On this, nearly everything has been said by van Gennep. His metaphor of society as a kind of house divided into rooms and corridors, the compartments carefully isolated and the passages between them protected by ceremonial, shows insight into the social aspects of pollution. So also does his insistence on the relative character of the sacred (Gennep, [1909] 1960: 12–13):

> Sacredness as an attribute is not absolute; it is brought into play by the nature of particular situations. . .. . Thus the 'magic circles' pivot, shifting as a person moves from one place in society to another. The categories and concepts which embody them operate in such a way that whoever passes through the various positions of a lifetime one day sees the sacred where before he has seen the profane, or vice versa. Such changes of condition do not occur without disturbing the life of society and the individual, and it is the function of rites of passage to reduce their harmful effects.

Van Gennep saw that rites of transition treat all marginal or ill-defined social states as dangerous. His treatment of margins is fully compatible with the sociological approach to pollution. But van Gennep's ideas must be vastly expanded. Not only marginal social states, but all margins, the edges of all boundaries which are used in ordering the social experience, are treated as dangerous and polluting.

Rites of passage are not purificatory but are prophylactic. They do not redefine and restore a lost former status or purify from the effect of contamination, but they define entrance to a new status. In this way the permanence and value of the classifications embracing all sections of society are emphasized.

When we come to consider cosmological pollution, we are again faced with the problem unresolved by Lévy-Bruhl. Cosmological pollution is to the Westerner the most elusive, yet the most interesting case. Our own culture has largely given up the attempt to unify, to interpenetrate, and to cross-interpret the various fields of knowledge it encompasses. Or rather, the task has been taken over by natural science. A major part of pollution behavior therefore lies outside the realm of our own experience: this is the violent reaction of condemnation provoked by anything which seems to defy the apparently implicit categories of the universe. Our culture trains us to believe that anomalies are only due to a temporarily inadequate formulation of general natural laws. We have to approach this kind of pollution behavior at second hand.

The obvious source of information on the place of cosmic

abnormality in the mind of the primitive is again Lévy-Bruhl. Earthquakes, typhoons, eclipses, and monstrous births defy the order of the universe. If something is thought to be frightening because it is abnormal or anomalous, this implies a conception of normality or at least of categories into which the monstrous portent does not fit. The more surprising that anomaly is taken to be, the clearer the evidence that the categories which it contradicts are deeply valued.

At this point we can take up again the question of how the culture of civilization differs from that which Lévy-Bruhl called primitive. Recalling that dirt implies system and that pollution beliefs indicate the areas of greatest systematization, we can assume that the answer must be along the same lines. The different elements in the primitive world view are closely integrated; the categories of social structure embrace the universe in a single, symbolic whole. In any primitive culture the urge to unify experience to create order and wholeness has been effectively at work. In 'scientific culture' the apparent movement is the other way. We are led by our scientists to specialization and compartmentalism of spheres of knowledge. We suffer the continual breakup of established ideas. Lévy-Bruhl, looking to define the distinction between the scientific and the primitive outlook, would have been well served if he had followed Kant's famous passage on his own Copernican revolution. Here Kant describes each great advance in thought as a stage in the process of freeing 'mind' from the shackles of its own subjective tendencies. In scientific work the thinker tries to be aware of the provisional and artificial character of the categories of thought which he uses. He is ready to reform or reject his concepts in the interests of making a more accurate statement.

Any culture which allows its guiding concepts to be continually under review is immune from cosmological pollutions. To the extent that we have no established world view, our ways of thinking are different from those of people living in primitive cultures. For the latter, by long and spontaneous evolution, have adapted their patterns of assumption from one context to another until the whole of experience is embraced. But such a comprehensive structure of ideas is precarious to the extent that it is an arbitrary selection from the range of possible structures in the same environment. Other ways of dividing up and evaluating reality are conceivable. Hence, pollution beliefs protect the most vulnerable domains, where ambiguity would most weaken the fragile structure.

Emotional Aspects of Pollution Behavior

Pollution beliefs are often discussed in terms of the emotions which they are thought to express. But there is no justification for assuming that terror, or even mild anxiety, inspires them any more than it inspires the housewife's daily tidying up. For pollution beliefs are cultural phenomena. They are institutions that can keep their forms only by bringing pressure to bear on deviant individuals. There is no reason to suppose that the individual in a primitive culture experiences fear, still less unreasoning terror, if his actions threaten to modify the form of the culture he shares. His position is exactly comparable to a speaker whose own linguistic deviations cause him to produce responses which vary with his success in communicating. The dangers and punishments attached to pollution act simply as means of enforcing conformity.

As to the question of the rational or irrational character of rules of uncleanness, Robertson Smith is shown to have been partly right. Pollution beliefs certainly derive from rational activity, from the process of classifying and ordering experience. They are, however, not produced by strictly rational or even conscious processes but rather as a spontaneous by-product of these processes.

Bibliography

DOUGLAS, MARY (1966), *Purity and Danger: an Analysis of Concepts of Pollution and Taboo*, London, Routledge & Kegan Paul.

DURKHEIM, ÉMILE ([1912] 1954), *The Elementary Forms of the Religious Life*, London, Allen & Unwin; New York Macmillan. First published as *Les Formes élémentaires de la vie religieuse, le système totémique en Australie*. A paperback edition was published in 1961 by Collier.

ELIADE, MIRCEA ([1957] 1959), *The Sacred and the Profane: The Nature of Religion*, New York, Harcourt. First published in German. A paperback edition was published in 1961 by Harper.

FESTINGER, LEON (1957), *A Theory of Cognitive Dissonance*, Evanston, Ill., Row.

FRAZER, JAMES ([1890] 1955), *The Golden Bough: a Study in Magic and Religion*, 3rd ed., rev. & enl. 13 vols, New York, St Martin's; London, Macmillan. An abridged edition was published in 1922 and reprinted in 1955.

FRENKEL-BRUNSWIK, ELSE (1949), 'Intolerance of ambiguity as an emotional and perceptual personality variable', *Journal of Personality*, *18*, 108–43.

GENNEP, ARNOLD VAN ([1909] 1960), *The Rites of Passage*, London, Routledge; University of Chicago Press. First published in French.

HEBB, DONALD O. (1949), *The Oganization of Behavior: a Neuropsychological Theory*, New York, Wiley.

HEBB, DONALD O. (1958), *A Textbook of Psychology*, Philadelphia, Saunders.

LEACH, EDMUND R. (1961), *Rethinking Anthropology*, London School of Economics and Political Science Monographs on Social Anthropology, no. 22. London, Athlone.

LÉVI-STRAUSS, CLAUDE ([1958] 1963), *Structural Anthropology*, New York, Basic Books. First published in French.

LÉVY-BRUHL, LUCIEN ([1910] 1926), *How Natives Think*, London, Allen & Unwin. First published as *Les Fonctions Mentales dans les sociétés primitives*.

LÉVY-BRUHL, LUCIEN ([1922] 1923), *Primitive Mentality*, New York, Macmillan. First published in French.

OSGOOD, CHARLES E. and SEBEOK, THOMAS A. (eds) ([1954] 1965), *Psycholinguistics: a Survey of Theory and Research Problems*, Bloomington, Indiana University Press.

SMITH, WILLIAM ROBERTSON ([1889] 1927), *Lectures on the Religion of the Semites*, 3rd ed., New York, Macmillan.

STEINER, FRANZ (1956), *Taboo*, New York, Philosophical Library.

4

Couvade and Menstruation
The Relevance of Tribal Studies

We all have the same human body, with the same number of orifices, using the same energies and seeking the same biological satisfactions. Yet tribal rituals are highly selective in their treatment of these themes. I cannot think of any physical condition of which the ritual treatment is constant across the globe. Even fear of the dead, even corpse pollution which Malinowski thought to be a universal human experience, has not been taken up universally in ritual. There are cultures, such as the Mae Enga of the New Guinea Highlands, where contact with corpses does not have to be ritually cleansed though they cleanse themselves from sex pollution (Meggitt, 1964). While in other parts, say the Nyakyusa of Tanzania, elaborate washings, seclusions and fumigations are necessary to make the mourners and burial party fit for normal society again (Wilson, 1957). The same holds good for menstruation: in tribal society it is not universally hedged with ritual taboos. Each primitive culture makes its own selection of bodily functions which it emphasizes as dangerous or good. The problem then is to understand the principles of selection.

Another point to consider is that rituals are not fixed from time immemorial. They are not unchanging hard cores of some mystic cosmology. It is a mistake to think of people as being set somewhere below and apart from their cosmological ideas. To some extent they themselves (or we, ourselves) get this feeling of being controlled by an external, fixed environment of ideas. But the feeling is an illusion. People are living in the middle of their cosmology, down in amongst it; they are energetically manipulating it, evading its implications in their own lives if they can, but

using it for hitting each other and forcing one another to conform to something they have in mind. If we can realize how
much a language changes in a lifetime, without the speakers
recognizing their own contribution, we can realize how rituals
and beliefs change. They are extremely plastic. These two points
should be taken together: first, that rituals select some bodily
conditions and ignore others; second, that they are being
manipulated by people trying to live together. Jointly they provide a clue to the interpretation of ritual, for we should look for
circumstances that are not universal, not common to all mankind, to discover the principles of selection. These we are likely to
find in the social environment, the dimension in which people are
using everything they can, particularly mystic ideas, to influence
one another.

The next stage is to distinguish various levels of meaning.
Take a common bodily condition and consider the range of rites
which seek to control it: there will be several psychological
meanings, some potent for the person undergoing that condition
and others for persons responding as an audience. Rites dealing
with menstruation will use a cluster of culturally standardized
meanings concerning blood, womanhood, fertility, barrenness.
Then there will be sociological meanings: at one level there is
scope for using the situation to manipulate other people, that is
at the level of interpersonal relations; at a more inclusive social
level the ritual may be made to say something public about social
groupings and their relation to one another.

I propose to discuss some rituals concerning menstruation to
demonstrate these two distinct sociological dimensions of
meaning.

First, beliefs which claim that women are dangerous while
menstruating give scope for playing out interpersonal conflicts.
These beliefs give rise to rituals which seclude women or require
them to be purified before return to mixed society. In order to
understand any such belief you have to place yourself in the
shoes of a man whose career is in reality liable to be frustrated by
female wiles and infidelity. For such a man the danger beliefs can
be seized upon as a clear symbolic statement of several things he
believes to be true and important in the social sphere. Belief in
the dangers of menstruation may be useful.

(i) *To assert male superiority*. This is expressed in ideas about cleanness and impurity. To express female uncleanness is to express female inferiority, a point which it may be vitally important to get across to a particular wife in a given home at any time.

(ii) *To assert separate male and female social spheres*. Men may wish to set clear limits to female intrusion in male affairs or the beliefs may reflect the *de facto* existence of separate male and female spheres of interest. To require a menstruating woman to keep to female quarters can make this point quite effectively. To blame her carelessness in this respect for *his* failure in fishing or hunting or farming is a way of using the cosmos to constrain other people: the man does not directly blame the bad weather for driving the fish deeper into the stream or the game deep into the forest or for drowning or drying the crops. He argues that the weather was bad, but would not have been if menstruating women had kept to the bounds laid down for them. I have heard this being furiously argued by Lele in the Kasai.

(iii) *To attack a rival*. Women can fasten on these beliefs and use them against one another. Lele believe that food cooked by a menstruating woman is dangerous, and women are not above using these beliefs to fasten blame for family disasters on rival co-wives.

All this is straightforward and obvious. The case of menstruation rites is only one example of a whole range of danger beliefs which are used to underline roles and obligations and to maintain statuses. They not only express people's interest in these social distinctions and duties – they give a handle for coercing everyone into conforming to the pattern. For example, beliefs in dangers following adultery clearly have an expressive function and a coercive potential. Similarly for beliefs in pollution of homicide, pollution of strangers, pollution of royalty by commoners, and so on. Menstrual impurity is a consistent part of a wide general category of pollution beliefs.

In a recent publication (Douglas, 1966) I have seemed to subscribe to the view that danger beliefs have a positive role in

enforcing morality. I gave the impression that the beliefs are able
to hold down deviance and to enforce conformity to a common
code, setting an independent sanction on behaviour. Such a view
is certainly wrong. The beliefs are the product of common assent
to a set of norms: they express it publicly and visibly, but their
power to hold people to a code of behaviour is no more than the
power of those people's respect for that code. This, of course, sets
limits to the scope for manipulating a social situation by citing
danger beliefs. Other people who are not committed to that code
will not take the danger beliefs seriously.

There is another quite different way in which danger beliefs
can be used to manipulate a social situation.

(iv) *To lay claim to a special relation.* Among the Hadza, a
small, poor tribe of hunters in Tanzania, all social groupings are very fluid. A band loses members, gains others,
disbands, reconstitutes itself with a largely different
membership in a matter of weeks. At the group level
people come and go very freely and set little store on belonging to this or that social unit. But at the interpersonal level there are certain strong pressures. Men
want to have sexual access to women, this is a dominant
pre-occupation. But women are able to live independently
of men, for the division of labour is very weak, and they
can look after their own needs and those of their children except for getting meat and trade goods. On this
unsymmetrical basis of sexual and economic dependence of one sex upon the other, the marriage tie
is fragile and easily broken. Here a belief in the dangers
of menstruation serves to define the married couple. Dr
James Woodburn, from whose unpublished Ph.D thesis
this material is drawn (Woodburn, 1964) describes certain risks which the whole band is thought to run, if
the husband of a menstruating woman pursues his usual
occupations. While his wife is menstruating the husband
is restricted in two important respects: he may not touch
poisoned arrows and he may not put his arm into a
bees' nest. If he fails to observe these restrictions, the
poison on the arrows he touches will lose its efficacy
and all the honey in the bees' nests in the area will be eaten
by the bees. Other people have an interest in making

sure that a man does acknowledge and continues to acknowledge cohabitation by observing these restrictions: men do not want the poison of their arrows to be spoiled by being handled during gambling by such a man and both men and women would be alarmed at the prospect of all the honey in the district disappearing. The effect is that husband and wife are thus at these times both partially segregated from their sexual groups. While she menstruates, he abstains from certain manly activities. Dr Woodburn writes charmingly of this observance which withdraws both husband and wife from the wider community as a monthly reaffirmation of their union. But as I see it, the husband, whose claim to the woman is always open to challenge and who never knows from month to month how long she will accept him, this precarious husband is using danger beliefs to proclaim publicly his relationship. In ostentatiously *not* joining his comrades and not doing the usual day's round, sitting around while his wife also abstains from certain female occupations, he is being conspicuously public-spirited in trying to avert hardship from the community. But his primary interest is in drawing attention to some alleged physical aspects of the social link between spouses. He is calling on the physical universe to prove his claim to her. Given the lack of other definition of the marital role in this society, one can even imagine two rivals abstaining from work during a woman's menstruation, of competing to apologize for hunting and honey failures due to their carelessness on this point – just as rival lineage elders among the Lugbara put in claims for being responsible for illnesses among their followers in a ritual duel for the succession (Middleton, 1960).

This example of a social use for menstrual taboos suggests a parallel interpretation for couvade, the custom whereby a man takes to his bed while his wife is in labour of child-birth, and often simulates her pains. On this approach, I suggest it would be worth looking for a correlation between practice of the couvade, weak definition of marriage and a strong interest on the husband's part in asserting his claim to the wife and her child. In

England we might expect the couvade to be found in sectors of society where the husband is forced to be absent for long periods from home; in tribal society where the marriage tie is weak. The couvading husband is saying, 'Look at me, having cramps and contractions even more than she! Doesn't this prove I am the father of her child?' It is a primitive proof of paternity. It is apparent that I am here seeking to restore to sociological investigation the hypotheses entertained by Tylor and Bachofen and discussed by Crawley (1902). For these anthropologists the practice of the couvade was a missing link in the evolutionary sequence from matriarchal to patriarchal society. I am suggesting that it is a danger belief in the same class as those others by which individuals seek to manipulate their social environment.

I am now ready to turn to the next sociological level of interpretation. Here I am talking about grand public rituals which involve everyone, initiations, funerals, marriages, rituals of peace and war. These are the occasions for arousing emotion and fastening it on focal values: the propositions they make are general, consensus-producing statements about the essential nature of society. These are not the occasions which individual X can use for coercing his enemy, or rival, Y. I contend that if the universal human experience of sex is taken up at this level of ritual it is used to say something publicly, not about sex, but about society. I am going to take for my example the very difficult case of initiation rites in which the genital organs of boys are cut so that they bleed with the explicit intention of making a parallel to female menstruation. Bettelheim (1955: 260) has discussed two examples of this rite among the Murngin and Arunta Australian aborigines. He interpreted them as expressions of male envy of the female procreative role. Indeed, he has ample justification for this interpretation in the texts which he quotes and which give native statements consistent with his view. 'We make the boys bleed so that they become like women,' they say, over and over again in different forms. He concludes (p. 204):

Anthropological observations lend themselves better to the interpretation that initiation rites were designed to compensate for what might have been considered male physical deficiency in procreation, perhaps reinforced by women because of penis envy or resentment of menstruation, than to the more familiar anthropological and psychoanalytic interpretation.

And again:

> These practices suggest that human beings' envy of the genital apparatus of the other sex leads to the desire to acquire similar organs and to gain power and control over the genitals of the other sex. The former desire is represented in men by sub-incision and possibly also circumcision; in women it is shown in manipulation to enlarge the clitoris and labia.

His argument, which is well known, derived from insights gained in his clinic for schizophrenic children approaching adolescence. These children had never heard of Murngin aborigines, nor of Arunta, nor Arapesh or Wogeo. They invented actions which were startlingly close to the practice of induced genital bleeding in boys which figures prominently in the initi-ation rites of these tribes. They even gave the same reasons for doing so, reasons which Bettelheim sums up as male envy of the womb. There is no need in this paper to take Bettelheim's argu-ment to pieces and show why his generalizations about primitive personality development are unacceptable as stated. The point is to be grateful to him for drawing attention so graphically to the central problem of interpretation of ritual, that is, the relation between individual psychological needs and public social needs, both expressed by symbolic acts. Take the case of the couvade: some tribes practise a ritual which requires a man to lie-in while his wife is in child-labour and which is supported by beliefs that the outcome will be unfortunate if he does not lie in. Here is a publicly recognized standard ritual. Then take the cases reported by contemporary doctors in Europe of men who claim to feel labour pains while their wives are in labour. This is not a public ritual, but a private situation, a pain felt by an individual. What the two cases have in common, whether it is public and private couvade or public and private womb envy, is the subject of this paper. The first step is to understand what the public enactment is about. Is it intended to bring relief to those whose private mental condition is disturbed or would be disturbed and who may gain balance and reassurance by the enactment? In my opinion, no. This is not what public rituals are about, though incidentally they may achieve this effect. A public ritual, with all its attendant beliefs in danger if it is not performed, is the summation of a whole community's experience. It expresses a common, public concern, and uses whatever symbolic language is to hand for bringing the point home. No one is going to be able to foist his private anxieties on the community unless they correspond to everyone's private anxieties, arising out of a common situation. In the case of the couvade in modern Europe, it is easy to see why some men might resort to it spontaneously in their anxiety to lay claim to their wives, and easy to see why it has not become a common practice. It is not likely to appeal to men who have a marriage settlement deposited with the solicitor; nor men in tribes where dowry and marriage payments give the husband security. It could become much commoner at the spontaneous level in an England of the future in which the marriage bond were much looser, and then we could predict the pundits dreaming up physical dangers to the unborn child likely to be averted by the father lying-in. Already one notices a new emphasis on the father's role in the lying-in of the mother, and a new responsibility for the mental health of his children, an emphasis which I would expect to be increasing with the greater ease of divorce.

Rituals expressing envy of the womb are not susceptible of a parallel interpretation. In the case of the couvade, I am taking the sociological dimension at the interpersonal level and suggesting that couvade is like menstrual and adultery pollution, a belief used directly for manipulating social relations. But there is the other dimension, the graphic expression of social forms. To place Murngin and Arunta boys' initiation in this dimension we need to consider other kinds of bodily symbolism.

When the Dinka, a tribe of cattle-herders in the Sudan, sacrifice an ox, they prescribe a variety of different ways of killing it (Lienhardt, 1961). Each method is symbolically appropriate to what the sacrifice is intended to bring about. If it is a truce between two groups of kin separated by a blood feud, they cut the beast in half across the middle and divide the whole animal between both parties; the quarrel is no more to be a division between them. For some occasions they trample it to death, for others they suffocate it. If the sacrifice is to cancel the effects of incest, the animal is cut in half longways, through the genital organs. What is being carved upon the body of the animal is a division to be recognized in future between two lineages: formerly they begot children in one line, now they are divided as to begetting: hence the cut through the genital organs.

There is no difficulty in seeing the body of a sacrificial ox as an image of the body politic. The way it is carved up is clearly the diagram of a social situation. It is clear that what is enacted states something of common concern. We must be prepared to make the same interpretation when the symbolic statement is being carved upon human flesh. This is a central clue to the incision rites which use womb envy to express something about the constitution of society.

When I read Bettelheim's *Symbolic Wounds*, I asked myself why these aboriginal tribes should be so anxious to emphasize symmetry even where symmetry most manifestly is absent, and why in their initiation rites they should try to make the boys acquire procreative powers like women's. It struck me that the artificial creation of symmetry between the sexes might correspond to a dual division within the tribes. True enough, the Murngin are divided into moieties, that is into exogamous, woman-exchanging halves, and the Arunta have a section system, which basically means that moieties have themselves been divided into half again. It seemed plausible then to suggest that the symmetry of the sexes created by initiation expresses the duality of society. If everyone in the system has a strong stake in maintaining the exchanges between the two parts of society, and if this exchange requires that the two parts be symmetrical and equal, then the incision of boys would express a common social concern. I have not had a chance to develop this interpretation. It requires detailed re-examination of the social situation and of the texts about the initiation ceremonies in the tribes cited by Bettelheim. But to make it sound less far-fetched, I will mention two other cases in which male-genital bleeding is ritually required, explicitly as a parallel with female menstruation; two other cases in which the same ritual emphasis on the symmetry of the sexes is found in societies with division into moieties. I take Margaret Mead's account (1938, 1940) of the Mountain Arapesh of New Guinea and Ian Hogbin's first account (1934–5) of the neighbouring Wogeo.

The cosmology of the Arapesh associates all power and energy with sex; it emphasizes the equality of male and female sexual power and their equal dangers. Each sex is concerned to control its own sexual power in the interests of fertility and growth. Excessive sexual energy, if uncontrolled, is dangerous to all in contact with it. Not only is a woman dangerous in her sexuality and especially in menstruation to men and children, but a man too is dangerous to women. The sexual power is manifested in blood: the female nourishes the young in her womb with good blood, her menstrual blood is dangerous; the male has equivalent blood in the penis which is good, life-giving and which he draws to feed to his child, once born, in exact parallel to the feeding of the foetus in the womb. Female menstruation strengthens the woman, because it is a means of discharging from her body the dangerous fluids of the opposite sex received in intercourse. This natural purifying discharge men achieve artificially by letting blood from the penis. The centre of the initiation rite of boys is the incision of the penis. Here we have duality and symmetry clearly expressed in rite and cosmology. What of the social structure? We read that this reaches only a very low level of organization.

> The typical picture is a cluster of hamlets, bound together by ties of inter-marriage, ceremonial co-operation – but within which there is little genuine integration, no centralized system for punishing offenders, no institutionalized leadership, and no mechanism for preventing any one of the associated hamlets from forming stronger ties with hamlets outside the temporary aggregation. The entire region depends on kinship ties as the major social mechanism and the tendency, so conspicuous in Polynesia and in Africa, of elaborating kinship ties into effective political superstructures is lacking.

The Arapesh have two patterns which combine this low-level organization of kinship into a larger unit: one concerns initiation and one concerns feasting. Mead says, 'Arapesh have two sorts of dual organization, both are virtually functionless, except for their value in oratory; one is vaguely connected with feasting and the other as vaguely associated with the initiatory cult.' This was in 1938, and nowadays an anthropologist would have to go to some trouble to demonstrate that a reported lack of function and vagueness in institutions is not subjectively imparted by the observer. The Arapesh evidently felt strongly about their dual system for she goes on to report that when a local schism resulted in one locality being entirely represented in one half of the dual division associated with initiation, they split themselves into two again, 'taking as their totems two varieties of the emblem bird, the hawk'.

Hogbin tells us that the cosmology of the Wogeo is also energized by sexual powers.

> The chief source of peril is sexual intercourse, when contact is at a maximum. . . . The juices of the male then enter the female, and vice versa. Women are automatically cleansed by the process of menstruation, but men, in order to guard against disease, have periodically to incise the penis and allow a quantity of blood to flow. This operation is often referred to as men's menstruation. . . . Men also incise the penis after they have performed certain tasks which for magical reasons are held to be very dangerous.

These include building a new men's house, burying a corpse, going on a murder expedition, initiating a boy. They also let blood before risky work, to eliminate the danger. As to social organization, they are organized in small patrilineal clans. Cutting right across them are two exogamous matrilineal divisions.

Here is evidently very rich material for testing my hypothesis. I would not argue that all rites of incision express the symmetry of dual social divisions. But if it is explicitly stated that the incision of the male genital organ is performed to achieve symmetry with the female reproductive system then I would look for important interdependent dual social divisions whose symmetry I would suppose to be expressed in the ritual creating a symmetry of the sexes.

To conclude: if psychologists turn to tribal studies to gain insights into the behaviour of their patients, they will find it difficult to isolate any strictly psychological levels of meaning which derive from the common human experience of sex and reproduction. For in a tribal culture even these intimate experiences can be mediated to the individual through cosmological and ritual categories. Even the physiological differences between male and female can be masked by a categorization whose primary purpose is to reflect and sustain a particular social order. Therefore I maintain that there is very little validity in the argument which would interpret tribal rituals by the light of psychiatric clinical experience. Tribal rituals are either being used by one individual to coerce another in a particular social situation, or by all members to express a common vision of society. We cannot argue from the rituals of our mentally disturbed patients to those of functioning tribal systems. But there may be some validity in arguing the other way. When I suggested that the couvade may relate to the husband's insecure claim to the wife, I offered a social context in which the couvade might be found, either in established ritual or arising spontaneously from psychosomatic interactions. Could it be that the schizophrenic boy in Bettelheim's clinic, who wanted to menstruate like the adolescent girl, felt his *social* world threatened by a division based on sexual disparity? Then it would be the symmetry of his *social* world that he wished to restore by creating symmetry of the sexes within it? Not womb envy, but reversing the behaviour of the Arapesh community which, when it found itself lopsidely representing only one totem, divided itself into two, the schizophrenic boy could equally well be trying to prevent a splitting of his society.

In sum, my argument is that we can hope for insight into tribal rituals by studying their social dimensions and into psychosomatic phenomena which resemble tribal rituals by studying the social context, both at the level of social manipulation and at the level of expressing social forms.

Bibliography

BETTELHEIM, B. (1955), *Symbolic Wounds*, Chicago, Free Press.

CRAWLEY, E. (1902), *The Mystic Rose: a Study of Primitive Marriage*, London, Macmillan.

DOUGLAS, M. (1966), *Purity and Danger: an Analysis of Concepts of Pollution and Taboo*, London, Routledge & Kegan Paul.

HOGBIN, H. I. (1934–5), 'Native culture of Wogeo', *Oceania*, 5, 330, 315.

HOGBIN, H. I. (1970), *The Island of Menstruating Men: Religion in Wogeo, New Guinea*, Chandler Publishing Co.

LIENHARDT, R. G. (1961), *Divinity and Experience: the Religion of the Dinka*, London, Oxford University Press.

MEAD, M. (1938), 'The Mountain Arapesh. I: An importing culture', *Anthrop. Pap. Am. Mus. Nat. Hist.*, 36 (3), 160, 168.

MEAD, M. (1940), 'The Mountain Arapesh. II: Supernaturalism', *Anthrop, Pap. Am. Mus. Nat. Hist.*, 37 (3), 344.

MEGGITT, M. (1964), 'Male–female relationships in the highlands of Australian New Guinea', *American Anthropologist*, vol. 66.

MIDDLETON, J. (1960), *Lugbara Religion*, London, International African Institute.

WILSON, M. (1957), *Rituals of Kinship Among the Nyakyusa*, London, Oxford University Press for International African Institute.

WOODBURN, J. (1964), 'Social organisation of the Hadza of North Tanganyika', Ph.D. thesis, University of Cambridge.

5

Heathen Darkness

In the nineteenth century the heathen was thought to be sunk in darkness. Now there is a widespread idea that primitive peoples are and always have been religious. Sometimes the religious form is thought to be highly magical. Sometimes it is supposed to be ecstatic. But it seems to be an important premise of popular thinking about us, the civilised, and them, the primitives, that we are secular, sceptical and frankly tending more and more away from religious belief, and that they are religious. No discipline can hope to keep control over the popular uses of its work. But every now and again its assumptions need to be checked, not so much for the sake of the general public, who will always do what they like, but for the sake of the discipline itself.

Anthropologists are the specialists who provide assumptions about primitive cultures. They should ask themselves how much longer they are prepared to underprop unthinkingly the popular notion of primitive piety. When we look more closely at our information we find plenty of secular savages. Indeed, in certain tribal places there is a notable lack of interest in the supernatural. God is not suddenly dead with western civilisation. Science has not delivered the *coup de grâce*. Anthropologists should really think twice before they subscribe to this particular fantasy about the difference between Us and Them.

In my childhood, Sunday school and the Catholic Truth Society had modified the earlier idea of heathenism. Primitive man was said to be religious in his own way. Just as ethologists nowadays seek to discover something about our basic human nature by studying other primates, so these teachers argued that

73

if primitive man is religious, this is proof that modern irreligion fails to meet the requirements of our nature.

The late Reverend Professor Wilhelm Schmidt developed an extreme form of this line of reasoning. Tribal religions, he admitted, are not exactly monotheistic, but they show signs of having lost an earlier revelation closer to that of primitive Christianity. Like comparative philology at the same period, he saw the work of comparative religion as an unravelling of clues about the parent stock from which religious beliefs had evolved. And he certainly thought that the outcome would be encouraging for Christians in general and missionaries in particular.

At a later stage of education, a shock awaited those brought up with primitive piety as a plank in the platform of their religious convictions. For it soon emerged that the very same idea was a plank in the counter-propaganda of rationalists. Frazer's *Golden Bough* suggested that the mere primitiveness of religious belief proves it is destined to be left behind on the march to civilisation, along with other relics of savagery. For anyone interested enough to turn to the specialists to resolve the question, a further surprise was in store.

Anthropologists of the last quarter of a century seemed all set to show that primitives are religious and that their beliefs have a positive role in sustaining their society. Indeed, so far was the Sunday-school approach vindicated and developed that doubts were aired about how modern industrial society could hold the moral commitment of its members without religious symbols and dogmas. Voltaire's proposition about God's existence took a new form: if true religion does not exist, we may have to invent one.

In this spirit, several rationalist anthropologists of that generation experimented hopefully with movements to establish godless churches. Now the more existentialist theologians themselves are playing with the idea of churchless religions. But still the basic idea that primitives are religious sustains both sides of the argument. No one has any axe to grind in unearthing infidels with no faith of their own. No one is going to bother to contradict the following statement under the heading 'Africa' in the illustrated encyclopedia of the supernatural, *Man, Myth and Magic*:

The African, surrounded from birth by all the wonders and terrors of nature, logically pays more heed to sun, rain, storms, rivers and animals than we do, as these objects are his immediate friends and enemies. From the dawn of time primitive man discovered objects of reverence and fear all round him. The former had to be thanked; the latter placated. This was the origin of all religious activity and remains the cardinal principle of African paganism. . . . Nature worship, then, is perhaps the most significant aspect of African paganism, and it is found in a hundred different forms throughout the continent.

In my opinion it is less accurate to say that most Africans are nature-worshippers than to say that most London journalists are Greek Orthodox.

Here the problem of definition arises. Any one definition of religion will apply to a number of examples. But no one definition of religion will apply to all tribal societies in such a way as to show them all to be religious. This has helped to cloud the issue. You can take your choice of definition, but everyone is convinced in advance of universal primitive religiousness, and if they all choose their own definitions, there is no debate.

Most anthropologists will follow Tylor in defining religion as a belief in spiritual beings. Durkheim rejected this as neither inclusive nor exclusive enough. It includes hobgoblins, poltergeists and fairies, excludes the theology of Buddhism, and still does not bring within its scope those aspects of religion considered central in the alternative definitions.

Belief in spirits, as a definition, would seem only to recommend itself to specialists mainly concerned with setting and marking precise examination questions. Some philosophers, such as T. H. Green, felt the essence of religion was its ethical meaning. Matthew Arnold added 'morality tinged with emotion'. Many theologians find the emotional aspect the dominant one, and follow Rudolph Otto in basing religion on a special kind of feeling, the sense of awe and terror in the face of the numinous.

Others reckon themselves to be religious without being sure that they have ever experienced this feeling. Others again, such as Peter Berger, try to combine the sense of sacred awe with the definition of religion as an all-embracing explanatory system.

Luckmann uses the comprehensiveness of the explanatory system as the critical distinction between religious and other beliefs which are only partial in their scope.

This last approach, which I find very serviceable, allows us to forget about subjective emotions and the fact that some religions have very little to say about spiritual beings, and that much of what is believed about spiritual beings has little to do with religion. The person without religion would be the person content to do without explanations of certain kinds, or content to behave in society without a single unifying principle validating the social order. Our original problem would be put more clearly if we were to ask whether tribal societies sustain their social reality by creating all-embracing universes of meaning, or whether there are not some which get along with partial systems of explanation, and large areas of experience left unexplained and unjustified.

The next question is to ask whether this last possibility is ever considered, and here we are up against the problem of evidence. What would be valid evidence strong enough to challenge such a deeply entrenched paradigm? To use paradigm (T. S. Kuhn's expression for a set of scientific assumptions based on a crucial well-established piece of research) relates this matter clearly to the history and philosophy of science, where I believe it is relevant.

In some intellectual atmospheres the negative case rates as a rich and exciting discovery. Researchers and funds are poured in to exploit its meaning. But just imagine the anthropologist who, fresh home from the field, announces: 'My tribe hasn't got any religion.' There ought to be a Bateman cartoon to illustrate the dropped spectacles and raised eyebrows and the sense of horrid solecism. No one has interest in the news except to pass a harsh verdict on the man's fieldwork.

Pity the poor anthropologist who expected his fieldwork to yield the usual interesting information on ritual symbolism. If he comes home without it, his monograph will lack its crowning chapter. Knowing this only too well while he is in the field, he works towards a nervous collapse or an angry showdown with his hosts, whom he suspects of holding out on him. How can he be sure that his fieldwork is not at fault, or that their disinclination to reveal their religion is not due to secretiveness or deep reserve?

Will it be a matter of time? Madame Dieterlen said the Dogon only opened up after seven years of intense inquiry and that it took twenty years to get the full story.

If the anthropologist is in a hurry with his career, he cannot be blamed for turning to another problem, land tenure or politics. On this he soon becomes so much an expert that he never has time again to research into primitive religion. Thus unintentionally is a professional bias established. And thus is an interesting subject rendered sterile.

Let me here give a few examples which have actually been published. First, for the supposed inherent relation between religion and morality: there are primitives who can be religious without being moral and moral without being religious. Ralph Barton described a thoroughly mercenary, unscrupulous, unspiritual set of dealings between gods and men among the Ifugao of the Philippines. In their everyday life the Ifugao regard power of any sort as an opportunity for extortion, and the same ideas about bribery and corruption appear in their ideas of the supernatural world. When I first read this, as a student of anthropology, I rejected Barton as a superficial, ignorant, even prejudiced observer. But to sustain this judgment would entail drawing an arbitrary line between this and his highly perceptive observation of every other aspect of these people's lives. He was a brilliant fieldworker.

Fredrik Barth gives an account of a tribe of Persian nomads who are so lacking in religious feeling that any priest in a smart London parish would find his own congregation fervent by comparison. These Basseri nomads are nominal Moslems. They see themselves as slack in the practice of their religion, generally uninterested in religion as preached by occasional mullahs and quite indifferent to metaphysical problems. Though they neglect Moslem prayers, they use the Moslem calendar like an *Old Moore's Almanac*, as an index of future good or bad luck, and the extent of their respect for Friday observance is to fear bad luck if they should drive a herd on that day of the week.

Barth illustrates my general point in another way. He is obviously very worried about the possible judgment on the quality of his fieldwork that this missing chapter on ritual symbols may provoke. So he writes a detailed appendix in order to provide

77

evidence of the thoroughness of his investigation and the sensitivity of his awareness.

It could be argued, along Father Schmidt's lines, that these tribes have been converted away from their original beliefs by Moslem missionaries. Somewhere in their primitive past they may have had their own rich system of religious beliefs. Their present state is a result of the march of civilisation – in other words, we can get bogged down in a quibble about the word 'primitive', if we are really determined not to open up the subject.

All right, then: what about Godfrey Lienhardt's report that the Anuak, in the heart of the Sudan, pay little or no cult to their god? Their only ritual practitioner is a witch finder, their main concern to protect themselves from vengeful ghosts and malicious witches. Here the editor of *Man, Myth and Magic* would point out that I have omitted the definition of religion which would obviously include witchcraft and magic. As editor, Richard Cavendish writes in his introduction that 'Supernatural is a convenient word for a huge area of human speculation about things believed to exist beyond the threshold of our ordinary everyday existence, our normal trudging journey from birth to death.'

But most tribal societies which believe in ancestral ghosts and magic spells regard them as part of their ordinary day to day existence. Philosophers would be taxed to identify the supernatural in other cultures which do not make our traditional set of distinctions enclosing the concept of the natural.

If the definition of religion were to be based on magic beliefs and if these are defined, as surely they must be, as belief in the efficacy of symbol, hardly a doctor in general practice, still less in specialist consultation, would escape the title of magician. It would be hard to argue that religious faith is strong in a people who only believe that their enemies are using magic techniques against them, and that their experts have counter-remedies.

Magic spells may be part of an all-embracing system of explanation. Or they may often be a technology, recipes for success, empirically tried and rejected when they fail. This is how the Garia of Madang District on the north coast of New Guinea use their magic spells, with a thoroughly modern-sounding pragmatism. Peter Lawrence says there is no moral feedback in their cosmological system, no reward for virtue or punishment for wrong.

He writes, with a little note of surprise, that for them

spiritual values such as purity and sin were non-existent. There was no idea of rewards in the next world in return for good works or of separate destinations for 'good' and 'bad'. The affairs of the dead automatically regulated themselves. Even the initiatory taboos had no abstract ethical meaning . . . spatially the cosmos was conceived as a unified physical realm with virtually no supernatural attributes, in which human beings reacted not only with each other but also with deities, spirits and totems.

He goes on to describe their culture as one which glorifies personal success and where the only offence is that of failure.

Once the question has reached the surface of our attention, the credibility of these reports is obvious. Dozens of other reports of secular-minded primitives must be checked, odd conversations and unpublished memoirs. Missionaries who claim that their converts formerly lacked religious faith need not be suspected for that mere reason of less reliable knowledge than those who respect the faiths they seek to overthrow. If it be accepted that tribal societies display as much variety as we in their religious propensities, the really interesting questions arise.

It is hard to accept the full implications. For one, we must question the assumption that tribal religions are static and hidebound. The variety implies fluidity. At the professional level this poses tricky questions of interpretation for anthropologists. They cannot suppose that tribal social structures have not been developing, simplifying, growing more complex in one direction or another, switching between formality and informality as migrations and changes of dynasty involve other changes. Since the anthropologists expect to find some degree of fit between religious beliefs and the institutions they sustain, they are committed to supposing religious revolutions have been continually taking place. So the tension between ritualism of established authority and enthusiasm from the outlying borders of society, the dynamic of religious reform in European history, must have its counterpart in the unwritten history of any primitive tribe.

They, too, will have had their protestant ethic, their shakers and quakers and anti-sacerdotal movements. They will also have had their periods of scepticism and secularism. Why not? A modern study of comparative religion must do away equally with the notion of the global primitive and with the notion of the fixity of tribal beliefs.

In *The Secular City*, Harvey Cox makes the claim that the ancient Israelites were the first to secularise their religion. By 'secularise' he understands the detachment of God from nature, a de-localising of holiness from particular persons, things and places, bring God into history. A secular God is as mobile and all pervasive as the wandering people He had chosen. This view, subtly argued, is used to justify a new de-sacralisation of holy places and things in the modern city, where man is as mobile as any nomad.

But the message of my argument is less reassuring for the success of new interpretations of Christian belief. I would argue that there are different kinds of mobility and that different theological trends go with them. For the unattached, competitive individualism of modern industrial man the parallel is not the highly structured Israelite tribe in the desert. Each tribe moved as a unit and belonged in a clear overall pattern including them all. Modern mobility is far more obviously like the competitive individualism of some New Guinea tribes and some Persian nomads.

And the religious tendencies of these latter peoples are secular in a very common sense of the word: they are not interested in metaphysical speculation or union with the source of all being. You can sell them formulas for achieving personal success or warding off bad luck. But that is not the end of it for the comparison with primitive forms of piety.

Just as tribes are mobile in different ways, so are we. Our kinds of mobility are vastly various. The upward and outward movement of the young executive who leaves his local suburb and travels in ever-widening circles on international airlines is utterly different from the rootless and unattached mobility of the urban proletariat. A serious comparative religion would identify counterparts in this dimension of social relations and go on to classify forms of piety and impiety.

Here we are, in a period in which popular interest in religion is as lively as it has ever been. There is not only interest in occult-

ism, but frank enjoyment of symbolic forms as such. The Missa
Luba provide the background music to *If*; the middle act of
The Silver Tassie at the Aldwych was impressively rendered in
plain chant; *Easy Rider* combines sex movingly with rosary and
requiem in a New Orleans cemetery; Andy Warhol mixes a well-
intoned Kyrie with naked seduction in *Lonesome Cowboys*. The
Bread and Puppets Theatre and mystery plays of summer 1969
drew more seriously on religious symbols.

Anthropologists, worrying about how to attract research funds,
may not be necessarily right in assuming that every project has
to show some pay-off in the field of economic development. They
are in the same case as Catholic theologians who try to justify
religion by its role in the war on poverty and dare not suppose
that a certain expertise in symbolic matters will have its own pay-
off. If anthropologists are to learn from this popular, half-
conscious cogitation on the symbolic life, this regurgitation, both
mocking and wistful, of the symbols of the Christian heritage,
their first step must be to ditch the myth of the pious primitive.

Then, questions smothered by the heavy hand of functional-
ism could be revived again. Inevitably most fieldwork will
suddenly become out of date. If it has been asking questions and
setting up taxonomies that have nothing to do with ourselves, it
is probably due for overhaul anyway.

A silence lies between anthropology and the history of religion.
The first asserts that religious systems sustain social structures
and that social structures sustain beliefs. Historians, if they want
to apply these notions, ask what kind of social structures go with
what kinds of religious ideas. The anthropologist can start to
answer in terms of local and esoteric typologies. There are classifications of ancestor cults, nativistic movements or witchcraft
beliefs. But so far we lack a way of relating our materials to the
European experience. Unless we can think of tribes as secular, or
given to mystery cults, dualist philosophies, or heterodoxies
about the nature of grace and godhead, the questions that have
unleashed historic wars and mass executions, we have hardly
begun the anthropology of religion.

Bibliography

BARTH, F. (1964), *Nomads of South Persia: the Basseri Tribe of the
    Khamseh Confederacy*, London, Allen & Unwin.

BARTON, R. (1946), 'The religion of the Ifugaos', *American Anthropologist, 48*, 4.

BERGER, P. L. (1969), *The Social Reality of Religion*, London, Faber.

COX, H. (1965), *The Secular City*, Harmondsworth, Penguin.

KUHN, T. S. (1962), *The Structure of Scientific Revolutions*, University of Chicago Press.

LAWRENCE, P. (1964), *Road Belong Cargo: a Study of the Cargo Movement in South Madang District, New Guinea*, Manchester University Press.

LIENHARDT, G. (1962), 'The situation of death: an aspect of Anuak philosophy', *Anthropological Quarterly, 35*, 2.

6

Do Dogs Laugh?
A Cross-cultural Approach to Body Symbolism

The body, as a vehicle of communication, is misunderstood if it is treated as a signal box, a static framework emitting and receiving strictly coded messages. The body communicates information for and from the social system in which it is a part. It should be seen as mediating the social situation in at least three ways. It is itself the field in which a feedback interaction takes place. It is itself available to be given as the proper tender for some of the exchanges which constitute the social situation. And further, it mediates the social structure by itself becoming its image. Some of this I discussed in the *Journal of Psychosomatic Research* (Douglas, 1968a) and in *Purity and Danger* (Douglas, 1966). To adapt the signal box metaphor to show the full involvement of the body in communication we should have to imagine a signal box which folds down and straightens up, shakes, dances, goes into a frenzy or stiffens to the tune of the more precise messages its lights and signal arms are transmitting. This paper is offered as a background to those others in this conference which treat of specialised signalling systems such as the voice and the face. It is above all offered as a preface to Professor Jenner's discussion of *endogenous* factors. I will suggest a parallel set of social factors *exogenous* to the biological organism, feedback pathways which control the rhythm of social interaction.

A young zoologist who asked my advice about a study he was making of laughter in human and non-human species, complained that sociologists had given him very little help. Indeed it is very difficult for us to produce a theory or even a vague hypothesis on the subject. My own idea on the body's role in joke

83

symbolism is not easily adapted to an experimental approach to laughter (Douglas, 1968b). We know that some tribes are said to be dour and unlaughing. Others laugh easily. Pygmies lie on the ground and kick their legs in the air, panting and shaking in paroxysms of laughter (Turnbull, 1961). Francis Huxley noted the same bodily abandonment to convulsions of gaiety in Haiti (Huxley, 1966). But we have nothing to say about these differences that could help the zoologist. It is just as difficult for us to suppose that laughter in different tribes means the same thing, as to be sure that animals are laughing when they grin and splutter.

Bergson (1900) declared that laughter is the unique prerogative of humans. However, we have it from a biologist that dogs laugh as they play. Lorenz in *Man Meets Dog* (1954) describes the case:

> an invitation to play always follows; here the slightly opened jaws which reveal the tongue, and the tilted angle of the mouth which stretches almost from ear to ear give a still stronger impression of laughing. This 'laughing' is most often seen in dogs playing with an adored master and which become so excited that they soon start panting.

He suggests that the same facial expression marks the beginning of erotic excitement.

Here is a description of the beloved master playing with his dog. Thomas Mann (1961) describes ways of rousing and stimulating his dog.

> Or we amuse ourselves, I by tapping him on the nose, and he, by snapping at my hand as though it were a fly. It makes us both laugh. Yes. Bashan has to laugh too; and as I laugh I marvel at the sight, to me the oddest and most touching thing in the world. It is moving to see how under my teasing his thin animal cheeks and the corners of his mouth will twitch, and over his dark animal mask will pass an expression like a human smile.

The play produces in the dog 'a state of ecstasy, a sort of intoxication with his own identity so that he begins to whirl around on himself and send up loud exultant barks'. Both accounts take the laugh to be essentially a facial expression, but both, being good observers, note the panting, the more generally visible excite-

ment or ecstasy. I shall return to these two useful clues to the
nature of laughter. First, it is a process which begins in a small
way, observable on the face, and is capable of ending in involving
the whole body. Second, it is normally a social response; private
laughing is a special case. Here I should set out my assumptions
about a systematic approach to the body as a channel of communication. The upshot will be to throw doubt on the attempt to
isolate a complex such as laughter, or indeed facial expression,
for comparative study.

I see the relation of the spoken word to non-verbal communication as analogous to the relation between written word and the
physical materials and visible manner of its presentation. Cali-
fornian sociologists are paying attention now to the unspoken
part of any discourse, its reliance on shared, implicit assumptions
(Garfinkel, 1967). In the same way, a written document communicates through a physical, metaphysical and social dimension. The typography, arrangement of footnotes, layout of
margins and headings, acknowledgments, all witness to a set of
implicit meanings about the realm of discourse it belongs in. Its
physical embodiment indicates a social sphere to which it is
directed. In the same way, the body comes into play to support
the meanings of a spoken communication. Posture, voice, speed,
articulation, tonality, all contribute to the meaning. The words
alone mean very little. Verbal symbols depend on the speaker
manipulating his whole environment to get the meaning across.
We have to make a special effort if we wish to consider the
meanings conveyed by the typography of a literary text in isolation from the verbal message. The whole trend of our education has been the other way. We now realise that we have
unduly privileged the verbal channel and tended to suppose it
could be effective in disembodied form. In the same way we
should now make an effort to think of the body as a medium in
its own right, distinct from the words issuing from the mouth.
Speech has been over-emphasised as the privileged means of
human communication, and the body neglected. It is time to
rectify this neglect and to become aware of the body as the
physical channel of meaning.

My first assumption is that normally the physical channel
supports and agrees with the spoken one. The case in which the
channels contradict one another is a special one, for conveying

the special meanings of banter, irony, mistrust, etc. I have discussed this general concordance between channels of communication in *Natural Symbols* (1970). My second assumption follows: that conscious and unconscious bodily expressions need not be distinguished, since both exhibit the same tendency to reinforce speech. The degree of consciousness can be ignored. My third assumption is based on observation. The body is not always under perfect control. A screening process divests uncontrolled noises of meaning. The small hiccups, sneezes, heavy breathing and throat clearings can and must be screened out as irrelevant noise, not to be treated as part of the bodily channel's message. There are limits of tolerance. Once the limit is passed, the discourse has to be stopped. A prolonged sneezing fit or other uncontrolled bodily movement forces the owner of the interrupting machine to withdraw if the noises cannot be framed with an apology. I would like to ask the zoologists whether animals screen off bodily interruptions or whether Bergson should have selected this capacity to ignore them, rather than laughter, as the distinctively human accomplishment.

The fourth assumption is that there is a cross-cultural, universal language of bodily interruptions. Instead of being ignored, they can be deliberately brought back artificially into the discourse to convey well understood messages based on a hierarchy of bodily orifices. Back and lower orifices rank below frontal and upper. A development of Freudian symbolism to the social dimension fits the meanings in a quite straightforward way (Hallpike, 1969). Fifth, here we come to the crux of the matter. Laughter, though not controlled any more than any other upper/front eruptions such as coughing or breaking wind, is not screened off and ignored. Laughter is a unique bodily eruption which is always taken to be a communication. I suggest that this is because a laugh is a culmination of a series of bodily communications which have had to be interpreted in the usual way as part of the discourse. The finally erupting laugh cannot be screened off because all the changes in bodily posture preceding it have been taken as part of the dialogue.

If this approach can be developed it will give a sociological perspective to those working on the study of facial signals. At this stage my provisional answer to the young zoologist asking for guidance in the sociology of laughter is this. Laughter is too complex a process; at the same time it is too narrowly defined for identification. It would be better to start by considering the exogenous social factors which govern the thresholds of tolerance of bodily relaxation and control. These thresholds are set socially. In some social situations it is proper to take cognisance fully of bodily eruptions as part of the symbolising of familiarity and relaxation, in others the thresholds are lowered in response to the need to express formality and social distance.

If we ask of any form of communication the simple question, What is being communicated?, the answer is: information from the social system. The exchanges which are being communicated constitute the social system. Let us assume a sensitive feedback between all the parties to the social exchange. The body is expressing both the social situation at a given moment, and also a particular contribution to that situation. Inevitably, then, since the body is mediating the relevant social structure, it does the work of communicating by becoming an image of the total social situation as perceived, and the acceptable tender in the exchanges which constitute it. The possibilities of change and development arise in the first instance in the spontaneous bodily responses, precisely because they are treated as modifying messages by those who receive them. The uncontrolled frown or giggle can effectively rechannel all subsequent exchanges into a different set of pathways.

In its role as an image of society, the body's main scope is to express the relation of the individual to the group. This it does along the dimension from strong to weak control, according to whether the social demands are strong, weak, acceptable or not. From total relaxation to total self-control the body has a wide gamut for expressing this social variable.

What does it mean when one tribe laughs a lot and another tribe rarely? I would argue that it means that the level of social tensions has set low or high thresholds for bodily control. In the first case, the full range of the body's power of expression is more readily available to respond fully to a small stimulus. If the general social control settings are slack, the thresholds of tolerance of bodily interruption will be set higher. Comparisons of laughter should take account of the load of social meaning which the body has to carry. Where we seek to compare laughter, we should compare also the pressure on the individual from the social structure. The two cases of the Pygmies and the Haitians cited above are instructive. The first, living in the equatorial Congo forest, sparse and freely mobile, are free from obvious social pressure. The second were admittedly part of a modern police state which was at a low level of economic development. The people whom Francis Huxley studied in Haiti were haphazard in their means of livelihood and their obligations to one another were tenuous and short-lived. Both peoples seemed to use the full bodily range of expression for grief and joy. In *Natural Symbols* I have said more about the significance of such variations in the strength and permanence of social relations for bodily expression.

Another aspect of social organisation which is likely to be expressed in bodily symbolism is the length and complexity of messages. Social systems which vary on this point will have corresponding variations in the amount of pause that can be tolerated in the process of verbal communication. An important experiment on hesitation phenomena was reported by Professor Bernstein (1962). The speech of middle-class and working-class boys was timed. It was found that cutting across measured differences of intelligence, the middle-class boys were more tolerant of long pauses in the discourse. Bernstein argued that the hesitation phenomenon reflected an expectation on their part that speech was subject to a complex and therefore slow process of programming. I would like to see this experiment repeated and developed as a valuable clue to understanding non-verbal symbolic behaviour. I would also like to see something comparable devised for primates of like intelligence and different social organisation. For example, when full studies are made of savannah chimpanzees, the comparison with forest chimpanzees along the lines indicated here would be interesting. Since their social organisation would be likely to be more rigidly hierarchised in the savannah, we would predict more strictly defined and less variable responses, more control, longer pauses – less 'laughing'.

Note

I acknowledge here my thanks to Dr Robert Martin for his discussion of this chapter and his suggestion of how the question could be treated experimentally with chimpanzees.

Bibliography

BERGSON, H. (1900), *Le Rire: essai sur la signification du comique*, Paris, Presses Universitaires de France.

BERNSTEIN, B. (1962), 'Linguistic codes, hesitation phenomena and intelligence', *Language and Speech*, 5, 1, 31–46.

DOUGLAS, M. (1966), *Purity and Danger: an Analysis of Concepts of Pollution and Taboo*, London, Routledge & Kegan Paul.

DOUGLAS, M. (1968a), 'The relevance of tribal studies', *J. Psychosom. Res.*, *1*, 12.

DOUGLAS, M. (1968b), 'The social control of cognition: some factors in joke perception', *Man. J. Roy. Anthrop. Inst.*, *3*, 3, 361–76.

DOUGLAS, M. (1970), *Natural Symbols, Explorations in Cosmology*, London, Barrie & Rockliff.

GARFINKEL, H. (1967), *Studies in Ethnomethodology*, New Jersey, Prentice-Hall.

HALLPIKE, C. R. (1969, 'Social hair', *Man. J. Roy. Anthrop. Inst.*, *4*, 2, 256–64.

HUXLEY, F. (1966), *The Invisibles*, London, Hart-Davies.

LORENZ, K. (1954), *Man Meets Dog*, London, Methuen.

MANN, T. (1961), 'A man and his dog' in *Stories of a Lifetime*, London, Secker & Warburg.

TURNBULL, C. M. (1961), *The Forest People*, London, Chatto & Windus.

7

Jokes

Anthropologists tend to approach ritual joking from scratch, with merely an introspective glance at the cases in which they themselves feel impelled to joke. Consequently they have treated joking rituals as if they arise spontaneously from social situations and as if the anthropologist's sole task is to classify the relations involved. The jokes have not been considered as jokes in themselves, nor has our own cultural tradition been applied to interpreting the joke situation. Certain new trends invite us now to make a more open approach. Anthropology has moved from the simple analysis of social structures current in the 1940s to the structural analysis of thought systems. One of the central problems now is the relation between categories of thought and categories of social experience. Joking as one mode of expression has yet to be interpreted in its total relation to other modes of expression.

Such an approach suggests that the alternatives of joking and of not joking would be susceptible to the kind of structural analysis which Leach (1961: 23) has applied to controlled and uncontrolled modes of mystical power. His original model for this was the linguistic patterning of voiced and unvoiced consonants; his sole concern to show that the contrasts were used in regular patterns. It was not relevant to his argument to ask whether the patterning of contrasted elements in the system of communication was arbitrary or not. But it is possible that the patterning of articulate and less articulate sounds corresponds to a similar patterning in the experiences which they are used to express. This question raises the general problem of the relation between symbolic systems and experience. It is true that in language the process of symbolic differentiation may start with arbitrarily selected elements at the simple phonemic level and combine them into consistent patterns. But at more complex levels each sign carries into the patterning an ever richer load of association. To return to Leach's case of modes of mystical power, I have elsewhere argued (Douglas, 1966: 101–3) that the discrimination of articulate and inarticulate forms of mystical power is not arbitrary. The use of spell and rite is attributed to people occupying articulate areas of the social structure, the use of unconscious psychic powers to others in inarticulate areas. There is a play upon articulateness and its absence, both in the kinds of mystic power being wielded and in the areas of the social structure to which they are allocated. The same appropriateness of symbolic forms to the situations they express can be illustrated with ritual joking. I am confident that where the joke rite is highly elaborated, joking is not used merely diacritically to contrast with seriousness, but that the full human experience of the joke is exploited. If we could be clear about the nature of joking, we could approach the interpretation of the joke rite at a more profound level than hitherto.

Fortunately, a new, more general trend enables this generation to make a fresh approach to joke rites. At the turn of the century when European thought turned an analytic eye upon humour, anthropologists were either antiquarians or specialists, or both. It would not have been in the tradition to look to recent thinkers for illumination. When Radcliffe-Brown wrote on joking relations in the 1940s (Radcliffe-Brown, 1940: 1949) it was still natural that he should not have taken account of Bergson or Freud. Still less would he have turned to the surrealist movement, whose passionate frivolity would estrange one who wished above all to establish the scientific status of his subject. He therefore wrote on the subject of joking in a very desiccated perspective. But there is a great difference in the form in which Freud's ideas are now available to the ordinary public. For us, thanks largely to the surrealists, it is not possible to read new fiction, to go to the theatre, to read the catalogue of any exhibition of painting or sculpture without taking note of an attitude which derives from the thinkers of the beginning of this century. Awareness of the contrast between form and formlessness, and awareness of the subjective character of the categories in which experience is structured have become the cultural premisses of our age. They are no longer erudite pre-occupations of the learned, but get expressed at an entirely popular level. Continual experimentation with form has given us now an intuitive sympathy for symbolic behaviour which is, after all, a play upon form. What is implicit in some other cultures has become an implicit part of our own. At the same time we can also bring to bear a tradition of explicit analysis. Thus we can have insights at the two levels necessary for understanding joking.

African joking institutions combine the following elements: first, a crude scatology; second, a range of specific relationships; and third, certain ritual occasions (namely funerals and purifications) expressed scatologically. The subject is therefore closely related to ritual pollution in general. I myself am drawn to it because I hope that it will prove possible to distinguish jokes from pollutions by analysing some aspects of humour. This is a task which I shirked in my essay on ritual pollution (1966).

As a key question in this exercise I take Griaule's controversy with Radcliffe-Brown about the whole status of so-called 'joking relationships'. According to Griaule (1948), the Dogon joking partners do not exchange witticisms but rather gross insults. Although Dogon find these exchanges very hilarious, Griaule found it arbitrary to fasten on the laughter-provoking aspect of a complex institution. Now what is the difference between an insult and a joke? When does a joke get beyond a joke? Is the perception of a joke culturally determined so that the anthropologist must take it on trust when a joke has been made? Is no general culture-free analysis of joking possible? When people throw excrement at one another whenever they meet, either verbally or actually, can this be interpreted as a case of wit, or merely written down as a case of throwing excrement? This is the central problem of all interpretation.

First, let me bracket aside the whole subject of laughter. It would be wrong to suppose that the acid test of a joke is whether it provokes laughter or not. It is not necessary to go into the physiology and psychology of laughter, since it is generally recognised that one can appreciate a joke without actually laughing, and one can laugh for other reasons than from having perceived a joke. As the two experiences are not completely congruent, I shall only touch on laughter incidentally. Here I am following Bergson, whose essay on laughter was first published in 1899 in the *Revue de Paris*, and Freud (1916), whose analysis of wit, first published in 1905, says very little about laughter.

Both Bergson and Freud assume that it is possible to identify a structure of ideas characteristic of humour. If this were a valid assumption, all that would be necessary here would be to identify this joke form in the African joke rite. But in practice, it is a very elusive form to nail down. We face the dilemma either of finding that all utterances are capable of being jokes, or that many of those which pass for jokes in Africa do not conform to the laid-down requirements. My argument will be that the joke form rarely lies in the utterance alone, but that it can be identified in the total social situation.

Bergson and Freud are in fact very close: the difference between them lies in the different place of joke analysis in their respective philosophies. Bergson's reflections on laughter are a distillation of his general philosophy on the nature of man. He takes humour as a field in which to demonstrate the superiority of intuition to logic, of life to mechanism. It is part of his general protest against the threatened mechanisation of humanity. According to Bergson the essence of man is spontaneity and freedom: laughter asserts this by erupting whenever a man behaves in a rigid way, like an automaton no longer under intelligent control. 'Humour consists in perceiving something mechanical encrusted on something living' (1950: 29). It is funny when persons behave as if they were inanimate things. So a person caught in a repetitive routine, such as stammering or dancing after the music has stopped, is funny. Frozen posture, too rigid dignity, irrelevant mannerism, the noble pose interrupted by urgent physical needs, all are funny for the same reason. Humour chastises insincerity, pomposity, stupidity.

This analysis is adequate for a vast number of funny situations and jokes. There is no denying that it covers the style of much African joking, the grotesque tricks of Lodagaba funeral partners (Goody, 1962) and the obscene insults of Dogon and Bozo joking partners (Griaule, 1948). But I find it inadequate for two reasons. First, it imports a moral judgment into the analysis. For Bergson the joke is always a chastisement: something 'bad', mechanical, rigid, encrusted is attacked by something 'good', spontaneous, instinctive. I am not convinced either that there is any moral judgment, nor that if there is one, it always works in this direction. Second, Bergson includes too much. It is not always humorous to recognise 'something encrusted on something living': it is more usually sinister, as the whole trend of Bergson's philosophy asserts. Bergson's approach to humour does not allow for punning nor for the more complex forms of wit in which two forms of life are confronted without judgment being passed on either. For example, Bemba joking partners (Richards, 1937) exchange elaborate references to the relationship between their clan totems; members of the Crocodile clan, for instance, point out to members of the Fish clan that fishes are food for crocodiles, but the latter riposte that crocodiles are therefore dependent on fishes. These are jokes which allegorise the political interdependence of the clans.

If we leave Bergson and turn to Freud, the essence of wit is neatly to span gulfs between different ideas. The pleasure of a joke lies in a kind of economy. At all times we are expending energy in monitoring our subconscious so as to ensure that our conscious perceptions come through a filtering control. The joke, because it breaks down the control, gives the monitoring system a holiday. Or, as Freud puts it, since monitoring costs effort, there is a saving in psychic expenditure. For a moment the unconscious is allowed to bubble up without restraint, hence the sense of enjoyment and freedom.

The late Anton Ehrenzweig (1953) extended the Freudian analysis of wit to aesthetic pleasure. In appreciating a work of art there is a perception of form, and underlying the articulate or dominant form there are other submerged forms half-perceived. These are inarticulate areas, sub-patternings or reversals of the main theme. Ehrenzweig argues that the perception of inarticulate forms is itself a direct source of pleasure. The inarticulate forms are experienced as an image of the subconscious. As they are perceived there is a release of energy, for they allow the subconscious itself to be expressed. Aesthetic pleasure would then have this in common with the joy of a joke; something is saved in psychic effort, something which might have been repressed has been allowed to appear, a new improbable form of life has been glimpsed. For Bergson it is lifeless encrustation which is attacked in the joke, for Freud the joke lies in the

release from control. If I may sum up the differences of emphasis
between Bergson and Freud I would suggest that for Bergson the
man who slips on a banana peel would be funny because he has
lost his bodily control and so becomes a helpless automaton: for
Freud this man would be funny because his stiff body has for two
seconds moved with the swiftness of a gazelle, as if a new form of
life had been hidden there. In short, they have a common
approach which Freud uses more abstractly and flexibly. For
both the essence of the joke is that something formal is attacked
by something informal, something organised and controlled, by
something vital, energetic, an upsurge of life for Bergson, of
libido for Freud. The common denominator underlying both
approaches is the joke seen as an attack on control.

Here we can see why scatology is potentially funny. Take any
pun or funny story: it offers alternative patterns, one apparent,
one hidden: the latter, by being brought to the surface impugns
the validity of the first. Bergson said: 'Est comique tout incident
qui appelle notre attention sur le physique d'une personne alors
que le moral est en cause' (1950: 391). Reference to the physical
pattern of events takes the dignity out of the moral pattern, yes.
But this is not all. The symbols are not necessarily loaded the
same way. Freud's approach is more complex because it allows
that the relation of physical and moral could equally well be the
other way round. What is crucial is that one accepted pattern is
confronted by something else.

All jokes have this subversive effect on the dominant structure
of ideas. Those which bring forward the physiological exigencies
to which moral beings are subject, are using one universal, never-
failing technique of subversion. But it would be a great mistake
to think that humour can be reduced to scatology. Beidelman
(1966) seems to do this, I think unintentionally, when he reduces
Kaguru joking relations to cosmological ideas about dirt and sex.
Structural analysis does not work by reducing all symbols to one
or two of their number; rather, it requires an abstract statement
of the patterned relations of all the symbols to one another. The
same applies to moral bias. It may be incidentally worked into
the structure of many jokes, but it is not the essence of joking.
Compare the *Comedy of Errors* with *Le Jeu de l'amour et du
hazard*. In the latter, Beaumarchais makes the girl of noble birth
pretend to be her own handmaid so as to spy on her suitor; he

adopts the same trick to observe her unrecognised. The joke lies in the ridiculous display of valet and handmaid disguised as lord and lady. In Bergson's terms the essence of the joke is that 'something living', natural nobility, triumphs over 'something encrusted', false imitation of breeding. Shakespeare, on the other hand, does not moralise when he successfully entangles the separate worlds of twin brothers and their twin servants and disengages them at the end. His is no less a comedy for all that the social messages are weaker.

By this stage we seem to have a formula for identifying jokes. A joke is a play upon form. It brings into relation disparate elements in such a way that one accepted pattern is challenged by the appearance of another which in some way was hidden in the first. I confess that I find Freud's definition of the joke highly satisfactory. The joke is an image of the relaxation of conscious control in favour of the subconscious. For the rest of this article I shall be assuming that any recognisable joke falls into this joke pattern which needs two elements, the juxtaposition of a control against that which is controlled, this juxtaposition being such that the latter triumphs. Needless to say, a successful subversion of one form by another completes or ends the joke, for it changes the balance of power. It is implicit in the Freudian model that the unconscious does not take over the control system. The wise sayings of lunatics, talking animals, children and drunkards are funny because they are not in control; otherwise they would not be an image of the subconscious. The joke merely affords opportunity for realising that an accepted pattern has no necessity. Its excitement lies in the suggestion that any particular ordering of experience may be arbitrary and subjective. It is frivolous in that it produces no real alternative, only an exhilarating sense of freedom from form in general.

Social Control of Perception

While hailing this joke pattern as authentic, it is a very different matter to use it for identifying jokes. First we should distinguish standardised jokes, which are set in a conventional context, from spontaneous jokes. Freud's claim to have found the same joke pattern in all joking situations hides an important shift in levels of analysis. The standard joke, starting for instance with 'Have you heard this one?' or 'There were three men, an Irishman, etc.', contains the whole joke pattern within its verbal form. So does the pun. The joke pattern can easily be identified within the verbal form of standard jokes and puns. But the spontaneous joke organises the total situation in its joke pattern. Thus we get into difficulties in trying to recognise the essence of a spontaneous joke if we only have the utterance or the gesture and not the full pattern of relationships. If the Kaguru think it witty to throw excrement at certain cousins or the Lodagaba to dance grotesquely at funerals or the Dogon to refer to the parents' sexual organs when they meet a friend, then to recognise the joke that sends all present into huge enjoyment we need not retreat into cultural relativism and give up a claim to interpret. The problem has merely shifted to the relation between joking and the social structure.

The social dimension enters at all levels into the perception of a joke. Even its typical patterning depends on a social valuation of the elements. A twentieth-century audience finds the Beaumarchais comedy weak because it one-sidedly presents the aristocrats' manners as live and their servants' manners as lifeless imitations. But to an eighteenth-century audience of French aristocrats any dramatist presenting both lords and commoners as equally lively in their own right would have had, not a comedy, but a theme of social reform to tempt only a Bernard Shaw in his most tendentious vein. In every period there is a pile of submerged jokes, unperceived because they are irrelevant or wrongly balanced for the perspective of the day. Here let me try to save the definition of the joke pattern from the charge that it does not include modern forms of humour, such as the shaggy dog story or the sick joke. The shaggy dog is only told in a society which has been satiated with joke stories. The joke of the tale that goes on in a declining spiral to a nadir of pointlessness lies in the dashed expectations of the listeners: the humour is not in the verbal utterances but in the total situation in which it is a practical joke. The sick joke expresses a parallel sophistication in joke forms. It plays with a reversal of the values of social life; the hearer is left uncertain which is the man and which the machine, who is the good and who the bad, or where is the legitimate pattern of control. There is no need to labour the point that such a joke form relates to a particular kind of social experience and could not be perceived by those who have not been exposed to a thoroughgoing relativising of moral values.

So much for the social control of perception. As to the permitting of a joke, there are jokes which can be perceived clearly enough by all present but which are rejected at once. Here again the social dimension is at work. Social requirements may judge a joke to be in bad taste, risky, too near the bone, improper, or irrelevant. Such controls are exerted either on behalf of hierarchy as such, or on behalf of values which are judged too precious and too precarious to be exposed to challenge. Whatever the joke, however remote its subject, the telling of it is potentially subversive. Since its form consists of a victorious tilting of uncontrol against control, it is an image of the levelling of hierarchy, the triumph of intimacy over formality, of unofficial values over official ones. Our question is now much clearer. We must ask what are the social conditions for a joke to be both perceived and permitted. We could start to answer it by examining the literature of various joking situations. My hypothesis is that a joke is seen and allowed when it offers a symbolic pattern of a social pattern occurring at the same time. As I see it, all jokes are expressive of the social situations in which they occur. The one social condition necessary for a joke to be enjoyed is that the social group in which it is received should develop the formal characteristics of a 'told' joke: that is, a dominant pattern of relations is challenged by another. If there is no joke in the social structure, no other joking can appear.

Take as an example Fredrik Barth's (1966) analysis of the social situation on board a Norwegian fishing boat. Here the skipper is in full charge of the crew until the boats are lowered into the water. Then the net boss takes over. Before that point the net boss is not subject to the skipper as are other crew members. He is there on the boat, nominally under the skipper, but potentially a source of authority which will supplant the skipper for a brief period. There is in this social pattern the perfect joke form. All the time that the skipper and the other members of the crew are busily expressing superordination and subordination within the frame of common commitment to the enterprise, the net boss expresses his detachment and individuality by witty sallies. As soon as he takes over responsibility, however, his joking stops short. The essential point is that the joking by the net boss expresses a pattern of authority which arises out of the technicalities of fishing: it does nothing to create the situation, it merely expresses it.

Take as a second example the rather unexpected story about laughter in the beginning of The *Iliad*. At first sight the social situation seems to be all wrong, if my account of a proper joke form is accepted. Thersites, a common soldier, insults the Greek leaders; Odysseus strikes him brutally with a metal studded rod; Thersites is crushed and the troops have a hearty laugh at his expense. On this showing there seems to be no joke to provoke the laughter, for the Greek leaders represent the dominant elements in the social structure. Odysseus's act merely asserts their authority. But this would be to take the story out of context. The Greek leaders' plan to mount a new attack on Troy is about to be thwarted by their men. The argument between Odysseus and Thersites takes place when the former has been trying single-handed to check a wild dash for the ships by hordes of men who have been nine years away from home. In the context of threatened mob rule, the leaders are not the dominant element in the pattern, but the weak, endangered element. One could say that everyone laughs with relief that their scramble for home is not allowed to overwhelm the delicate balance of power between a handful of leaders and a mass of followers. Thersites, the rude and ugly cripple, usually takes Odysseus and Achilles for his butts; this time the pattern is reversed. The men laugh to find themselves on the side of the leaders, in reverse of their behaviour a short time before.

As a final example, I would like to turn to the parables in the New Testament to suggest that when the social structure is not depicted, it is unlikely that we can perceive 'told' jokes even when the joke form is clearly present in the verbal utterance. Many of the parables have an obvious joke pattern: the kingdom of heaven likened to a mustard seed (Luke 13: 19; Mark 4: 31–2), the prayers of the complacent Pharisee placed second after the humble prayer of the publican (Luke 18: 10–14), the guest who takes the lowest place and is brought up to the top, to cite a few. Many incidents in the Gospel narrative itself also have a joke form, the wedding at Cana to take only one. But whereas the Gospel incidents present little difficulty in the light of the messages that 'the things that are impossible with men are possible with God' (Luke 18: 27), some of the parables do. Why was the poor fellow with no wedding garment bound and cast into the place of darkness with weeping and gnashing of teeth (Matthew 22: 11–14)? Why was the unjust steward commended for making friends with Mammon (Luke 16: 1–9)? How does this accord with the message of love and truth? I suggest that the difficulties arise because we are lacking signals from the social situation. Suppose that the Galilee audience, as soon as it heard 'Let me tell you a parable' settled into the same expectant joking mood that we do on hearing 'Do you know the riddle about . . .?' Then we could interpret the parables frankly as jokes, told at a rattling pace, with dramatic pauses for effect, each reaching higher and higher climaxes of absurdity and ridicule. The punishment of the man with no wedding garment then appears as a necessary correction to the obviously funny story of the rich man whose social equals, having refused his invitation to a feast, found their places were filled by beggars from the street (Matthew 22: 2–10). Could the kingdom of heaven be filled with any kind of riff-raff then? No – that would be to miss the point of the story. True, the socially uppermost are not necessarily the best qualified for the kingdom of heaven. But to correct the wrong impression about riff-raff, a new joke has to be introduced against the gate-crasher. There will be more to say later about the joke form as a vehicle of religious thought.

I hope that I have established that a joke cannot be perceived unless it corresponds to the form of the social experience: but I would go a step further and even suggest that the experience of a joke form in the social structure calls imperatively for an explicit joke to express it. Hence the disproportionate joy which a feeble joke often releases. In the case of a bishop being stuck in the lift, a group of people are related together in a newly relevant pattern which overthrows the normal one: when one of them makes the smallest jest, something pertinent has been said about the social structure. Hence the enthusiasm with which a joke at the right time is always hailed. Whatever happens next will be seen to be funny: whether the lowliest in the no longer relevant hierarchy discover the right switch and becomes saviour of the mighty, or whether the bishop himself turns out to be the best mechanic, the atmosphere will become heady with joy, unless the bishop has made the mistake of imposing the external hierarchy.

To the pleasure of the joke itself, whatever that may be, is added enjoyment of a hidden wit, the congruence of the joke structure with the social structure. With laughter there is a third level of appositeness: for disturbed bodily control mirrors both the joke structure and the social structure. Here there is the germ of an answer to the puzzle of why tickling should provoke laughter, discussed by Koestler (1964).

Tickling, says Koestler, using the same Bergson-Freud analysis of wit, is funny because it is interpreted as a mock attack. The baby laughs more when it is tickled by its own mother than by a stranger; with strangers one can never be sure (Koestler, 1964: 80–2). But to the uncertainty about whether a stranger is really making a serious or a mock attack add the fact that there is no social relation with strangers. Hence the wit is not in play in the social dimension to anything like the same extent. From the content of the joke, to the analogy of the joke structure with the social structure, on to the analogy of these two with the physical experience, the transfer of formal patterns goes on even to a fourth level, that revealed by Freud. A joke unleashes the energy of the subconscious against the control of the conscious. This, I argue, is the essential joke experience, a fourfold perception of the congruence of a formal pattern.

Jokes as Rites

In classing the joke as a symbol of social, physical and mental experience, we are already treating it as a rite. How then should we treat the joke which is set aside for specified ritual occasions?

Once again, as with standardised and spontaneous jokes, it is necessary to distinguish spontaneous rites from routinised or standard rites. The joke, in its social context as we have discussed it so far, is a spontaneous symbol. It expresses something that is happening, but that is all. The social niche in which it belongs is quite distinct from that of ritual which is enacted to express what ought to happen. Similarly, the spontaneous rite is morally neutral, while the standard rite is not. Indeed, there is a paradox in talking about joke rites at all, for the peculiar expressive character of the joke is in contrast with ritual as such. Here I need to return to the general idea of joke structure derived from

Freud, and to contrast the way a joke relates disparate ideas with the way a standard ritual does the same.

A standard rite is a symbolic act which draws its meaning from a cluster of standard symbols. When I use the word 'rite' in what follows, I combine the action and the cluster of symbols associated with it. A joke has it in common with a rite that both connect widely differing concepts. But the kind of connection of pattern A with pattern B in a joke is such that B disparages or supplants A, while the connection made in a rite is such that A and B support each other in a unified system. The rite imposes order and harmony, while the joke disorganises. From the physical to the personal, to the social, to the cosmic, great rituals create unity in experience. They assert hierarchy and order. In doing so, they affirm the value of the symbolic patterning of the universe. Each level of patterning is validated and enriched by association with the rest. But jokes have the opposite effect. They connect widely differing fields, but the connection destroys hierarchy and order. They do not affirm the dominant values, but denigrate and devalue. Essentially a joke is an anti-rite.

I have analysed elsewhere (Douglas, 1966: 114–28) rituals which use bodily symbolism to express ideas about the body politic. The caste system in India is a case in point. The symbolism underlying the ideas about pollution and purification has something in common with wit; it transfers patterns of value on a declining slope of prestige from one context to another with elegant economy. The lowest social ranks in the caste system are those required to perform social functions equivalent to the excretory functions of the body. There is the basis for a joke in the congruence of bodily and social symbolism, but the joke is absent since two patterns are related without either being challenged. The hierarchy is not undermined by the comparison, but rather reinforced.

Totemic systems make play with formal analogues. The same patterns are transposed from context to context with exquisite economy and grace. But they are not funny. One of the essential requirements of a joke is absent, the element of challenge. I give an example from Madame Calame-Griaule's recent book (1966) on Dogon language. She has analysed something that might be called a kind of linguistic totemism. The Dogon use a limited number of classes of speech as a basis for classifying wide ranges of other experience. With speech of the market place, for instance, are classified commerce and weaving. There is an obvious analogy from two kinds of constructive interaction. Here we have economy in connecting up disparate activities, but no humour. Take the class of speech that Dogon call 'trivial speech', the speech of women. This includes certain forms of insect, animal and human life. The controlling idea for the class associated with 'trivial speech' is dissipation. The work in this class is the sower's broadcasting of seed; the red monkey who comes to eat the crops after the farmer has planted is the appropriate animal in the class; the despised Fulani herder who pastures his cattle on the stubble after harvesting it is the human associated with it. The insect is the grasshopper, alleged to defecate as fast as it eats, an obvious type of fruitless effort. The references to despised forms of activity and to uncontrolled bowel movements has a derogatory implication for the idle chatter of women. The range of behaviour on which the pattern of 'trivial speech' is imposed degenerates from human Dogon to human Fulani, from human to animal pest, then to insect pest and finally to the excretory functions of the body. As the classification moves down from one context to the next, it slights and devalues. There is the possibility of a joke here. If it were challenging the known pretensions of women to utter important speech, it would have the making of a joke. But, given the low place of women in Dogon esteem, it is more likely to be the deadly earnest affirmation of male superiority, in which case this classification supports the established social order. The message of a standard rite is that the ordained patterns of social life are inescapable. The message of a joke is that they are escapable. A joke is by nature an anti-rite.

When joking is used in a ritual, it should be approached none the less as a rite. Like any other rite the joke rite is first and foremost a set of symbols. Its symbolism draws on the full experience of joking, just as communion rites draw on the full experience of eating, right down to the digestive process, and sexual rites and sacrifice draw on the experience of sex and death. So we should expect the joke rite to exploit all the elements of the joke in its essential nature. This will give the full explanation of ritual joking. Jokes, being themselves a play upon forms, can well serve to express something about social forms. Recall that the joke connects and disorganises. It attacks sense and hierarchy. The joke rite then must express a comparable situation. If it devalues social structure, perhaps it celebrates something else instead. It could be saying something about the value of individuals as against the value of the social relations in which they are organised. Or it could be saying something about different levels of social structure; the irrelevance of one obvious level and the relevance of a submerged and unappreciated one.

John Barnes (1954: 43) used the term 'network' to indicate an undifferentiated field of friendship and acquaintance. In his Morgan Lectures, Victor Turner has suggested that the word 'community' could be applied to this part of social life. In 'community' the personal relations of men and women appear in a special light. They form part of the ongoing process which is only partly organised in the wider social 'structure'. Whereas 'structure' is differentiated and channels authority through the system, in the context of 'community', roles are ambiguous, lacking hierarchy, disorganised. 'Community' in this sense has positive values associated with it; good fellowship, spontaneity, warm contact. Turner sees some dionysian ritual as expressing the value of 'community' as against 'structure'. This analysis gives a better name to, and clarifies, what I have elsewhere crudely called the experience of the non-structure in contrast to the structure (Douglas, 1966: 102). Laughter and jokes, since they attack classification and hierarchy, are obviously apt symbols for expressing community in this sense of unhierarchised, undifferentiated social relations.

Peter Rigby (1968) has developed this approach in his survey of all types of relationship in which joking is required in Gogo culture. He starts with interclan joking, then goes on to affinal joking, grandparent/grandchild joking, and finally joking between mother's brother and sister's sons and between cross-cousins. Each kind of joking has its own rules and quality of joke required. He concludes from his survey that he needs the concept of 'community' as distinct from 'structure' in order to interpret this pattern of behaviour: 'In Gogo society it is relationships with and through women which establish the "community"; that is affinal, matrilateral and uterine kin' (Rigby, 1968: 152).

Interclan links and links with aliens and enemies are included in a general class along with links through women. Starting from an ego-centred universe of kin, the Gogo have developed a cosmic model: joking categories are contrasted with control categories; joking categories are links or mediators between different organised domains. Gogo use the idea of joking categories to express the fading out of social control at all points and in all directions. It is a boundary image, but the boundaries are fuzzy and face two ways; one is structured, the other is unstructured. Boundaries connect as well as separate. Women are the boundaries of the patrilineal lineage. Affines stand out of reach of clan and lineage control but they are links. Clans are bounded as clans, but are linked by exogamy. 'Grandfathers are links or mediators with the unstructured world of the spirits of the dead who are not distinguished on the basis of lineal descent' (Rigby, 1968: 152).

Here we have an analysis which brings out cosmological implications hidden in the nature of joking. A joke confronts one relevant structure by another less clearly relevant, one well-differentiated view by a less coherent one, a system of control by another independent one to which it does not apply. By using jokes at social boundary points the Gogo are being witty at several levels: they comment on the nature of society, and on the nature of life and death. Their joke rites play upon one central abstraction, the contrast of articulation, and they develop the application of this symbol with the energy of inveterate punners. At the division of meat at a funeral, the heirs are told by the elders to speak clearly: if they mumble the sister's son will take everything (Rigby, 1968 : 149). Here is an explicit reference to articulateness in speech as the symbol of structured relationships and inarticulateness as the symbol of the personal, undifferentiated network.

The interpretation of the Gogo joke rites as an abstract statement of two kinds of social interaction is highly satisfactory. The interpretation of Kaguru joke rites as an expression of an association made between sex, filth and liminality I find dubious. According to Beidelman, the Kaguru use joking to express 'liminal' relations, that is ambiguous ones. The range of relationships in which Kaguru require joking is much the same as the range of Gogo joking relations. It would seem plausible that the ego-oriented view of social life (as either differentiated by a pattern of control or undifferentiated), is enough to warrant joking between these categories, and that dirt is an apt enough expression of undifferentiated, unorganised, uncontrolled relations.

It still remains to distinguish jokes in general from obscenity as such. They are obviously very close. A joke confronts one accepted pattern with another. So does an obscene image. The first amuses, the second shocks. Both consist of the intrusion of one meaning on another, but whereas the joke discloses a meaning hidden under the appearance of the first, the obscenity is a gratuitous intrusion. We are unable to identify joke patterns without considering the total social situation. Similarly for obscenity, abominations depend upon social context to be perceived as such. Language which is normal in male company is regarded as obscene in mixed society; the language of intimacy is offensive where social distance reigns and, similarly, the language of the dissecting room where intimacy belongs. Inevitably, the best way of stating the difference between joking and obscenity is by reference to the social context. The joke works only when it mirrors social forms; it exists by virtue of its congruence with the social structure. But the obscenity is identified by its opposition to the social structure, hence its offence.

In the modern industrial world the categories of social life do not embrace the physical universe in a single moral order. If there is a social offence, there are moral implications such as cruelty, impiety, corruption of the innocent, and so on. But the social offence is not thought to release floods, famines or epidemics. Obscenity for us is a mild offence, since it can now be accounted for entirely in terms of offence against social categories. This leaves us unqualified to comprehend the much greater offence of obscenity in a primitive culture. For there the categories of social life co-ordinate the whole of experience: a direct attack on social forms is as disturbing as an attack on any of the symbolic categories in which the social forms are expressed – and vice versa. The idea of obscenity then has a much greater range and power, and the response it triggers is stronger. It is better to use a quite different word, such as abomination or ritual pollution, for the primitive cultures' equivalent to obscenity and to look for a much more whole-hearted and systematic wiping out of the offence than we can muster for dealing with obscenity.

Abomination is an act or event which contradicts the basic categories of experience and in doing so threatens both the order of reason and the order of society. A joke does nothing of the sort. It represents a temporary suspension of the social structure, or rather it makes a little disturbance in which the particular structuring of society becomes less relevant than another. But the strength of its attack is entirely restricted by the consensus on which it depends for recognition.

The Joker

Now we should turn to the role of the joker. He appears to be a privileged person who can say certain things in a certain way which confers immunity. He is by no means anything like a taboo breaker whose polluting act is a real offence to society. He *is* worth contrasting with persons undergoing rituals of transition, mourners and initiands. Symbolically, they are in marginal states, passing from one clearly defined status to another. They are held to be dangerous to themselves and to others until they have gone through the whole ritual of redefinition. In the symbolisation of the social structure, they have let go their moorings and are temporarily displaced. But the joker is not exposed to danger. He has a firm hold on his own position in the structure and the disruptive comments which he makes upon it are in a sense the comments of the social group upon itself. He merely expresses consensus. Safe within the permitted range of attack, he lightens for everyone the oppressiveness of social reality, demonstrates its arbitrariness by making light of formality in general, and expresses the creative possibilities of the situation.

From this we can see the appropriateness of the joker as ritual purifier. Among the Kaguru, certain common sexual offences such as sexual intercourse between affines are thought to bring illness, sterility or death on the kin of the two offenders. There are other graver sexual offences, but these relatively minor ones can be ritually cleansed by the joking partners of the transgressors (Beidelman, 1966: 361–2). A similar responsibility falling on joking partners among the Dogon led Griaule to describe their partnership as cathartic (1948). Rites of purification are a very widespread responsibility of joking partners in central and east Africa, as Stefaniszyn (1950) has pointed out. I myself commented (Tew, 1951) that the joking aspects of the relationships could not be understood without an analysis of the relation

between joking and purification. Now I suggest that the rel
evance of joking to purification emerges as another elaborate
ritual pun. These rites make a double play on the joke experi
ence: laughter itself is cathartic at the level of emotions; the joke
consists in challenging a dominant structure and belittling it; the
joker who provokes the laughter is chosen to challenge the rel
evance of the dominant structure and to perform with immunity
the act which wipes out the venial offence.

The joker's own immunity can be derived philosophically from
his apparent access to other reality than that mediated by the
relevant structure. Such access is implied in the contrast of forms
in which he deals. His jokes expose the inadequacy of realist
structurings of experience and so release the pent-up power of
the imagination.

Perhaps the joker should be classed as a kind of minor mystic
Though only a mundane and border-line type, he is one of those
people who pass beyond the bounds of reason and society and
give glimpses of a truth which escapes through the mesh of
structured concepts. Naturally he is only a humble, poor brother
of the true mystic, for his insights are given by accident. They do
not combine to form a whole new vision of life, but remain
disorganised as a result of the technique which produces them
He is distinctly gimmicky. One would expect him to be the
object of a hilarious mythology, as among the Winnebago, but
hardly the focus of a religious cult. And yet there he is
enshrined – Proteus in ancient Greece; the elephant god who
gives luck and surprises in Hinduism; and the unpredictable
disruptive, creative force called Legba in Yoruba religion
(Wescott, 1962). Needless to say, he is always a subordinate deity
in a complex pantheon. The joker as god promises a wealth of
new, unforeseeable kinds of interpretation. He exploits the
symbol of creativity which is contained in a joke, for a joke
implies that anything is possible.

It is much easier now to see the role of the joker at a funeral
By restraining excessive grief he asserts the demands of the
living. I would expect joking at funerals to be more possible and
more required the more the community is confident that it will
turn the mourner's desolation into a temporary phase. Then the
question is: who must joke and what should be his precise
degree of relationship with the bereaved and the dead? The

central African joking partner is a friend cultivated by gifts and hospitality, and is by definition not a close kinsman : his role at a funeral is to cheer the bereaved and to relieve them of the polluting duties of burial. There are here the elements of another ritual pun; for it is the kin who are ritually endangered by contact with the dead, the kin who are involved in the social structure of inheritance and succession, and it is the personal friend, the joking partner, who is uninvolved in the social structure and is the person who is immune from pollution of death.

There are many ways in which it can be appropriate to joke at a funeral. When a man dies his friends fall to reviewing his life. They try to see in it some artistic pattern, some fulfilment which can comfort him and them. At this moment obvious inconsistencies and disharmonies are distressing. If he is a great man, a national figure, of course his achievements are cited, but it seems important to be able to say that in his private life he also had fulfilled his family roles. If he is an ordinary citizen then the assessment of his success goes on entirely at the level of family and community. He is judged as a man, not as an item of social structure.

The role of the joker at the funeral could call attention to his individual personality. Indeed, in the Jewish *shib'ah*, a week of mourning after burial, the friends who come in to comfort the bereaved and praise the departed, invariably find themselves joking at his expense. Thus they affirm that he was an individual, not only a father or brother in a series of descending generations, but a man. So much for the social symbolism.

On the subject of funeral joking it is tempting to consider some metaphysical implications. A joke symbolises levelling, dissolution and recreation. As a symbol of social relations it is destructive (somewhat like fire?) and regenerative (somewhat like water?). The joke, working on its own materials, mimics a kind of death. Its form in itself suggests the theme of rebirth. It is no coincidence that practical jokes are common in initiation rites, along with more concrete expressions of dying and being reborn. When Jan Vansina underwent the Bushong boys' initiation (1955) he was continually involved in practical joking, either at the expense of non-initiates or at the expense of the group of novices to which he belonged. One after another the much dreaded ordeals were revealed to be only tricks.

Metaphysical Jokes

If the joke form can symbolise so much, it could be capable of saying something about death itself in the context of religion.

We have traced the pun from its social to its psychological form, from these to its physical expression in laughter, and from the spontaneous symbol of social relationships to the standardised joke rite, expressing the value of less articulate sectors of social relationships compared with formalised structures. At funerals it expresses the value of the man himself, or the value of disinterested friendship or the value of the level of community in which most of a man's life is effective. It seems, after all this, not too bold to suggest that by the path of ritual joking these African cultures too have reached a philosophy of the absurd. By revealing the arbitrary, provisional nature of the very categories of thought, by lifting their pressure for a moment and suggesting other ways of structuring reality, the joke rite in the middle of the sacred moments of religion hints at unfathomable mysteries. This is the message which Turner attributes to the practical joke at the centre of the cult of Chihamba performed by the Ndembu tribe in Zambia.

First the initiates pay homage to the great white spirit, Kavula, as the source of all power; then as they approach his tabernacle, they are told to strike his effigy under a white cloth with their rattles, and then that they have killed him. Soon after they are told that they are innocent, and that he is not dead, and the paraphernalia under the white cloth is revealed to be no more than some everyday implements. Everyone then laughs joyfully. Following an elaborate exegesis, Turner (1962: 87) says:

> we have in Chihamba the local expression of a universal-human problem, that of expressing what cannot be *thought of*, in view of thought's subjugation to essences. It is a problem which has engaged the passionate attention of ritual man in all places and ages. It is a problem, furthermore, which has confronted artists, musicians and poets whenever these have gone beyond the consideration of aesthetic form and social manners.

It is unfortunate that Turner presented his novel interpretation of a primitive cult in neo-scholastic terms. The only serious consideration which his study has received attacks this presentation.

Horton (1964) argues that the whole complex of ontological problems with which Turner has saddled Ndembu theologians, the
distinction between the act-of-being itself (an act) and the concept of being (an essence) only makes sense in the terms of
Thomist-Aristotelian philosophy. He deftly applies the logical
positivist criticism to this approach. Further, Horton rejects the
idea that 'a dominant concern to "say the unsayable" about the
ultimate ground of all particular forms of existence' can be
found in all African religions (1964: 96–7), still less, as Turner
says, universally in all religions whatever.

  These criticisms by-pass the main challenge of Turner's thesis.
Merely to dare to interpret a ritual mock-killing of a god in one
particular African religion as an attempt to express unfathomable mysteries about the inadequacy of the categories of thought
for expressing the nature of existence is bold enough. Leave out
Turner's claim that this is a universal human pre-occupation; it
may be or it may not be. Forget his presentation in scholastic
terms; it could as well have been presented through Kant or
Kierkegaarde or modern phenomenologists as through Aquinas.
It is still a daring claim that he makes for the profound meaning
of an African joke rite. For all the subtlety and complexity with
which he spins out the symbolism, my own first response was one
of doubt. It was the first serious suggestion by a contemporary
anthropologist that rituals which have no formal philosophical
exegesis in their native culture could be concerned with problems
about the relation of thought to experience which are, undeniably, a universal pre-occupation of philosophy. After reflecting
on the use of the joke rite in Africa, I am now much more
convinced that Turner may be right. African cultures have clearly reached an apotheosis of wit by playing upon the joke at
various levels of meaning. It is not a great leap from attributing
to the joke rite a subtle image of society to attributing also to it
an image of the conditions of human knowledge.

  But this is not the point at which I would wish to end this
article. There is another implication which should be under-
lined: the social control of experience. It is here argued that the
patterning of social forms limits and conditions the apprehension
of symbolic forms. This may be extended from the perception of
the joke form to the perception of other patterns, hierarchy, part-
whole relations, unity, schism, incorporation, exclusion. The con-

trol exerted by experience in the social dimension over the perception of conceptual patterns is already taken into account in learning theory and in religious sociology. This study of the joke rite suggests that the achievement of consonance between different realms of experience is a source of profound satisfaction. It suggests that the drive to reduce dissonance may work at a more abstract level than has been recognised hitherto. The exercise of tracing the analogies drawn in joke rites gives additional meaning to Kandinsky's famous saying that the impact of an acute triangle on a circle produces an effect no less powerful than the finger of God touching the finger of Adam in Michelangelo's famous fresco.

Notes to this Edition

Early versions of this article received valuable criticism from the Makerere Conference on Joking Relationships, in December 1966 and from the Muirhead Society, Birmingham.

Professor John Beattie has pointed out that the difference I make between Freud and Bergson is almost indiscernible and with this criticism I agree.

Dr Audrey Richards makes a more serious criticism that my use of her writings on the Bemba distorts the information. Either I should leave them out or say a great deal more about them, giving a survey of all the occasions in which formalised joking occurs in Bemba socety. It is quite incorrect to say that 'the jokes categorise the political interdependence of the clans' since the clans are neither corporate nor interdependent, nor do they have any function except the regulation of exogamy and the right to appoint to one or two court offices. She has agreed to publishing the following useful note for which I am extremely grateful:

> I realise that you have not really concentrated on the reciprocal clan relationships. You say that the use of these jokes 'categorises the interdependence of the clans' using the Bemba, but I do not think that they are interdependent now except at the court when the clan membership of the bakabilo has a good deal of significance, and of course they remain exogamous for some extraordinary reason considering that they have really *no* other corporate functions as regards commoners.
>
> Of course the reciprocal clan relationships cannot fit in with your view that 'whatever the joke, however remote its subject, the

telling of it is potentially subversive' and further that it 'destroys harmony and order'. But you could expand your idea to say that in the case of the royal Crocodile clan, this would be true, although it would be untrue of the other clans. When the head of the Fish clan dances in front of the Chitimukulu, threatening him with a broad-bladed fishing spear and insulting him, there is just this element of the subversive in everyone's behaviour. Everyone present enjoys the situation and comes round to watch the affair and to laugh. The chief does not enjoy it although he smiles in a sickly way. He takes special routes across the river in order to avoid having his goods plundered by members of the Fish clan. He told me it was very tiresome and that he thought that now the Europeans were there, they ought to put an end to such 'things of the past'. I suppose it depends on whether your theory needs for its support an account of the emotions of the people actually expressed at the time as well as the descriptions of Banungwe relations.

As regards commoners, the parallels between the behaviour of marriageable classes, for example, cross-cousins, is rather striking and in some cases was made explicit to me but only by old men. One man said to me that *Bunungwe* were enemies whom we married when we first came into the country. (I think I mention this in my article but do not seem to have any copy at all.) Cross-cousins joke in this way together and can snatch each others' goods. *Banungwe* joke and take each others' things once a month when the new moon comes – but bury each other which of course cross-cousins do not do. The joking is stereotyped for clan opposites but not for cross-cousins.

Bibliography

BARNES, J. A. (1954), 'Class and committees in a Norwegian island parish', *Hum. Relat.*, 7, 39–58.

BARTH, FREDRIK (1966), *Models of Social Organisation* (Occasional Papers Royal Anthropological Institute, 23), London, Royal Anthropological Institute.

BEIDELMAN, T. O. (1966), '*Utani:* some Kagura notions of death, sexuality and affinity', *SWest. J. Anthrop.*, 22–4, 354–80.

BERGSON, HENRI (1950), *Le Rire: essai sur la signification du comique*, first published Paris, Presses Universitaires de France.

CALAME-GRIAULE, G. (1966), *Ethnologie et langage: la parole chez les Dogon*, Paris, Gallimard.

DOUGLAS, M. (1966), *Purity and Danger: an Analysis of Concepts of Pollution and Taboo*, London, Routledge & Kegan Paul.

EHRENZWEIG, ANTON (1953), *The Psychoanalysis of Artistic Vision ana Hearing: a Theory of Unconscious Perception*, London, Routledge & Kegan Paul.

FREUD, SIGMUND (1916), *Wit and its Relation to the Unconscious* (trans A. A. Brill), London, Fisher & Unwin.

GOODY, J. R. (1962), *Death, Property and the Ancestors*, London Tavistock Publications.

GRIAULE, MARCEL (1948), 'L'Alliance cathartique', *Africa, 16*, 242–58.

HORTON, R. (1964), 'Ritual Man in Africa', *Africa, 34*, 85–104.

KOESTLER, A. (1964), *The Act of Creation*, London, Hutchinson.

LEACH, E. R. (1961), *Re-thinking Anthropology* (London School of Economics Monographs in Social Anthropology, 22), London Athlone Press.

RADCLIFFE-BROWN, A. R. (1940), 'On joking relationships', *Africa, 13* 195–210.

RADCLIFFE-BROWN, A. R. (1949), 'A further note on joking relationships', *Africa, 19*, 133–40.

RICHARDS, A. I. (1937), 'Reciprocal clan relationships among the Bemba', *Man, 37*, 188–93.

RIGBY, P. (1968), 'Joking relationships, kin categories and clanship among the Gogo', *Africa, 38*, 133–55.

STEFANISZYN, B. (1950), 'Funeral friendship in central Africa', *Africa, 20*, 290–306.

TEW, MARY (1951), 'A further note on funeral friendship', *Africa, 21* 122–4.

TURNER, V. W. (1962), *Chihamba, the White Spirit* (Rhodes-Livingstone Papers, 33), Manchester University Press.

VANSINA, J. (1955), 'Initiation rituals of the Bushong', *Africa, 25* 138–52.

WESCOTT, J. (1962), 'The sculpture and myths of Eshu-Elegba the Yoruba trickster: definition and interpretation in Yoruba iconography', *Africa, 32*, 336–65.

Critical Essays

Introduction

The late Franz Steiner once said that he could never bring himself to use the verb 'to express'. Indeed, it opens the way to at least three fallacies. The first starts with over-extending the contrast (necessary to any exegesis) between the expression and the idea expressed. Let me hasten to separate my range of problems from those in which such a distinction is necessary and right. In any restricted programme of interpretation, the analysis of a medium of discourse such as speaking, riddling, myth, clothing, food, there must be the vocabulary for referring the sign to that which it signifies. This is the straight translation job. In my own essay on 'Deciphering a Meal', in the third section of this book (chapter 16), I am involved in the de-coding process as wholeheartedly as anyone. In what follows here I am warning against the fallacy of allowing the language of translation to carry abroad hidden and false assumptions about the relations between media of expression. If we say that speech and writing are media, and also radio and television and gifts of fruit or flowers, we are using the metaphor of a vehicle of conveyance, channel or band or code. Along and through it something else, the message, seems to pass. But if the idea of a medium be extended to all bodily behaviour and all social relations, as it readily can be, the puzzle arises as to what are the messages conveyed.

The fallacy is particularly clear when among all the realisations of a social situation one level is singled out to be privileged above the others. It may be right to say that a handshake expresses 'how do you do', but equally the words express the handshake, or a smile can do for either. If the gesture, the smile and the words express a general willingness for acquaintanceship, then so do the hundred acts of recognition spread over time express the friendship. But it is also true to say that they constitute it. The relationship is non-existent if it never takes any material form. The gestures, verbal and other, are constitutive of social reality. There is no one moment that can be picked out and said to carry the expressive function on its own. The verb 'to express' tempts the sociologist to reify or freeze one part of the action, arbitrarily dub it 'the expression', and so create a puzzle as to what it expresses. We are thus landed with an artificially foregrounded subject matter, symbolism, essential clues thrown into shadow. The solution is to drop the transportation metaphor and to take all the expressions of a situation, at all levels, as equally contributing to it, making it actual.

The other two fallacies arise once expression has been distinguished from what it expresses. For then a choice appears between competing views of reality. On one view, symbol is the reality, the rest is machinery for producing it. This is the front stage bias. The so-called symbolic system, whether a logically intricate set of kinship terms, or names of herbs, animals or totems, is taken to be the enduring image. Such significance as can be attributed to the rest is somehow summed or incorporated in its expression. No one holds exactly this view, but it sustains some protagonists in the long argument about the status of kinship terms. Let David Schneider (1972) speak, who has been giving doughty battle on the subject:

> For Morgan, as for many people even today, words meant things, concrete objects, and they had either one and only one meaning or a primary meaning which could be distinguished from secondary, metaphoric, extended, or connotational meanings. On premises such as these it seemed obvious to Morgan that the mode of classification could be read directly from the kinship terminology; that is, those positions on the genealogical grid which were grouped together under one kinship term could be distinguished from those positions on the genealogical grid grouped under a different kinship term and so on. Hence kinship terminology was *the* key to the mode of classification and in fact, practically the only key, since the kinship

terms meant (either only or primarily) specific relationships of blood or marriage. The taxonomy, then, was derived from no other source than the kinship terminology.

He rightly suggests that the same fallacy obscures the interpretation of religion. Ethnoscientists fall into it likewise when they concentrate on verbal behaviour, isolate it and elevate its power to carry meaning. As Robin Horton (1967) points out, it is a trap into which primitive cultures fall readily. Comparing the magical use of verbal and non-verbal forms, he sets up a scale of attributed concreteness and effectiveness, running from the spoken word to the written word, to the magical object.

One may still ask, however, why magicians spend so much time choosing objects and actions as surrogate words, when spoken words themselves are believed to have a magical potential. The answer, I suggest, is that speech is an ephemeral form of words, and one which does not lend itself to a great variety of manipulation. Verbal designation of material objects converts them into a more permanent and more readily manipulable form of words. . . .

But certainly Robin Horton would never argue that only traditional thought falls into the error of attributing concreteness to verbal formula. It is usual to think of this as a characteristic of primitive religions. The following remarks by Godfrey Lienhardt (1956) make the application to our scientists clear enough:

Since for Max Muller God was an idea rather than an active power, he was surprised by a characteristic of primitive religion which he nevertheless intelligently noted – its preference for the concrete, its attachment to material symbols. He noted that there were two distinct tendencies to be observed in the growth of ancient religion . . . on the one side, the struggle of the mind against the material character of language, a constant attempt to strip words of their coarse meaning, and fit them, by main force, for the purposes of abstract thought. But . . . on the other side, a predilection for the material sense instead of the spiritual.

The same cap fits the anthropologist as the people he studies. Anyone who cares to follow up David Schneider's description of the modern anthropologist will recognise a predilection for concretising written words and treating them as the only hard and solid objects of study. This anthropologist starts by saying that the only accessible reality lies in the words of classificatory systems. He goes on to write as if this externally visible and audible reality represents another more real but hidden one, the categories inside the heads of the informants. The system of classification is credited with autonomy and fixity, neither of which it plausibly has. According to this presentation the rest of human behaviour is a bloodless affair, without strife or feeling. These anthropologists spiritualise social life, like vegetarians who depreciate their own carnal existence by feeding on only fruit and seeds. On their record, an awful lot of human behaviour is discarded as unworthy of a scholar's time. This view has something of the attraction of plastic flowers. The verb to express allows the transient to be fixed. Life moves too fast for easy analysis. Exclusive focusing upon expression and its logical categories detaches from the flux of living something that will stay still long enough to be contemplated. The echo of scholastic theology is heard. To concentrate research upon the logical categories and their expression has the satisfaction of seeming to confront mind in its pure state. But if this is the goal that draws the scholar, why not plunge straight into the *Principia Mathematica* and, going back and forward from there, become a pure logician? I would not deny that the analysis of logical forms, in kinship terminology or religious categories, in folklore or studies of riddles, is an arduous, technical and highly important task. But the anthropologists who train to specialise in it must also be interested in how the category systems are generated. The subject needs both kinds of approach, and neither should exclude the other, nor remain unaware of how they are related.

The back-stage bias takes the reverse view of the same issues. From this angle, the symbolic system is what appears on the surface. It is mere show, an illusion. Only the work is real which produces it. The mumming performed on stage is hardly relevant: the real stuff of sociological concern lies in the dealings that go on back-stage. Sidney and Beatrice Webb are reported to have enjoyed an evening at Covent Garden calculating from the average box-office takings what the dancers earned. These anthropologists likewise are content with the truth which can be reached after stripping off the fancy dress and laying bare the

transactions between management and artists. A strong movement in anthropology would focus exclusively on transactions,
following on the development of exchange theory in political
science and psychology.

In sum the terminology which separates symbolic orders from
the rest of the action fits either of two rival positions in anthropology and is therefore hard to dislodge. But they both leave
important issues unformulated. Many pay lip-service to the unity
of experience, claiming that their approach does it no violence.
But they underestimate the challenge of attempting to control
the sociological vision in both dimensions. The pioneers who
attempt the enormously difficult synthesis are easily belittled by
those who stay with either logic or transactions. But soon they
will develop their own critical canons and common terminology.
Surely, as their work converges on a technical plane, they will
become, like the Oxford anthropologists under Professor Evans-
Pritchard in the 1950s, a self-recognising élite, turning inwards
to bound their field of interest and hammer out their validating
procedures, and it will greatly advance the subject when they
do – but I will not be there.

In the meanwhile, the review essays in this section plead for
the symbolic system always to be presented with a scrutiny of the
social system in which it is generated. It would be a pity to take
them for factious requests for validation in a narrow tradition of
English empiricism. It is true that they praise the insight into
socio-economic relationships of my contemporaries here, while
pointing to the sociological gaps in the work of some overseas
anthropologists. But at the time of their writing it seemed necessary to insist that the sociological dimension is not easy to fill in.
They say that interpretation which spans many levels of experience is more convincing than one supported with a shallower
depth of documentation and that those who shirk the sociological route suffer a grave problem of validation. Re-read, the
reviews show the need for a better vocabulary for discussing the
generation of meaning. The vocabulary should clearly recognise
that society is entirely constituted by exchanges, verbal and
material, that are loaded with significance. It should not minister
to our bias for splitting behaviour into levels of more or less
symbolic value. Splitting is necessary for examining particular
segments. But it should not carelessly relegate precious infor-

mation to the waste-bin. Any one realisation of society is sustained by many others. The present analytic challenge is to identify and isolate for scrutiny areas of experience that are sufficiently coherent and well-bounded for the ethnographer to record all and only the information necessary to convince colleagues by his interpretation.

Front-stage and back-stage are opposed preferences held by the social scientists. If they raise ancient questions of philosophy concerning illusion and reality, sign and signified, they are by no means remote or lacking practical effect. According to such predilections teachers guide their students, and thesis subjects are defined. But the matter goes deeper still. The historians of European thought commonly attribute to Descartes the philosophy based on a dichotomy between ideas and the external world. They suggest that but for him the division between mind and matter would never have stayed to bedevil us. But he had merely found that the older one between substance and form needed to be questioned. And before the school men were Aristotle and Plato themselves. The essay reprinted here on the Dogon reminds us that a people who use oracular techniques of divination are likely to be landed with their own dichotomies between different kinds of reality. Instead of rebuking Descartes, it would be constructive to admit that thinking about the process of thinking encourages the tendency to treat thought as something apart. When anthropology can recognise that thought is the central organising activity, that all social activity is symbolic, and that all behaviour contributes to the constituting of reality, it will be ready for a big theoretical revolution. From there, the next conclusion is that all apprehended reality is socially constituted. And then at last there is scope for the questions about different kinds of socially constituted reality, questions which afford escape from negative relativism.

Bibliography

HORTON, ROBIN (1967), 'African traditional thought and Western science', *Africa*, 37, 2, 50–187.

LIENHARDT, R. G. (1956), 'Religion', in *Man, Culture and Society*, ed.

H. L. Shapiro, New York, Oxford University Press, ch. xiv, p. 313ff.

SCHNEIDER, D. (1972), 'What is kinship all about?' in *Kinship Studies in the Morgan Centennial Year,* ed. P. Reining, Anthropological Society of Washington, D.C., pp. 32–63.

8

If the Dogon . . .

There are German scholars who so much admire Shakespeare that they sometimes call him 'our Shakespeare'. I have something of this feeling about the Dogon. Yet, would Dogon studies strike this note of sympathy if they had been actually carried out by the English? If the Nuer had been studied by the Missions Griaule how much more would we know about them today. How much poorer our knowledge of Dogon culture, if we ourselves had studied them.

Some of the differences between the two schools of ethnography depend on concentration of time and effort. It is true that Evans-Pritchard was only able to study the Nuer for a very short time. The poverty of their recorded cosmology partly reflects this. Compare his two brief visits with the many years of dedicated teamwork of the Missions Griaule. But it is certain too that very different points of view inspired the two kinds of ethnography. What would we know of the Nuer if they had been in the French Sudan – and of the Dogon if they had been on the banks of the White Nile? It is hard to imagine because the Dogon now seem so unmistakably French, so urbane, so articulate, with such philosophical insight. The very themes central to their philosophy are themes in the main stream of Greek and Christian thought. For example, their reflections on sexual dualism echo those of Plato in very similar vein. And their use of anthropomorphic symbolism for the corpus politic and the mystical body is a preoccupation of Christian philosophers as well. Nuer myths, by contrast, are as crude as their way of life. Their manners are blunt, not to say rude. Their cosmological ideas are confused. To complete the contrast, the Dogon work out their metaphysics in terms of speech symbolism, the Nuer use more concrete cattle symbolism. The man whose personality and initiative give him a little leadership they call 'the bull of the herd'. The British, too, use a bovine metaphor to designate the man whose confident buying gives a lead to the stock market. 'The market is "bullish",' they say, or: 'Today bulls were active.' The Nuer may one day feel satisfaction that the national sobriquet of their ethnographers is John Bull. Thus while the Dogon seem pre-eminently susceptible to the literary and aesthetic investigation at which the French excel, the Nuer seem only apt for the discoveries in primitive politics and kinship which interest the British. Yet I long to subject each tribe to a fusion of the British and French techniques of research.

Of all the plays of Shakespeare it is said to be *Hamlet, Prince of Denmark* for which the Germans feel such strong affection. Of all the books on the Dogon it is Mme Calame-Griaule's *Ethnologie et langage* which draws me to Dogon studies. This great book is not a linguist's book about a language. Rather it is an account of Dogon reflections on language in general and their own language in particular. Out of their reflections on speech, the Dogon have created a symbolic structure uniformly embracing their entire universe. The grain of millet in its husk – the human foetus in the uterus –, the world in its atmospheric envelope, are each analogues of the others. The constituent materials and morphology of speech are seen to correspond to those of cereals, of man, of woven cloth, of the whole cosmos. The same intricate harmony of images is drawn down and across from one level of experience to the next. Reading it is like gazing through a microscope at a flourishing form of life, confusingly alien and familiar. The lens through which the Dogon see themselves is their theory of speech.

Many primitive cultures use one relatively narrow range of experience for developing a symbolic code. Nilotic peoples do this to some extent with cattle symbolism. Lienhardt has shown how such primary experiences as those of colour are mediated for Dinka children by prior reference to cattle colours; a man's image of himself is mediated by his identification with an ox, his experience of society is summed up in a series of animal sacrifices which give material for profound reflections on the nature of life and truth (Lienhardt, 1961). Ndembu develop something comparable by reflecting on the common qualities of juicy elements in men and trees; different coloured saps are classified with blood and milk and bile, and from their likenesses a cosmic harmony is derived (Turner, 1966). The Bushmen, reflecting on the morphology of human and animal bodies, have developed what Lévi-Strauss has called anatomical totemism. And so on. But the originality of the Dogon in this list is that the intellectual unity which they confer on experience is derived from reflecting on the nature, power and effects of language.

On first view this would presuppose a degree of self-consciousness about the processes of thought which would lift their culture clear out of the class of primitives. It is not fantastic to hope that the fully recorded epistemology of an ancient West African culture should produce a kind of break-through for us. It could at least produce a new perspective such as that produced in European art at the turn of the century by the impact of African sculpture. If traditional African art had an effect on the artistic vision of Europe at that time, it was because it was welcomed in French artistic circles. Conversely I predict that if African linguistics are to make a stir in modern Europe, the greatest impact is likely to be through Anglo-Saxon appreciation. For we regard ourselves as the home of several kinds of linguistic studies. Linguistic philosophy, let's face it, was born in Austria but naturalised British. Linguistics have several roots in our country, though the richest flowering has been in the United States. I can bring home to you our special claim on the Dogon by mentioning a few points of controversy to which their reflections make a definite contribution.

First, consider the support they lend to Malinowski. His main contribution to linguistics was to discover the relevance of social context. The stone he thus threw into the pond has made big ripples, but there are a few linguists who are not convinced. In this argument the Dogon come down clearly on the side of Malinowski. They have no doubt that language is a social activity and should be analysed as such. 'Dans la mesure où tout acte social suppose un échange de paroles, où tout acte individuel est lui-même une manière de s'exprimer, la "parole" est parfois synonyme d'action' (Calame-Griaule, 1965:24).

Second, linguistic philosophy started by analysing statements and considering the relation between statements and facts on which they impart information. Following this track they come to the position at which they have forgotten that some statements do not convey information but are performances of actions. J. L. Austin (1962) drew the attention of his colleagues to the class of performative sentences in which the utterance is the performance of an act.

> For example, some performative statements are contractual:
> 'I do take this woman to be my lawful wedded wife.'
> 'I bet you sixpence it will rain tomorrow.'
> Some are declaratory:
> 'I name this ship *Queen Elizabeth*.'
> 'I declare war.'

The Dogon do not need to be reminded of this faculty of speech. 'Acte et parole sont liés dans la pensée dogon, c'est pourquoi on appellera aussi symboliquement "parole" le résultat de l'acte, l'oeuvre, la création matérielle qui en résulte' (Calame-Griaule, 1965: 24). Dogon would even enlarge the performative class of speech to include insults and blessings (Calame-Griaule, 1965: 422–9), which they consider to have immediate material efficacy.

In these two instances the Dogon are on the side of contemporary thought. The things that our philosophers and linguists are now remarking are things the Dogon know well. But this is because among ourselves the movement to greater and greater specialisation has run itself to a halt in certain directions. We are forced to return to more naive approaches. It is not so remarkable that a traditional African philosophy should be found to enshrine some old truths we have forgotten.

More impressive is Dogon subtlety in respect of truth. As is well known, the Dogon divide their universe between Nommo and Yourougou. Nommo is the heavenly power who represents right, reason, society, ritual and order in all its forms. Yourougou or the Pale Fox is his brother, fallen from grace by an initial act of disobedience. He represents enigma, disorder. Dogon classify speech into twenty-four forms belonging to Nommo and twenty-four belonging to the Fox. The analysis of this classification shows the speech attributed to the Fox is the obverse of the speech attributed to Nommo. And it is fascinating to note that truth is associated with the Fox: that is, truth in all its forms, both unexpressed and truth expressed. Formal judgments are the speech of Nommo. They lay down the law, as it were. But the speech which predicts the future and the speech which sifts the truth from lies belong to the Fox. Here we can hail a really sophisticated approach to the sociology of truth.

Franz Steiner pointed out a similar native wisdom when he analysed Chagga concepts of truth (1954). A true statement, for the Chagga, had to be formally vested with an extra charge of value. For them the true word differs from ordinary speech in much the same way as we would distinguish sworn affidavits from other kinds of statement. Lienhardt, taking up this line of thought (1961), has observed an elaboration of the difference between ritual truth and actual truth among the Dinka. If the Dinka perform a sacrifice to turn aside the ill-effects of quarrelling, the sacrificer is likely, in his oration, to deny the existence of past quarrels. As Lienhardt says, he is not attempting to deceive divinity or hoping to get away with a false representation of what has happened. The ritual and prayer are used to control experience, to put an imprint on men's minds of what their life should be like and to bridge the gap between actual behaviour and moral intentions. So the Chagga give us sworn truth which is more fully guaranteed than ordinary statements, and the Dinka recognise ritual truth which may be very different from remembered experience.

Both these approaches allow less validity for the statements which are not ritualised. To this extent I find them naive and superficial. The Dogon recognise another kind of reality, that which is not expressed in ritual. For them formal judgments, curses and blessings are efficacious rites. They belong to Nommo. But truth belongs to the Fox. This is a marvellous insight. They recognise oracular truth and locate it somewhere beyond formal appearances. The truth of the Fox is discovered in oracles and it is held a truer truth than the judgments of priests and elders. This Fox should be a great surrealist figure, for he challenges the validity of realist perspectives. The Pale Fox is an obvious emblem for André Breton since he honours the riches and truth of the imagination. May we claim him also as an emblem for English anthropology? It is flattering, no doubt, to see ourselves in the guise of diviners. But here is the source of the paradoxical affinity which I see between our way of thinking and that of the Dogon.

Any culture which admits the use of oracles and divination is committed to a distinction between appearances and reality. The oracle offers a way of reaching behind appearances to another source of knowledge. We can therefore place Dogon thought in a historical perspective. For this is a perennial problem of philosophy. It is as alive today as it was for Parmenides and Plato.

As I understand Dogon philosophy, they place the world of appearances under the control of Nommo. It is a well-defined, well-illumined field. Their theory of speech and of thought is part of a crudely mechanistic physiology and psychology of hot and cold emotions. Their formal sociology deals only with external behaviour and it treats formal judgments and ritual statements in a formalistic way. An example of their concrete treatment of the world of appearances is the physical efficacy they attribute to speech. At the level of language analysis, I find the Dogon have only used their complex classification to produce another highly structured type of symbolic patterning, a totemism of linguistics, as it were. At the level of socio-linguistics, again, I find their insights less subtle and profound than I had hoped. Socio-linguistics is specially concerned with what is not said, the suppressed idea, the unexpressed choices which control use of verbal forms. The object of all behavioural sciences is to go behind the external forms of behaviour and discover other information than that which is overtly expressed.

At first sight Dogon formal theory of language is extremely simple on these points. Dogon comments on silence, hesitation and confused speech are not specially profound. They seem to be more concerned to classify their material rather than to solve any problem. The speech of the drunkard has neither oil nor grain, it has more beer than water and goes in gusty zigzags. The deaf-mute is like a child who has never acquired control of speech. The stutterer is not much better. False promises are equivalent to theft. The Dogon seem not to admit that it is possible for one sort of speech to rise up in the mind while another issues involuntarily from the mouth. They could not begin to discuss Benjamin Lee-Whorf's hypotheses about how language may shape our inchoate thoughts, since they do not recognise one except as the manifestation of the other. Their mechanical linguistic theory cannot deal with the case of a thinker deceived by the structures of his own words. Mme Calame-Griaule (1965: 546–7) notes this rigidity: '... on peut craindre que trop de codifications n'aboutissent à un formalisme stérile, qui ramènerait la société au péril d'immobilisme qu'elle voulait justement éviter. Nous pouvons nous demander quelle place la société dogon fait à la liberté.'

She indicates that the answer to this lies in the theory of divination. The oracle, by the obscure sign language of the Fox, aims at freedom from the formal conditions of knowledge. The oracle gives access to a form of reality which is free from the restrictive frame of time. The fox, by his initial incest with his mother, defied the order of the generations and so of time itself: thus he can read the future. Death lies in the domain of the Fox and the Fox knows secret remedies and poisons by which life and death can be controlled. It is clear that the Dogon are not misled by their solidly material theory of speech into seeing no difference between symbols and symbolised. Half of their coding system deals formally with knowledge of the world of appearances and half of it attempts to find short cuts by another method. The clear words of Nommo are contrasted with those of the Fox, which include false promises, contradictions, stuttering, and dreaming. Nommo is respectable, while the Fox is a shady character.

Thus the Dogon are as convinced as Plato that the world of appearances and sensation is not the whole of truth. They recognise another kind of reality. Plato used the metaphor of the prisoners in the cave who took their shadows to be real. They disbelieved the man who had been in the daylight of logic and philosophy, but he alone understood how the shadows were cast. For Plato the world of appearance is confused and shadowy and the world of ideas is bright. The Dogon reverse the light and shade. They situate real truth (the sifting of lies and contradictions) in the shadowy realm of the Pale Fox. Formal appearances they place in the daylight world of Nommo.

I ask you here to note the extraordinary sympathy between the Dogon and the surrealists, a sympathy of both methods and aims. André Breton was a poet, reflecting on the conditions of poetic inspiration. His problem was to go behind the screen of realist control and release the imagination. Stimulated by Freud's work on dreams, he also reversed Plato's pattern of light and shade. Wakefulness, logic and necessity for him distort and limit human experience. Revelation comes with dreams in the night, by means of nonsense, disjunction, total relaxation of control. There is not time to quote here his account of how he developed techniques for escaping the dreary perspectives of realism (Breton, 1924: 30–5). But one is struck at once by their close relation to techniques of oracular consultation.

From here we can place the British anthropologists in a new light. Apparently so down to earth, so practical, so interested in realist themes – now we turn out to be allies of the surrealists on the one hand, and of the Pale Fox of the Dogon on the other. For we also are passionately interested in getting behind the screen of appearance. All our professed interest in politics and kinship is an interest in the machinery that casts the shadows on the wall. The field in which our efforts have been most successful is in trying to discover the social determinants of cosmology. We have done regrettably little in the recording of cosmologies, but something more in what can be called pre-cosmology.

There is one field which is characteristically ours. That is the question of how mystical powers are distributed. There are at base only two classes of mystical power. On the one hand there is mystical knowledge, the power to see and reveal. On the other hand there is power to do harm or good to fellow men. The allocation of these powers is undoubtedly the part of cosmology which excites our interest. It is the mechanism which links cosmos to social structure. If we could understand this link, we could explain the intricate peculiarities of a particular cosmology by the channelling of energies in the particular social system. This is not the same as treating the cosmology as a mirror-image of the society. It is not showing the congruence of the infrastructure with superstructure. The programme is more ambitious – an attempt to discover how the two are generated. We start by assuming that society consists of individuals who seek to manipulate any given situation to their private intentions. Thus we have concentrated largely on the drive for power and legitimacy.

Durkheim rivetted our attention on cosmology as a source of legitimation. Evans-Pritchard has been called the Stendhal of anthropology. Certainly he has revealed the secrets of men's hearts. He first showed how Azande used oracles to manipulate social situations. He also saw that accusations of witchcraft are found in limited niches of the social structure. Since then, our best work has followed on these lines. I cite the work of Turner in Ndembu (1961) and Middleton in Lugbara (1960) on how divination serves political ends. And the work of Gellner on the Islamic cosmology of Berbers of Morocco. He found the alleged distribution of *baraka* or divine power is sensitively attuned to the distribution of political strength and has a practical effect in reinforcing the strong. Not only is *baraka* on the side of the big battalions, but they become even bigger as change of allegiance is justified by the appearance of *baraka* on the winning side. The exact mechanism of how *vox populi* becomes *vox dei* is our favourite puzzle. As to witchcraft, we should one day be able to map the areas of social structure in which men are likely to blame their misfortunes on others, and those in which the victim is held responsible for his own misfortunes.

In 'Spirits, witches and sorcerers in the supernatural economy of the Yakö', Daryll Forde has sought to show the human concerns for health and prosperity which energise the cosmological system. Here he was countering a tendency to attribute all cosmological variations too narrowly to variations in the social dimension. But elsewhere he has probably come closest to formulating a testable hypothesis on the relationship between cosmology and social structure. In *The Context of Belief* he suggests that the peculiarly fragmented and uncoordinated character of the Yakö cosmology and the lack of sharp definition given to the principal mystic forces which control their lives may be related to characteristics of their social structure: 'Where the field of interaction of the individual is both wide and heterogeneous as a result of activities and interests in a series of distinct, non-congruent units' (Forde, 1958b: 208–11), we may expect that beliefs in mystical forces are not closely co-ordinated in a harmonious and complex cosmology.

Now to draw the parallel between our consuming interest in pre-cosmology and those of the Dogon Pale Fox. Denise Paulme, in an important article (1937), tells us that any fine evening a number of Dogon men can be seen stooping over the flat sandy rocks outside the village. They are preparing their divining tables. They represent a man's personal problems by drawing a rectangular box with three sub-sections, one for heaven, one for

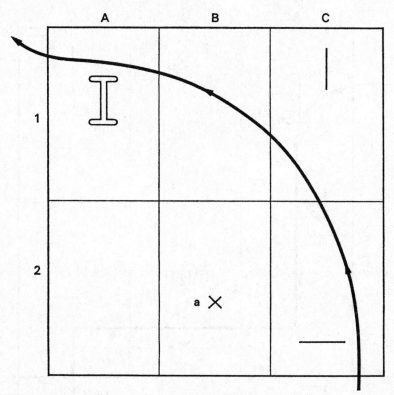

Figure 8.1
Question: Will the pale fox tell the truth?
Answer: Yes, because the tracks lead upwards

man and one for the Fox. The box of heaven has an upper half for dealing with all the divine powers and their attitudes to the consulter, and a lower half for dealing with his specific ritual duties. The rectangle for man has an upper section dealing with outsiders and enemies, and a lower section dealing with the consulter's own family. The upper section of the rectangle for the Fox deals with death in general, and the power part with the grave of the consulter himself. Here is a reduced and entirely abstract model of the universe. In these empty squares a man fills in little pebbles and sticks, to represent his personal problems. He diagrammatises the interplay of his ambition and his conscience. Psychologists use something of the same technique in devising

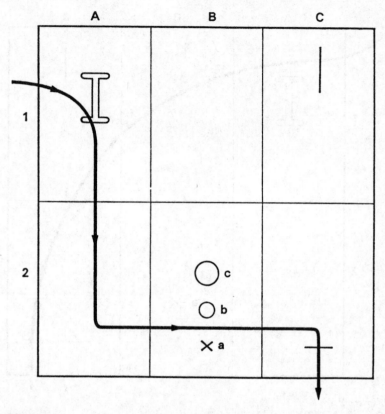

Figure 8.2
A member of the family will die. The tracks bypass B1 into B2, the enquirer's house, and come out by C2, squashing the object representing the graveyard. In B2 objects are placed to stand for the enquirer (a), his mouth (b) and his food (c)

games for child analysis. But I am struck with the efficiency and economy of the Fox oracle. Note that the symbols used for posing the problem are lifted out of their general context. They are stripped bare – mere tools for setting a limited question. Then note, and most important of all, that having posed the question the enquirer goes to bed. In the night the Pale Foxes will come and make mute signs with their paws on the sand and thus the truth will be revealed. The consulter abandons conscious control of the oracle. He does not expect that his rational analysis will

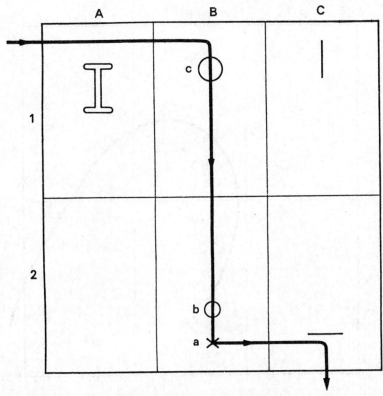

Figure 8.3
The enquirer will die. The tracks have squashed (c), the object
representing food in general in B1, gone on to tread on the enquirer's own food (b) in B2 and finally knocked over the stick
representing the enquirer himself (a), walking off through the graveyard in C2

yield results. He is even ready to admit that the way the problem
has been posed is all wrong. If one Fox runs along the divining
table from heaven to the grave, and another runs the other way,
he is forced to reconsider the whole matter and pose it again the
next day. In many ways the process of consultation reminds me
of the nightly examination of conscience recommended by St
Ignatius. But the Ignatian system put great stress on duty and
rational control. The Fox oracle, with its homage to the free
imagination, could have spiritual advantages. Perhaps the Fox

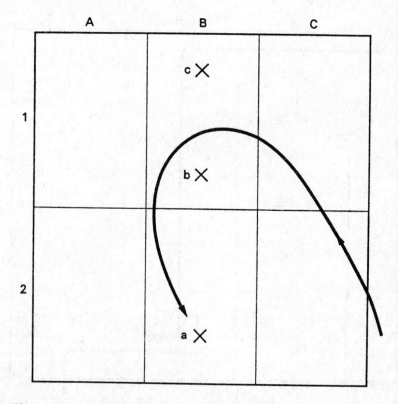

Figure 8.4
Question: Should the enquirer (a) ask the girl (b) to marry him?
The answer is favourable: the tracks encircle both (a) and (b). It
would have been negative if the tracks had gone between them. The
girl's family are represented by the cross at (c) in B1

oracle fits closer to the religious genius of St Francis of Assisi
who used little oracles to teach his monks humble dependence on
the will of God.

In reading of the techniques of the Fox oracle I am haunted by
the correspondence between this and the techniques of certain
surrealists. Artistic creation bristles with technical and personal
problems and the great work of art is always one in which the
artist has succeeded in organising both himself and his technical
apparatus at the same time. I do not understand Raymond
Roussel's poetry. But two of his books in prose, *Locus Solus* and

Impressions d'Afrique are wonderfully rich fantasies. They serve as a perfect illustration for my theme. He has described for us his elaborate technique in *Comment j'ai écrit certains de mes livres*. He would construct a kind of acrostic or *métagramme* as he called it. 'Je choisissais deux mots presque semblables (faisant penser aux métagrammes). Par exemple *billard* et *pillard*. Puis j'y ajoutais des mots pareils mais pris dans deux sens différents, et j'obtenais ainsi deux phrases presque identiques' (Roussel, 1963: 11). Then he would use these two phrases, so close in sound, but different in meaning as a problem for his imagination. Somehow within these artificial constraints a story had to be worked out. At first, when he was a very young writer, he set himself the task of opening his tale with the phrase in its more obvious meaning, and closing it with the same phrase in the more recondite sense. In between the two phrases the story hardly mattered. He used banal little Breton folk tales. The result was not a literary masterpiece – more a clever parlour trick, rather as Dr Johnson said of women novelists: If we are amazed at a dog standing on its hind legs it is not because it does it well, but that it does it at all! However, the young Roussel was cast down because his techniques did not bring him instant glory. Observe that one thing was missing from his early experiments. He had discovered a technique of creative writing but he had not learnt to use it to express his own preoccupations. As I see his early work, he was at the same point at which the late Marcel Griaule and Denise Paulme were in 1937 when they recorded the system of divination by the Fox. The technique was well demonstrated, but only by the use of hypothetical examples. They neither knew how the Dogon used it to solve *their* dominant preoccupations, *nor* how to use it to solve their *own* problems as investigators.

The cold neglect of his work drove Raymond Roussel to intensify his efforts. His technique became more elaborate and more supple. He used it to bore a narrow well into his imagination and then watched artesian waters gush up. The two books I admire give passionate expression to the writer's own personal concerns. They consist of loosely strung together episodes. Each describes the creation of a work of art which brings glory and renown to its author. Sometimes the episodes describe a man watching a crowd which is admiring a work of art, which portrays a crowd admiring a work of art, which portrays . . . and so on.

Generally the work of genius consisted in discovering how to make a work of art create itself. The inventor pushes a lever and starts the machinery working of its own accord. Michel Butor in his critical essay on Roussel has made it abundantly clear what personal driving force lies behind these stories. Here we have a writer who found a technique which harnessed the guiding power of his own ambition to his problems as a creative artist. Granted that he was one of the most richly imaginative writers of his generation, we only need to note three things about his technique: one, the violence done to the association between word and meaning, between symbol and thing symbolised; second, his adherence to rigid, artificial constraints; third, the indirect approach to the problem. This last is the true surrealist respect for the unfettered imagination. Somehow the work of art must be made free to produce itself. Note also that many of the fantastic inventions which Roussel described are no more and no less than oracular techniques which produce mysterious writings or hidden truths.

Now, finally, I must try to convince you that British anthropology is not inspired by down to earth concern with problems of colonialism. We must be classed along with other allies of the Fox, both in our aims and our techniques.

To start with the techniques, we reduce the universe to small-scale abstract models, such as genealogies and tables of village composition. These do not serve a love of genealogical lore for its own sake. They are designed to isolate the dynamic conflict of politics and conscience. Take, for example, Marwick's interpretation of Cewa witchcraft in 1952. He suspected that accusations of witchcraft expressed rival claims for political control. To demonstrate this he needed to depict the structure of political units: hence the need for lineage tables. Similarly, John Middleton in 1960 had an insight about how the ancestral cult of the Lugbara interacted dynamically with their witch beliefs. Above all, the insight itself derived from reflecting on the struggle for power and the channelling of private ambition through the lineage structure.

These techniques require a suspension of respect for the symbolic order. Raymond Roussel tore words apart and stripped them of fixed associations, to make them tools for richer uses. Less savagely than James Joyce, he treated words irreverently.

He would take a common phrase and chop it up phonetically into different units. From the phrase 'Napoléon Empereur', he got *nappe, ollé, ombre,* and these gave him the image of a Spanish dancer (*ollé*) on a table, so clearly seen that even the shadow (*ombre*) of the crumbs on the cloth (*nappe*) were visible. He thus made a practice of ignoring the stock meanings attached to verbal symbols and finding alternative readings. Surely the Dogon who consults the Fox oracle is also led to analyse his stock allegiances and confront himself with alternative readings of a situation. In a very sensitive perception, Denise Paulme suggests that the oracle consulter is torn between two desires. He must pose his problem unequivocally so as to get a clear answer for himself. But he must choose ambiguous symbols so as to disguise his problem from inquisitive eyes. Such a procedure would lead these tribal philosophers far into the problem of the relation between appearance and reality. No wonder their treatment of it in their cosmology is so sophisticated. Let me claim as much sophistication for the British anthropologists.

We also show little respect for symbols and try to prize them apart from the reality they represent. For example, David Tait in 1950 published an analysis of Dogon social structure with detailed lineage diagrams. By means of this tool of enquiry he discovered that Dogon social reality is less symmetrical than Dogon official theory claims. He found, for instance, that the arrangement of paired joking clans is not symmetrical. We should not be surprised, of course, that the pressure of living distorts the actual pattern from its ideal form. But the question then becomes more acute: What is the actual experience to which corresponds the Dogon ideal pattern of symmetrical pairs of twins? One final point as to technique: Only the oblique approach will yield the results we seek. The scrupulous setting down of informants' views merely sets up the screen which must then somehow be passed or penetrated. The kind of truths we seek to reveal are hidden from informants themselves. Hence our attempts to develop a foxy cunning in checking statements against action. In the nursery stories about Brer Fox, remember that he always 'laid low and said nuffin'. We try likewise to lie low and to eschew direct questions. We aim to let the informants reveal, by contradiction and inconsistency, the practical social uses to which their cosmological schemes are put.

So much for technique. I hesitate whether to count Professor Lévi-Strauss among the followers of the Fox. Obviously he too is passionately interested in going behind the screen and finding hidden meanings. He is a great diviner. His techniques are as rigid and as oblique as any and he certainly succeeds in catching the informant unawares. Above all, he seeks to reveal the mechanism which casts the shadows on the wall. His prodigious achievement has dealt precisely with the relation between infrastructure and superstructure. On all these counts he is with us up to the hilt, only one detail is missing. He works at the cognitive level of experience. He is not interested in the self-regarding passions. I feel he is hardly at all concerned with the effect of men's ambition and remorse on society and its cosmos. This is the crucial difference between his work and the kind of English anthropology in Africa that I am talking about. Working on this same problem of Plato's World of Forms, he stays with Plato and we stay, perhaps benightedly, with the Fox.

To conclude. The ethnographers of the Dogon and the Nuer are following different trails and use different techniques to pursue different kinds of quarry. Their combined research would open a new era of advance in these sciences. The French would map the marvellous world of forms, whilst the English would burrow underground. Who are these sorcerers whom the Dogon fear? Who is accused and why, and what is the result of an accusation? What is the real balance of power which is expressed in the honouring of twins and the rejection of odd numbers? Where is authority most precarious? What is the ladder to advancement? In these subterranean corridors we are more at home.

Note

Based on a paper given on 9 March 1967 at the École Pratique des Hautes Études (VIth Section, Sorbonne). I wish to record my gratitude to Mme Denise Paulme for her discussion. I am grateful to the Société des Africanistes for permission to reproduce Figures 8.1–4 from Paulme (1937).

Bibliography

AUSTIN, J. L. (1962), *How to Do Things with Words, The William James Lectures at Harvard, 1955*, Oxford University Press.

BRETON, A. (1924), *Manifeste du surréalisme*, Paris.

BUTOR, M. (1966), *Essais sur les modernes*, Paris.

CALAME-GRIAULE, G. (1965), *Ethnologie et langage. La parole chez les Dogon*, Paris.

EVANS-PRITCHARD, E. (1937), *Witchcraft, Oracles and Magic among the Azande*, Oxford, Clarendon Press.

FORDE, D. (1958a), 'Spirits, witches and sorcerers in the supernatural economy of the Yokö', *Journal of the Royal Anthropological Institute*, 88, 2, 165–78.

FORDE, D. (1958b), *The Context of Belief, a Consideration of Fetishism among the Yakö*, The Frazer Lecture for 1957, Liverpool University Press.

GELLNER, E. (1961), 'Role and organisation of a Berber Zawiya', London, Ph. D. Thesis. (1969), *Saints of the Atlas*, London, Weidenfeld & Nicolson.

GRIAULE, M. (1937), 'Notes sur la divination par le chacal', *Bulletin du Comité d'Études Historiques et Scientifiques et l'Afrique Occidentale Française*, 20, 1–2, 113–41.

LIENHARDT, G. (1961), *Divinity and Experience, the Religion of the Dinka*, London, Oxford University Press.

MARWICK, M. G. (1952), 'The social context of Cewa witch beliefs', *Africa*, 22, 120–35, 215–33.

MIDDLETON, J. (1960), *Lugbara Religion*, London, Oxford University Press.

PAULME, D. (1937), 'La divination par les chacals chez les Dogon de Sanga', *Journal de la Société des Africanistes*, 7, 1–15.

ROUSSEL, R. (n.d.), *Locus Solus* [Paris].

ROUSSEL, R. (n.d.), *Impressions d'Afrique* [Paris].

ROUSSEL, R. (1963), *Comment j'ai écrit certains de mes livres* [Paris].

STEINER, F. (1954), 'Chagga truth', *Africa*, 24, 364–9.

TAIT, D. (1950), 'An analytical commentary on the social structure of the Dogon', *Africa*, 20, 3, 175–99.

TURNER, V. W. (1961), 'Ndembu divination: its symbolism and techniques', (*Rhodes-Livingstone Paper*, 31), Manchester University Press.

TURNER, V. W. (1966), 'Colour classification in Ndembu ritual', *Anthropological Approaches to the Study of Religion*, general editor M. Banton, ASA, 3, London.

WHORF, B. L. (1956), *Language, Thought and Reality, Selected Writings of Benjamin Lee Whorf*, J. B. Carroll (ed.), Cambridge, Mass., Harvard University Press.

9

The Healing Rite

The healing power of symbols is central to the whole subject of symbolic meaning. Now that Turner's four volumes on Ndembu are published (1957; 1962; 1967; 1968), we should see where we stand, as anthropologists, on ritual healing. In the long run nearly everything he has written is concerned with the efficacy of symbols. This is partly because Ndembu rituals claim to have power to heal the body as well as to enlighten the mind; consequently every piece of the jigsaw puzzle of how to interpret their symbolic acts contributes to understanding the great moments when sickness is brought under priestly control. So the climax of the sequence of Ndembu studies is the performance of *ihamba*, the rite which cures one Kamahasanyi of his lassitude and backache by extracting from his body the tooth of an angry dead hunter's ghost. His body purged thus of a symbol of jealous backbiting is itself the symbol of the village which is purged, by the same ritual, of intrusive elements in its system. It is also a symbol of the matrilineal principle reaffirmed in its purity and solidarity – to the confusion of intrusive patrilateral segments and unbrotherly brethren. The rite is not only symbolic in the expressive sense. It even brings about the required changes at the physical and social levels.

To show how a rite can achieve all this the anthropologist requires a detailed analysis of the social structure as well as an analysis of the symbolic system. To provide such detailed analyses of life crises, afflictions and of how the Ndembu ritualise them, creates thorny problems of interpretation. Only when the descriptions are on record and the interpretations justified is

Turner ready for a summing up and demonstration. His *Drums of Affliction* is the climax to which the previous studies lead.

The two books under review relate to one another and to previously published Ndembu studies as follows. First in 1957 came *Schism and Continuity*. This was an analysis of the Ndembu social system. It described how the pulls of matrilineal descent and village membership create personal dilemmas. Here was elaborated the concept of social drama, a ritual resolution of conflict and an affirming of community values. This is the base line, as it were, for subsequent studies of ritual. Then came *Chihamba, the White Spirit* (1962) a short book describing a particular cult. Now we have in *The Forest of Symbols* (1967) a set of papers which originally appeared in various books and journals. Four deal with the interpretation of ritual symbols; two with rituals of healing, one with hunting ritual, one with witchcraft and sorcery and two with initiation. One of the latter, on boys' circumcision, is entirely new and has not been published elsewhere. Then in 1968, published by the International African Institute, another volume, *The Drums of Affliction*, deals specifically with ritual healing. There is some overlap between the two last books. The first contains two chapters on healing while the second has a long section on girls' puberty ritual which might well have gone into the first. Turner (1968: 198) explains the principle by which he includes life crisis rituals in the book on rites of affliction by a valuable essay on ritual legitimation. While affliction rituals, as distinct from life crisis rituals,

> are *ad hoc* and unpredictable in their origin and represent responses to unprecedented events, the latter accompany the passage of an individual, or a set of similarly circumstanced individuals, from one social status to another. It is on such occasions of life crises, when fairly elaborate *rites de passage* are performed, that the legitimacy of certain crucial principles of Ndembu society is most fully and publicly endorsed. In the rituals of affliction we see these principles under challenge; in the life crisis rituals we see them being renewed and replenished.

Thus there is a true sense in which the study of healing symbols would not be complete without examining the whole context in which symbols are generated and applied. For the same reason, the book dealing specifically with healing condenses a great deal of the previous material on social structure and on interpretation.

It is extremely valuable to have in the 1967 volume articles which have been scattered and relatively inaccessible. It is also of first importance to have within one set of covers a self-sufficient account of the healing rites of one culture. Without further introduction *The Drums of Affliction* can be put into the hands of anthropologists, psychologists, medical sociologists or anyone interested in the subject. The achievement is so extensive that I cannot take up points of detail without losing proportion. Let me say something general about the scope and originality of the project which is now complete. No one else has done quite this: to push as far as possible the relation of the symbolic to the social order, showing how each gives form to the other in a dynamic intermingling of meanings. In this example we have the answer to the ticklish problem of validation. Anthropologists are rightly always worried by the danger of subjectively imposing their categories on the material to be analysed. How can we control this subjective factor? Turner's answer is to require a convincing demonstration of how the cultural categories sustain a given social structure. It should never again be permissible to provide an analysis of an interlocking system of categories of thought which has no demonstrable relation to the social life of the people who think in these terms. For example, my own discussion of animal categories in the Old Testament, an analysis of Leviticus 11 in *Purity and Danger* (1966), cannot be acceptable on the standards laid down.

Of course Turner is also original in the quality of his fieldwork. In systematic coverage he is unrivalled. The reading may be repetitive, but this is inevitable for one alive to the need to prove that he has not imposed his own patterns on his material. There is pawky humour, tender observation of personality and many switches of style, expository, narrative and even lyrical. But these books do not make easy reading. Turner always requires us to be projected into the Ndembu social world. He expects us to understand the micro-history and current micro-social structure of Ndembu villages. Then from a strictly local point of departure he proceeds to analyse their treatment of the common themes of birth, sex, authority and death. I pride myself on being specially interested in central African ethnography, so it is from a critical vantage point that I confess that his interpretations seem to be as objectively valid as they can be (given the elementary stage of theoretical understanding of the subject). Indeed, my own professional concerns about Turner's reporting are quite the other way. His villages are located, mapped, their history recorded. The inhabitants are placed on genealogical charts. Their ambitions and conflicts with one another are the essential background to learning the meaning of the rituals. Their names are no doubt scrambled, but to little purpose since each individual seems to be entirely and unmistakably identifiable. What will they feel like when they read these pages in years to come? (Turner, 1968: 197, 192).

> Kamahasanyi, sterile as he was, weak, effeminate, formerly suspected of sorcery, slightly paranoid . . .

> For Kamahasanyi appeared to have passive homosexual tendencies, which suggested there might be a conflict between masculine and feminine strivings in his unconscious psyche. It is not perhaps too surprising that he had undergone several performances of Ihamba, a ritual which might be considered to provide masochistic gratifications and to imitate, in its emissions of blood, agonised writhings and final expulsion of an object from within the body, certain of the features of parturition.

It may be as well for Turner that Kamahasanyi has no descendants to come to Chicago to avenge their father's dignity.

The study of colour symbolism has been justly celebrated ever since a paper on it was read to the Association of Social Anthropologists in 1963 (Turner, 1965). Curiously enough, Turner himself has been in a poor position to exploit fully the tight little complex of meanings he discovered in the ritual combination of black, red and white. He was primarily engaged on the exercise I have just described, that of raising the whole standard of fieldwork, of validation of ethnographers' interpretations, of analytically relating the social and cultural processes. This task, once achieved, makes possible more condensed presentations for future fieldworkers whose range of relevance has been established once and for all. However, it is quite certain that the colour meanings are only one important set. If Turner had been the old style cultural anthropologist he would have delved until he revealed other equally tightly organised sets and demonstrated their structural interrelationships. His special originality is to have come close enough to the field of action to show how meanings arise spontaneously in the minds of people, then are polished up and brought out to express great public occasions. Layer after layer of meaning accrues to each symbol as its application is extended. At each context a social consensus isolates a particular sense. Obviously the working out of the lexical consistency and the syntactic flexibility of the whole ritual language would be a very complex task. Turner could hardly have had time to achieve this as well as what he has done. We seem to have come a long way since Leach (1958: 151–2) was able to write that it is

> surely useless to enquire just why one set of symbolisations is employed in preference to another? Europeans wear black for mourning, Chinese white. In each case the special status of the mourner is indicated by the wearing of a special dress. But the question of *why* one culture selects black for this purpose and another white is surely both irrelevant and unanswerable.

Leach of course is assuming that the answer that is not irrelevant is in terms of the total patterning of symbols in the culture. But by demonstrating how these arise Turner is able legitimately to raise interesting questions about the experiences that generate both thought and society – the enterprise which Lévi-Strauss says only a fool or a genius could attempt (Lévi-Strauss, 1962: 173).

It is very revealing to compare Turner's work on the efficacy of symbols with that of Lévi-Strauss on the same theme. Admittedly, for Turner it is the main interest and for Lévi-Strauss a subsidiary one. But each has written about the calling of the diviner in strikingly different vein. Both would agree that his stock-in-trade is a set of symbolic structures which tend towards creating harmony between different layers of experience. Both would agree that the diviner cures by locating discrepancies and by realigning the patient's subjective attitudes to an acceptable pattern of symbols. Lévi-Strauss's model is the wonder-working shaman of the American shamanist tradition. He dazzles by the skill of his conjuring and the force of his personality. He achieves his cures by producing a social consensus in favour of himself and at the expense of rivals. It is very much a question of outwitting and out-shining (Lévi-Strauss, 1958: 198). 'Quesalid did not become a great shaman because he cured his patients; he cured his patients because he had become a great shaman.' The passage quoted goes on to say that the diviner's own neurotic imagination provides a symbolic mode in which normal thought can fathom the problem of illness. The symbolic systems which the shaman employs draw their emotional force from their correspondence with the psychological and physical experiences of the patient. In another essay on the effectiveness of symbols Lévi-Strauss shows how the shaman works directly on the psyche of his patients (1958: ch. 10). The intervening social structure plays no role in investing the symbols with their emotional power: doctor and patient might be alone (for all explanatory purposes) in an imagined universe constructed by the shaman specially for the séance.

Victor Turner's shaman is also a conjuror; he produces by sleight of hand objects from the sufferer's body. But his style so eschews the flamboyantly magical that he rather suggests a psychiatric social worker. His task is to size up a social problem in terms of an accepted and usual pattern of symbols, and then to encourage his clients to conform to the moral norms of their culture. To this end he gets them to dramatise their situation in an established ritual idiom. At the same time he skilfully manipulates their relationships. Any personal charisma is masked. According to Turner's account, knowing how the social structure works and is symbolised is much more important for the Ndembu shaman than to make a brilliant dazzle.

Place the Anglo-Saxon and the Gaul side by side and we have two anthropologists speaking to us in just such contrasted styles about the way to understand symbols. But any *ad hominem* conclusion is very out of place. They are talking about two different cultures, oceans apart. Each anthropologist forms his bias in association with his informants. The culture interacts with the researcher and to disallow this factor is to lose the rightful impact of his teaching. No doubt at all, ritual healing and social structure are very different, between America and Africa. If Lévi-Strauss had been instructed at an impressionable age by Ndembu teachers he would have written differently. He would surely have been as apt a pupil as Turner for the scholarly Windson,

F*

Muchona, Ihembi and the others. Take the portrait of Muchona, contrasted with his rival (Turner, 1967: 132, 134):

> Kasonda was worldly and a shade spiteful, *au fait* with the seamier side of Ndembu (and indeed human) nature. He took a rancorous zest in the struggle for headmanship, prestige and money that were the bane of village life. Muchona, for all his battling against witchcraft and the moody, punitive dead, had a curious innocence of character and objectivity of outlook. I was to find that in the balance mankind came off well for Muchona. Between these men lay the gap that has at all times divided the true philosopher from the politician. . . . Living as he had done on the margins of many structured groups and not being a member of any particular group, his loyalties could not be narrowly partisan, and his sympathies were broader than those of the majority of his fellow tribesmen. His experience had been richer and more varied than that of most Ndembu, though all Ndembu, being hunters and semi-nomadic cassava cultivators travel considerable distances during their lives.

This was one of the men who held seminars for the anthropologist on the intricate meanings of colours and rituals. Writing of him as a practitioner, Turner is concerned to point out his courage and gentleness (1967: 137, 138):

> Muchona was treating a woman who was suffering from delusions as a result of puerperal fever. My friend was impressed by what he considered the 'compassionateness' of Muchona's demeanour. Gone was the rather uneasy pertness and comicality of his usual manner; in its stead was an almost maternal air – kind, capable hands washing with medicine, a face full of grave concern. My friend commented on the 'heroism' with which Muchona, at one phase of the ritual, ventured out alone into the ghost-ridden graveyard, far from the firelight, to exorcise the agencies of evil that were making the poor victim writhe and babble nonsense. He subdued his fear to his curative vocation.

In our 'seminars', Muchona seldom betrayed the emotional bases of his calling. A new and exhilarating intellectual dimension had opened up to him as well as to myself in our discussions of symbolism. At such times he had the bright hard eye of some raptor, hawk or kite, as he poised over a definitive explanation. Watching him, I sometimes used to fancy that he would have been truly at home scoring debating points on a don's dais, gowned or perhaps in a habit. He delighted in making explicit what he had known subliminally about his own religion. A curious quirk of fate had brought him an audience and fellow enthusiasts of a kind he could never have encountered in the villages.

Returning to the comparison with Lévi-Strauss and American shamanism, we should recall the difficulties that Lowie voiced about Durkheim's theory of totemism (Lowie, 1925). To Durkheim's thesis that religious beliefs expressed and sustained society, Lowie riposted that Crow religion was emphatically individualistic. But there is no doubt that Crow social organisation, at least at the level of kinship, was nowhere near as highly systematised as that of the Australian aborigines. It thus seems fair to suppose that Durkheim would never have developed the full theme of *The Elementary Forms of the Religious Life* if he had only had access to Crow and other Plains Indian material. So it is interesting to suppose that Turner's approach to rites of affliction, so strongly Durkheimian in feeling, would never have been developed if he had worked under the instruction of American Indian shamans. It may well be possible that a therapeutic tradition in which the patient and doctor construct their own world of fantasy for comprehending the illness may work in a particular kind of social structure and not in others. In two accounts of ritual efficacy (1958: chs 9 and 10) Lévi-Strauss can proceed as if no restrictions from the social structure need to intervene between the individual patient and the pattern of efficacious symbols spun for him by the diviner. There seem to be no limits to what an imaginative and histrionic performer can induce his community to believe. A Zuni boy accused of sorcery cures his alleged victim by spinning fantastic tales. He is quite explicitly said to be inventing his tall stories and the problem to be explained is how he himself comes to believe in his own fiction (1958: 189–92). The Cuna shaman's song (1958: 205–26) describes the dangers faced by the unborn baby in its mother's womb. Lévi-Strauss does not say that any song which endows the labouring woman's body with cosmic significance would equally well affect her emotional power to respond. Indeed, he stresses (pp. 217–8) that the cure requires that she and her community should believe in the mythology. The social processes by which belief is engendered and sustained are not described. Yet it must be quite misleading for an anthropologist to give the impression that efficacious symbols can always be woven out of private fantasy without reference to the social system. The relevance of this for Ronald Laing's psychiatric work is obvious.

No one has done more than Lévi-Strauss to display the interlocking categories of culture. These constitute a public symbolic system which is available for everyone to draw upon who is a member of the culture. He shows how they are based upon basic social categories and how they schematise all the material aspects of life into patterns of meaning. Lévi-Strauss does not take culture to be a static thing. Everything he has written shows his interest in how changes in the social structure such as the erosion of the moiety system or of clans or variations in the division of labour go with corresponding alterations in the cosmological scheme. Therefore he postulates an interaction between individual and society and some kind of mediation of the social system on the kinds of symbolic patterns which the public culture can generate.

When it comes to ritual healing and the efficacy of magic, however, he takes this narrower and less sociological view. It would almost seem as if the healer were free to be a *bricoleur*, fitting together the bits of the local stock of symbols into the patterns that will most impress his audience and his patient. Yet the rest of his writing implies that the *bricolage* is controlled by the exigencies of a particular social structure in which the patient is involved. The symbols the diviner chooses to apply must be those which allow everyone concerned to perceive a desirable social configuration and, having recognised it, to achieve it. Therefore the healer is not working simply on the psyche of the patient, in terms of their widest social concerns. His business is with how they internalise the values of their society. Useless for him to propose heroic sacrifice if it is not already validated; useless to open new perspectives of hitherto unimagined love and harmony which leave his audience unconvinced. If his therapy works it is because the symbols are creative instruments of a particular social structure. It is precisely here that Turner makes his special contribution.

Lévi-Strauss first aroused intense excitement by announcing what he was going to do by applying structural analysis to mythology (1955). He then proceeded to apply it, in volume after volume (1964, 1966, 1968). The anticipatory demand was already created. Clearly Turner's intellectual odyssey has been rather the other way. He approached his material with openness, ready to find what it contained. The surprises in it probably surprised himself. The very integrity with which he has developed his insights has limited their impact. Here we have a Ndembu-style philosopher, relatively home-spun, making a tremendous contribution to discussions going on in the glare and noise of a more spectacular forum. To make sure that it is fully used is the challenge for us.

Bibliography

DOUGLAS, MARY (1966), *Purity and Danger: an Analysis of Concepts of Pollution and Taboo*, London, Routledge & Kegan Paul.

DURKHEIM, É. (1915), *The Elementary Forms of the Religious Life*, London, Allen & Unwin.

LEACH, E. R. (1958), 'Magical hair', *J. R. Anthrop. Inst.*, 88, 147–63.

LÉVI-STRAUSS, C. (1955), '*The structural study of myth*. In Myth: a symposium,' *J. Am. Folkl.*, 78, 428–44.

LÉVI-STRAUSS, C. (1958), *Anthropologie structurale*, Paris, Plon.

LÉVI-STRAUSS, C. (1962), *La Pensée sauvage*, Paris, Plon.

LÉVI-STRAUSS, C. (1964), *Le Cru et le cuit* (Mythologiques *1*), Paris, Plon.

LÉVI-STRAUSS, C. (1966), *Du Miel aux cendres* (Mythologiques *2*), Paris, Plon.

LÉVI-STRAUSS, C. (1968), *L'Origine des manières de table* (Mythologiques *3*), Paris, Plon.

LOWIE, R. H. (1925), *Primitive Religion*, London, Routledge & Kegan Paul.

TURNER, V. W. (1957), *Schism and Continuity in an African Society: a Study of Ndembu Religious Life*, Manchester University Press.

TURNER, V. W. (1962), 'Chihamba, the White Spirit' (*Rhodes-Livingstone Paper, 33*), Manchester University Press.

TURNER, V. W. (1965), 'Colour classification in Ndembu ritual: a problem in primitive classification' in M. Banton (ed.), *Anthro-*

pological *Approaches to the Study of Religion* (Ass. Social Anthrop. Monogr., 3), London, Tavistock.

TURNER, V. W. (1967), *The Forest of Symbols: Aspects of Ndembu Ritual*, New York, Cornell University Press.

TURNER, V. W. (1968), *The Drums of Affliction: a Study of Religious Process among the Ndembu of Zambia*, Oxford, Clarendon Press.

10

The Meaning of Myth

Social anthropology, as we know it, was born of a professedly empirical approach. And it was first developed in Britain. These two marks, of being British and empirical, are not accidentally linked. This is the home of philosophical scepticism, an attitude of thought which has insulated us more effectively than the North Sea and the Channel from Continental movements of ideas. Our intellectual climate is plodding and anti-metaphysical. Yet, in spite of these traditions, we cannot read much of Lévi-Strauss without feeling some excitement. To social studies he holds out a promise of the sudden lift that new methods of science could give. He has developed his vision so elaborately and documented it so massively from so many fields of our subject that he commands our attention.

He has developed most explicitly in connection with myth his ideas of the place of sociology within a single grand discipline of Communication. This part of his teaching draws very broadly on the structural analysis of linguistics, and on cybernetics and communication theory in general, and to some extent on the related theory of games. Briefly, its starting-point is that it is the nature of the mind to work through form. Any experience is received in a structured form, and these forms or structures, which are a condition of knowing, are generally unconscious (as, for example, unconscious categories of language). Furthermore, they vary little in modern or in ancient times. They always consist in the creation of pairs of opposites, which are balanced against one another and built up in various (algebraically representable) ways. All the different kinds of patterned activity can be analysed according to the different structures they produce. For example, social life is a matter of interaction between persons. There are three different types of social communication. First, there is kinship, the structure underlying the rules for transferring women; second, there is the economy, that is the structure underlying transfer of goods and services; third, there is the underlying structure of language. The promise is that if we can get at these structures, display and compare them, the way is open for a true science of society, so far a will-o'-the-wisp for sociologists.

So far myth has not been mentioned. Lévi-Strauss recognizes that its structures belong to a different level of mental activity from those of language, and the technique of analysis must be correspondingly different. The technique is described in his 'Structural study of myth' (1955) and is also made very clear in Edmund Leach's two articles (1961, 1962) in which he applies the technique to the Book of Genesis. It assumes that the analysis of myth should proceed like the analysis of language. In both language and myth the separate units have no meaning by themselves, they acquire it only because of the way in which they are combined. The best comparison is with musical notation: there is no musical meaning in a single isolated note. Describing the new science of mythologics which is to parallel linguistics, Lévi-Strauss unguardedly says that the units of mythological structure are sentences. If he took this statement seriously it would be an absurd limitation on analysis. But in fact, quite rightly, he abandons it at once, making great play with the structure underlying the meaning of a set of names. What are sentences, anyway? Linguists would be at a loss to identify these units of language structure which Lévi-Strauss claims to be able to put on punched cards and into a computing machine as surely and simply as if they were phonemes and morphemes. For me and for most of us, computer talk is a mysterious language very apt for prestidigitation. Does he really mean that he can chop a myth into semantic units, put them through a machine, and get out at the other end an underlying pattern which is not precisely the one he used for selecting his units? The quickness of the hand deceives the eye. Does he further believe that this underlying structure is the real meaning or sense of the myth? He says that it is the deepest kind of sense, more important than the uninitiated reader would suspect. However, I do not think it is fair to such an ebullient writer to take him literally. In other contexts it is plain that Lévi-Strauss realizes that any myth has multiple meanings and that no one of them can be labelled the deepest or the truest. More of this later.

From the point of view of anthropology, one of his novel departures is to treat all versions of a myth as equally authentic or relevant. This is right, of course. Linguistic analysis can be applied to any literary unit, and the longer the better, so long as there is real unity underlying the stretches of language that are analysed together. Why stop short at one of Shakespeare's historical plays? Why not include the whole of Shakespeare? Or the whole of Elizabethan drama? Here Lévi-Strauss gives one of his disturbing twists of thought that make the plodding reader uneasily suspect that he is being duped. For by 'version' we find that Lévi-Strauss means both version and interpretation. He insists that Freud's treatment of the Oedipus myth must be put through the machine together with other earlier versions. This challenging idea is not merely for the fun of shocking the bourgeois mythologist out of his search for original versions. Freud used the Oedipus myth to stand for his own discovery that humans are each individually concerned with precisely the problem of 'birth from one' or 'birth from two' parents. On Lévi-Strauss's analysis of its structure, this problem is revealed as underlying the Oedipus cycle. So there is no inconsistency between Freud and Sophocles. But the reference to Freud interestingly vindicates Lévi-Strauss on a separate charge. Some must feel that the themes which his technique reveals are too trivial and childish either to have been worth the excavation, or to have been worth the erecting of an elaborate myth series in the first place. But after Freud no one can be sure that an individual's speculation about his own genesis is a trivial puzzle without emotional force.

I admit that the use of all interpretations of a great myth might not always so triumphantly vindicate this method. Meyer Fortes (1959) treated Oedipus rather differently in *Oedipus and Job in West Africa*. Compare St Augustine, Simone Weil (1950), and Edmund Leach (1962) on the Biblical story of Noah drunk in the vineyard: for one the drunken, naked Noah is Christ humiliated; for the other he is the dionysian mysteries too austerely rejected by the Jewish priesthood, and for the last the tale is a trite lesson about Hebrew sexual morality. I will say more below of how these 'versions' would look coming out of the mythologic computer. At this stage of the discussion we should treat the computer as a red herring and forget for the moment the quest for the real meaning. We can then begin seriously to evaluate Lévi-Strauss's approach to mythology.

First, we should recognize his debt to the dialectical method of Hegelian-Marxist philosophy. The dialectic was Hegel's speculation about the nature of reality and about the logical technique by which it could be grasped. When Lévi-Strauss says that mythic thought follows a strict logic of its own, he means a Hegelian logic of thesis, antithesis, and synthesis, moving in ever more complex cycles to comprehend all the oppositions and limitations inherent in thought. According to Lévi-Strauss, the structure of myth is a dialectic structure in which opposed logical positions are stated, the oppositions mediated by a restatement, which again, when its internal structure becomes clear, gives rise to another kind of opposition, which in its turn is mediated or resolved, and so on.

On the assumption that it is the nature of myth to mediate contradictions, the method of analysis must proceed by distinguishing the oppositions and the mediating elements. And it follows, too, that the function of myth is to portray the contradictions in the basic premises of the culture. The same goes for the relation of myth to social reality. The myth is a contemplation of the unsatisfactory compromises which, after all, compose social life. In the devious statements of the myth, people can recognize indirectly what it would be difficult to admit openly and yet what is patently clear to all and sundry, that the ideal is not attainable.

Lévi-Strauss does not stick his neck out so far as to say that people are reconciled better or worse to their makeshift arrangements and contradictory formulae – but merely that myth makes explicit their experience of the contradictoriness of reality.

A summary of 'La Geste d'Asdiwal' best demonstrates how this is to be understood. It is a cycle of myths told by the Tsimshian tribes. These are a sparse population of migratory hunters and fishers who live on the Pacific coast, south of Alaska. They are culturally in the same group with Haida and Tlingit, northernmost representatives of Northwest Coast culture. Topographically their territory is dominated by the two parallel rivers, Nass and Skeena, which flow southwest to the sea. In the summer they live on vegetable products collected by women, and in winter on marine and land animals and fish killed by the men. The movements of fish and game dictate their seasonal movements between sea and mountains, and the northern and southern rivers. The Tsimshian were organized in dispersed matrilineal clans and lived in typical Northwest Coast composite dwellings which housed several families. They tended to live with their close maternal kin, generally practising avunculocal residence at marriage and the ideal was to marry a mother's brother's daughter.

The myth begins during the winter famine in the Skeena valley. A mother and daughter, separated hitherto by their marriages but now both widowed by the famine, set out from east and west, one from upstream and one from downstream of the frozen Skeena, to meet each other half-way. The daughter becomes the wife of a mysterious bird who feeds them both and when she gives birth to a miraculous child, Asdiwal, its bird father gives him a magic bow and arrow, lance, snow-shoes, cloak, and hat which make him invisible at will, invincible, and able to produce an inexhaustible supply of food. The old mother dies and the bird father disappears. Asdiwal and his mother walk west to her natal village. From there he follows a white bear into the sky where it is revealed as Evening-Star, the daughter of the Sun. When Asdiwal has succeeded, thanks to his magic equipment, in a series of impossible tasks, the Sun allows him to marry Evening-Star, and, because he is homesick, to take his wife back to the earth generously supplied with magic food. On earth, because Asdiwal is unfaithful to her, his sky wife leaves him. He follows her half-way to the sky, where she kills him with a thunderbolt. His father-in-law, the Sun, brings him to life and they live together in the sky until Asdiwal feels homesick again. Once home, Asdiwal finds his mother is dead and, since nothing keeps him in her village, he continues walking to the west. This time he makes a Tsimshian marriage, which starts off well, Asdiwal using his magic hunting-weapons to good effect. In the spring he, his wife, and her four brothers move along the coast northwards, towards the River Nass, but

Asdiwal challenges his brothers-in-law to prove that their sea-hunting is better than his land-hunting. Asdiwal wins the contest by bringing home four dead bears from his mountain hunt, one for each of the four brothers, who return empty handed from their sea expedition. Furious at their defeat, they carry off their sister and abandon Asdiwal, who then joins some strangers also going north towards the Nass for the candlefish season. Once again, there are four brothers, and a sister whom Asdiwal marries. After a good fishing season, Asdiwal returns with his in-laws and wife to their village, where his wife bears them a son. One day, however, he boasts that he is better than his brothers-in-law at walrus-hunting. Put to the test, he succeeds brilliantly, again infuriating his wife's brothers, who abandon him without food or fire to die on a rocky reef. His bird father preserves him through a raging storm. Finally, he is taken by a mouse to the underground home of the walruses whom he has wounded. Asdiwal cures them and asks in exchange a safe return. The King of the Walruses lends Asdiwal his stomach as a boat, on which he sails home. There he finds his faithful wife, who helps him to kill her own brothers. But again Asdiwal, assailed by home-sickness, leaves his wife and returns to the Skeena valley, where his son joins him. When winter comes, Asdiwal goes hunting in the mountains, but forgetting his snow-shoes, can go neither up nor down and is changed into stone.

This is the end of the story. In the analysis which follows, Lévi-Strauss draws out the remarkably complex symmetry of different levels of structure. Asdiwal's journeys take him from east to west, then north to the Nass, then southwest to the sea fishing of walrus, and finally southeast back to the Skeena River. So the points of the compass and the salient points of order of Tsimshian migration are laid out. This is the geographical sequence. There is another sequence concerned with residence at marriage, as follows.

The two women who open the tale have been separated by the daughter's virilocal residence at marriage. Living together, they set up what Lévi-Strauss calls a 'matrilocal residence of the simplest kind, mother and daughter'. Lévi-Strauss counts the first marriage of the bird father of Asdiwal as matrilocal. Then the sky marriage of Asdiwal himself with Evening-Star is counted as matrilocal, and matrilocal again the two human marriages of Asdiwal, until after he has come back from the walrus kingdom, when his wife betrays her brothers. So, Lévi-Strauss remarks that all the marriages of Asdiwal are matrilocal until the end. Then the regular pattern is inverted and 'patrilocalism triumphs' because Asdiwal abandons his wife and goes home, accompanied by his son. The story starts with the reunion of a mother and daughter, liberated from their spouses (and paternal kin in the case of the daughter), and ends with the reunion of a father and son, liberated from their spouses (and maternal kin in the case of the son). To the English anthropologist some of this symmetry and inversion seems rather far-fetched. The evidence for counting the bird marriage as matrilocal is dubious and the sky marriage is plain groom service. The rejection of the third wife is hardly 'patrilocalism'. But more about inversion below. I want to go into details of another sociological sequence which produces two more pairs of oppositions which are also inverted at the end.

The same symmetry is traced in the cosmological sequence. First, the hero sojourns in the sky where he is wounded and cured by the sky people; then he makes an underground sojourn where he finds undergound people whom *he* has wounded, and whom *he* cures. There is a similar elaboration of recurring themes of famine and plenty. They correspond faithfully enough to the economic reality of Tsimshian life. Using his knowledge of another myth of the region, Lévi-Strauss explains their implication. The Northwest Coast Indians attribute the present condition of the world to the disturbances made by a great Crow, whose voracious appetite initiated all the processes of creation. So hunger is the condition of movement, glut is a static condition. The first phase of the Asdiwal tale opposes Sky and Earth, the Sun and the earthly human. These oppositions the hero overcomes, thanks to his bird father. But Asdiwal breaks the harmony established between these elements: first he feels homesick, then, once at home, he betrays his sky wife for a terrestrial girl, and then, in the sky, he feels homesick again. Thus the whole sky episode ends on a negative position. In the second phase, when Asdiwal makes his first human marriage, a new set of oppositions are released: mountain-hunting and sea-hunting; land and sea.

Asdiwal wins the contest as a land-hunter, and in consequence is abandoned by his wife's brothers. Next time Asdiwal's marriage allies him with island-dwellers, and the same conflict between land and sea takes place, this time on the sea in a boat, which Asdiwal has to leave in the final stage of the hunt in order to climb onto the reef of rock. Taken together, these two phases can be broken down into a series of unsuccessful mediations between opposites arranged on an ever-diminishing scale: above and below, water and earth, maritime hunting and mountain-hunting. In the sea hunt the gap is almost closed between sea- and mountain-hunting, since Asdiwal succeeds where his brothers-in-law fail because he clambers onto the rock. The technique by which the oppositions are reduced is by paradox and reversal: the great mountain-hunter nearly dies on a little half-submerged rock: the great killer of bears is rescued by a little mouse; the slayer of animals now cures them; and, most paradoxical of all, the great provider of food himself has provender become – since he goes home in the stomach of a walrus. In the final dénouement, Asdiwal, once more a hunter in the mountains, is immobilized when he is neither up nor down, and is changed to stone, the most extreme possible expression of his earthly nature.

Some may have doubted that myths can have an elaborate symmetrical structure. If so, they should be convinced of their error.

Lévi-Strauss's analysis slowly and intricately reveals the internal structure of this myth. Although I have suggested that the symmetry has here and there been pushed too hard, the structure is indisputably there, in the material and not merely in the eye of the beholder. I am not sure who would have argued to the contrary, but myths must henceforth be conceded to have a structure as recognizable as that of a poem or a tune.

But Lévi-Strauss is not content with revealing structure for its own sake. Structural analysis has long been a respectable tool of literary criticism and Lévi-Strauss is not interested in a mere literary exercise.

He wants to use myth to demonstrate that structural analysis has sociological value. So instead of going on to analyse and compare formal myth structures, he asks what is the relation of myth to life. His answer in a word is 'dialectical'. Not only is the nature of reality dialectical, and the structure of my myth dialectical, but the relation of the first to the second is dialectical too.

This could mean that there is a feedback between the worlds of mythical and social discourse – a statement in the myth sets off a response which modifies the social universe, which itself then touches off a new response in the realm of myth, and so on. Elsewhere, Lévi-Strauss (1962: 283–4) has shown that this complex interaction is indeed how he sees the relation between symbolic thought and social reality. And he even attempts to demonstrate with a single example how this interaction takes place (1963b; cf. 1962, ch. IV). But in his analysis of myth itself he leaves out this meaning of dialectic. This is a pity, but perhaps inevitable because there is so little historical information about the tribes in question, and still less about the dating of different versions of the myth.

Rather, he develops the idea that myth expresses a social dialectic. It states the salient social contradictions, restates them in more and more modified fashion, until in the final statement the contradictions are resolved, or so modified and masked as to be minimized. According to Lévi-Strauss, the real burden of the whole Asdiwal myth and the one burning issue to which all the antinomies of sky and earth, land and sea, etc, are assimilated, is the contradiction implicit in patrilocal, matrilateral cross-cousin marriage. This comes as a surprise, since there has never been any mention whatever of matrilateral cross-cousin marriage in the myth of Asdiwal. But the Asdiwal story has a sequel. His son, Waux, grows up with his maternal kin, and his mother arranges for him to marry a cousin. He inherits his father's magic weapons and becomes, like him, a great hunter. One day he goes out hunting, having forgotten his magic spear which enables him to split rocks and open paths through the mountains. There is an earthquake. Waux sees his wife in the valley and shouts to her to make a sacrifice of fat to appease the supernatural powers. But his wife gets it wrong and thinks he is telling her to eat the fat, on which she proceeds to stuff herself until, gorged, she bursts and turns into a rock. Waux, now without either his father's spear or his wife's help, also turns into stone. With this story the

Asdiwal cycle is completed. Waux's wife dies of glut, thus reversing the opening gambit in which Asdiwal's mother is started on her journey by a famine. So the movement set going by famine ends in the immobility of fullness. Asdiwal's marriages were all with strangers, Waux makes the approved Tsimshian marriage with his maternal cousin, but she ends by ruining him; the myth makes thus the comment that matrilateral cross-cousin marriage is nothing but a feeble palliative for the social ills it seeks to cure.

Lévi-Strauss points out that the Tsimshian, along with other Northwest Coast cultures, do not benefit from the equilibrium which cross-cousin marriage could produce for them in the form of a fixed hierarchy of wife-givers and wife-receivers. They have chosen instead to be free to revise their whole system of ranking at each marriage and potlatch. So they are committed to deep-seated disequilibrium. Following Rodney Needham (1962), one suspects that this far-fetched reference to Lévi-Strauss's theory of elementary structures of kinship is misplaced. There is no reason to suppose that matrilateral cross-cousin marriage among the Tsimshian is prescribed. However, in reaching these basic antagonisms of social structure, Lévi-Strauss feels he has got to the rock bottom of the myth's meaning (1958a, pp. 27, 28).

> 'All the paradoxes ... geographic, economic, sociological, and even cosmological, are, when all is said and done, assimilated to that less obvious yet so real paradox which marriage with the matrilateral cousin attempts but fails to resolve ...'

A great deal of this myth certainly centres on marriage, though very little on the cross-cousin marriage which is preferred. Lévi-Strauss says that the whole myth's burden is a negative comment on social reality. By examining all the possibilities in marriage and showing every extreme position to be untenable, it has as its core message to reconcile the Tsimshian to their usual compromises by showing that any other solution they attempt is equally beset with difficulty. But as I have said, we cannot allow Lévi-Strauss to claim the real meaning of such a complex and rich myth. His analysis is far from exhaustive. Furthermore, there are other themes which are positive, not negative, as regards social reality.

In the first place, this area of Northwest Coast culture combines a very elaborate and strict division of labour between the sexes with a strong expression of male dominance. The myth could well be interpreted as playing on the paradox of male dominance and male dependence on female help. The first hero, Asdiwal, shows his independence of womankind by betraying his first wife. He is betrayed by his second wife, abandons his third wife, but in the sequel his son, Waux, dies because of his wife's stupidity and greed – so the general effect is that women are necessary but inferior beings, and men are superior. Surely this is a positive comment?

In the second place, the potlatch too is built on a paradox that the receiver of gifts is an enemy. One-up-manship, in potlatch terms, brings success, rank, and followers, but two-up-manship inflicts defeat on the opponent and creates hostility. Asdiwal went too far when he brought four huge bears down from the mountain to confront his empty-handed brothers-in-law. Here again, the myth is positive and true to life, so no wonder they abandoned him. The ambivalent attitude in Northwest Coast culture to the successful shaman is a third theme that can plausibly be detected in the myth. Great shamans are always victims of jealousy. Asdiwal, the great shaman, is abandoned. So the myth is plain and simply true to life.

I feel that we are being asked to suspend our critical faculties if we are to believe that this myth mirrors the reverse of reality. I shall return again to give a closer look at the social realities of Tsimshian life.

The ideas of reversal and of inversion figure prominently in Lévi-Strauss's argument. First, he suggests that the myth is the reverse of reality in the country of its origin. Then he has formulated a curious law according to which a myth turns upside down (in relation to its normal position) at a certain distance from its place of origin. These are both developed in the Asdiwal analysis. Third, a myth which appears to have no counterpart in the ritual of the tribe in which it is told is found to be an inversion of the rites of another tribe (cf. Lévi-Strauss, 1956). On this subject the stolid English suspicion of cleverness begins to crystallize.

If ever one could suspect a scholar of trailing his coat with his tongue in his cheek, one would suspect this law of myth-inversion. The metaphor is borrowed from optics, without any explanation of why the same process should be observed in the unrelated science of mythics (Lévi-Strauss, 1956:42):

> When a mythical schema is transmitted from one population to another, and there exist difference of language, social organization or way of life which makes the myth difficult to communicate, it begins to become impoverished or confused. But one can find a limiting situation in which, instead of being finally obliterated by losing all its outlines, the myth is inverted and regains part of its precision.

So we must expect that exported myths will give a negative or upside-down picture of what the original myth portrayed. Is the scholar being ingenuous, or disingenuous? He must recognize that opposition is a pliable concept in the interpreter's hands. The whole notion of dialectic rests on the assumption that opposition can be unequivocally recognized. But this is an unwarranted assumption, as appears from a critical reading of his treatment of a Pawnee myth (Lévi-Strauss, 1956).

To demonstrate the relation of myth to rite he takes the Pawnee myth of the pregnant boy. An ignorant young boy suddenly finds he has magical powers of healing and the makings of a great shaman. An old-established shaman, always accompanied by his wife, tries to winkle his secret from him. He fails, since there is no secret learning to transmit, and then ensorcells the boy. As a result of the sorcery the boy becomes pregnant, and goes in shame and confusion to die among wild beasts. But the beasts cure him and he returns with even greater power, and kills his enemy. The analysis distinguishes at least three sets of oppositions.

Shamanistic powers through initiation : without initiation
child : old man
confusion of sex : distinction of sex

Lévi-Strauss then invites us to consider what rite this Pawnee myth corresponds to. His problem, which seems very artificial, is that there is at first sight no correlated rite. The myth underlines the opposition of the generations, and yet the Pawnee do not oppose their generations: they do not base their cult associations on age-classes, and entry to their cult societies is not by ordeals or by fee; a teacher trains his pupil to succeed him on his death. But, as he puts it, all the elements of the myth fall into place confronted with the symmetrical and opposite ritual of the neighbouring Plains Indian tribes. Here the shamanistic societies are the inverse of those of the Pawnee, since entry is by payment and organization is by age. The sponsor and his sponsored candidate for entry are treated as if in a father-son relation, the candidate is accompanied by his wife, whom he offers for ritual intercourse to his sponsor. 'Here we find again all the oppositions which have been analysed on the plane of the myth, with inversion of all the values attributed to each couple.' The initiated and uninitiated are as father to son, instead of as enemies; the uninitiated knows less than the initiated, whereas in the myth he is the better shaman; in the ritual of the Plains Societies it is the youth who is accompanied by his wife, while in the myth it is the old man. 'The semantic values are the same but changed in relation to the symbols which sustain them. The Pawnee myth exposes a ritual system which is the inverse, not of that prevailing in this tribe, but of a system which does not apply here, and which belongs to related tribes whose ritual organization is the exact opposite.'

Mere difference is made to qualify as opposition. Some of the oppositions which Lévi-Strauss detects in myth are undeniably part of the artistic structure. But opposition can be imposed on any material by the interpreter. Here we have an unguarded example of the latter process. To me it seems highly implausible that we can affirm any opposition worthy of the name between cult organization with age-grading and entrance fees, and cult organization by apprenticeship without age-grading. Old male with wife versus young man without wife, and with confusion of sex, these seem equally contrived as oppositions. If the alleged oppositions are not above challenge, the whole demonstration of inversion falls to the ground.

Here we should turn to the relation of myth to literature in general. Lévi-Strauss recognizes that a myth is 'a work of art arousing deep aesthetic emotion' (Jakobson and Lévi-Strauss, 1962 : 5). But he strenuously rejects the idea that myth is a kind of primitive poetry (Lévi-Strauss, 1963a : 210).

Myth [he says] should be placed in the gamut of linguistic expressions at the end opposite to that of poetry. . . . Poetry is a kind of speech which cannot be translated except at the cost of serious distortions; whereas the mythical value of the myth is preserved even through the worst translation.

He goes on in terms more emotional than scientific to declare that anyone can recognize the mythic quality of myth. Why does he want so vigorously to detach myth criticism from literary criticism? It is on the literary plane that we have his best contribution to the subject of mythology. He himself wrote a splendid vindication of his own technique of literary analysis by working it out with Jakobson on a sonnet of Baudelaire (Jakobson and Lévi-Strauss, 1962). This essay is an exercise in what T. S. Eliot calls 'the lemon-squeezer school of criticism, in which the critics take a poem to pieces, stanza by stanza, line by line, and extract, squeeze, tease, press every drop of meaning out of it' (Eliot, 1957: 112). After reading the analysis, we perceive the poem's unity, economy, and completeness, and its tremendous range of implication.

When the lemon-squeezer technique is applied to poetry it has a high rate of extraction and the meaning flows out in rich cupfuls. Furthermore, what is extracted is not a surprise – we can see that it was there all the time. Unfortunately, something goes wrong when the technique is applied to myth: the machine seems to spring a leak. Instead of more and richer depths of understanding, we get a surprise, a totally new theme, and often a paltry one at that. All the majestic themes which we had previously thought the Oedipus myth was about – destiny, duty, and self-knowledge, have been strained off, and we are left with a worry about how the species began. When Edmund Leach applies the same technique to the Book of Genesis, the rich metaphysical themes of salvation and cosmic oneness are replaced by practical rules for the regulation of sex. When Lévi-Strauss has finished with the Tsimshian myth it is reduced to anxieties about problems of matrilateral cross-cousin marriage (which anyway only apply to the heirs of chiefs and headmen). It seems that whenever anthropologists apply structural analysis to myth they extract not only a different but a lesser meaning. The reasons for this reductionism are important. First, there is the computer analogy, for the sake of which Lévi-Strauss commits himself to treating the structural units of myth as if they were unambiguous. This takes us back to the basic difference between words and phonemes. The best words are ambiguous, and the more richly ambiguous the more suitable for the poet's or the myth-maker's job. Hence there is no end to the number of meanings which can be read into a good myth. When dealing with poetry, Lévi-Strauss gives full value to the rich ambiguity of the words. When dealing with myth he suggests that their meaning is clear cut, lending itself to being chopped into objectively recognizable, precisely defined units. It is partly in this process of semantic chopping that so much of the meaning of myth gets lost.

But there is another reason, more central to the whole programme. There are two possible objectives in analysing a piece of discourse.[1] One is to analyse the particular discourse itself, to analyse what has been said. The other is to analyse the language, seen as the instrument of what is said. No reason has so far been given to suppose that the structure of discourse is necessarily similar to that of language. But there is reason to point out that if the language analogy is adopted, research will look for a similar structure, a logic of correlations, oppositions, and differences (Ricoeur, 1963). We can say that the first kind of analysis, of what has been said in a discourse, aims at discovering a particular structure. This is what the literary critics do and what Jakobson and Lévi-Strauss did in 'Les Chats', and what Lévi-Strauss in practice does most of the time. This kind of analysis is not intended to yield a compressed statement of the theme. It is not reductionist in any sense. The other kind of analysis discovers a formal or general structure which is not particular to any given stretch of language. For instance, the alexandrine or the sonnet form is not particular to a given poem, and to know that a particular poem has been written in sonnet form tells you nothing about what that poem is about. In the same way, a grammatical structure is formal. A book of grammar gives the conditions under which communication of a certain kind can take place. It does not give a communication.

Lévi-Strauss claims to be revealing the formal structures of myths. But he can never put aside his interest in what the myth discourse is about. He seems to think that if he had the formal structure it would look not so much like a grammar book as like a summary of the themes which analysing the particular structure of a myth cycle has produced. Hence the reductionist tendency is built in to his type of myth analysis. He falls into the trap of claiming to discover the real underlying meanings of myths because he never separates the particular artistic structure of a particular set of myths from their general or purely formal structure. Just as knowing that the rhyme structure is a, b, b, a, does not tell us anything about the content of a sonnet, so the formal structure of a myth would not help very much in interpreting it. Lévi-Strauss comes very near this when he says (Lévi-Strauss, 1957) that the structural analysis of a Pawnee myth consists of a dialectical balancing of the themes of life and death. It might have been better to have said that it was a balanced structure of pluses and minuses, or of positives and negatives. If he had actually used algebra to present the pattern he discerned, then Edmund Leach might have been less tempted to speculate on the similarity of mythic themes all over the world. He himself had found a structure of pluses and minuses in the Garden of Eden myth (1961) and remarked that the recurrence of these themes of death versus life, procreation versus vegetable reproduction, have the greatest psychological and sociological significance. But I think that their significance is that of verb/noun relations in language. Their presence signifies the possibility of finding in them formal structures. But they are not the formal myth structures that we have been promised. These can hardly be knowable in ordinary language. If they are to be discovered special terms will have to be invented for recording them, comparable to the highly specialized terminology of grammar. To say simply that myth structures are built of oppositions and mediations is not to say what the structures are. It is simply to say that there are structures.

I will return later to the question of whether these formal myth structures are likely to be important for sociology. At this stage of publication (though three new volumes are in the press), Lévi-Strauss has not succeeded in revealing them. I should therefore do better to concentrate on the particular artistic structures he has revealed.

The meaning of a myth is partly the sense that the author intended it to convey, and the sense intended by each of its recounters. But every listener can find in it references to his own experience, so the myth can be enlightening, consoling, depressing, irrespective of the intentions of the tellers. Part of the anthropologist's task is to understand enough of the background of the myth to be able to construct its range of reference for its native hearers. To this Lévi-Strauss applies himself energetically, as for example when he finds that the myth of the creative Great Crow illuminates the themes of hunger and plenty in Tsimshian life.

From a study of any work of art we can infer to some extent the conditions under which it was made. The maidservant who said of St Peter, 'His speech betrays him as a Galilean', was inferring from his dialect; similarly the critic who used computer analysis to show that the same author did not write all the epistles attributed to St Paul. This kind of information is like that to be obtained from analysing the track of an animal or the finger-prints of a thief. The anthropologist studying tribal myths can do a job of criticism very like that of art critics who decide what 'attribution' to give to a painting or to figures in a painting. Lévi-Strauss, after minute analysis of the Asdiwal myth, could come forward and, like a good antiquarian, affirm that it is a real, genuine Tsimshian article. He can guarantee that it is an authentic piece of Northwest Coast mythology. His analysis of the structure of the myth can show that it draws fully on the premises of Tsimshian culture.

Inferences, of course, can also be made within the culture; the native listener can infer a moral, and indeed myths are one of the ways in which cultural values are transmitted. Structural analysis can reveal unsuspected depths of reference and inference meaning for any particular series of myths. In order to squeeze this significant out, the anthropologist must apply his prior knowledge of the culture to his analysis. He uses inference the other way round, from the known culture to the interpretation of the obscure myth. This is how he discerns the elements of structure. All would agree that this is a worth-while task. But in order to analyse particular structures, he has to know his culture well first.

At this stage we should like to be able to judge how well Lévi-Strauss knows the social reality of the Tsimshian. Alas, very little is known about this tribe. He has to make do with very poor ethnographic materials. There are several minor doubts one can entertain about his interpretation of the facts, but the information here is altogether very thin. A critic of Lévi-Strauss

(Ricoeur) has been struck by the fact that all his examples of mythic thought have been taken from the geographical areas of totemism and never from Semitic, pre-Hellenic, or Indo-European areas, whence our own culture arose. Lévi-Strauss would have it that his examples are typical of a certain kind of thought, a type in which the arrangement of items of culture is more important and more stable than the content. Ricoeur asks whether the totemic cultures are not so much typical as selected, extreme types? This is a very central question which every anthropologist has to face. Is *La Pensée sauvage* as revealed by myth and rite analysis typical, or peculiar, or is it an illusion produced by the method? Here we are bound to mention Lévi-Strauss's idea of mythic thinking as *bricolage*. The *bricoleur*, for whom we have no word, is a craftsman who works with material that has not been produced for the task he has in hand. I am tempted to see him as an Emmett engineer whose products always look alike whether they are bridges, stoves, or trains, because they are always composed of odd pieces of drainpipe and string, with the bells and chains and bits of Gothic railing arranged in a similar crazy way. In practice this would be a wrong illustration of *bricolage*. Lévi-Strauss himself is the real Emmett engineer because he changes his rules as he goes along. For mythic thought a card-player could be a better analogy, because Emmett can use his bits how he likes, whereas the *bricolage* type of culture is limited by pattern-restricting rules. Its units are like a pack of cards continually shuffled for the same game. The rules of the game would correspond to the general structure underlying the myths. If all that the myths and rites do is to arrange and rearrange the elements of the culture, then structural analysis would be exhaustive, and for that reason very important.

At the outset of any scientific enterprise, a worker must know the limitations of his method. Linguistics and any analysis modelled on linguistics can only be synchronic sciences. They analyse systems. In so far as they can be diachronic it is in analysing the before-and-after evolution of systems. Their techniques can be applied to any behaviour that is systematic. But if the behaviour is not very systematic, they will extract whatever amount of regularity there is, and leave a residue. Edmund Leach has shown that the techniques of Lévi-Strauss can be applied to early Greek myths, to Buddhist, and to Israelite myths. But I suppose he would never claim that the analysis is exhaustive. In the case of his analysis of Genesis, I have already mentioned above that the residue is the greater part.

Lévi-Strauss in his publications so far seems blithely unconscious that his instrument can produce only one kind of tune. More aware of the limitations of his analysis, he would have to restrict what he says about the attitude of mythic thought to time, past and future. Structural analysis cannot but reveal myths as timeless, as synchronic structures outside time. From this bias built into the method there are two consequences. First, we cannot deduce anything whatever from it about the attitudes to time prevailing in the cultures in question. Our method reduces all to synchrony. Everything which Lévi-Strauss writes in *La Pensée sauvage* about time in certain cultures or at a certain level of thinking, should be rephrased to apply only to the method he uses. Second, if myths have got an irreversible order and if this is significant, this part of their meaning will escape the analysis. This, as Ricoeur points out, is why the culture of the Old Testament does not fit into the *bricolage* category.

We know a lot about the Israelites and about the Jews and Christians who tell and retell these stories.[2] We know little about the Australian aborigines and about the no longer surviving American Indian tribes. Would this be the anthropologist's frankest answer to Ricoeur? We cannot say whether the *bricolage* level of thought is an extreme type or what it is typical of, for lack of sufficient supporting data about the examples. But we must say that the *bricolage* effect is produced by the method of analysis. For a final judgment, then, we can only wait for a perfect experiment. For this, richly abundant mythical material should be analysed against a known background of equally rich ethnographic records. We can then see how exhaustive the structural analysis can be and also how relevant its formulas are to the understanding of the culture.

Notes

1 In what follows I am indebted to Professor Cyril Barrett, S. J. for criticism.

2 Edmund Leach makes the following point in an editorial note: Lévi-Strauss's own justification for *not* applying his method to

G

Biblical materials seems to rest on the proposition that we do not know enough about the ancient Israelites! See *Esprit*, November 1963, p. 632 but cf. Leach (1966) *passim*.

Bibliography

ELIOT, T. S. (1957), *On Poetry and Poets*, London, Faber & Faber.

FORTES, M. (1959), *Oedipus and Job in West African Religion*, Cambridge University Press.

JAKOBSON, R. and LÉVI-STRAUSS, C. (1962), ' "Les Chats" de Charles Baudelaire', *L'Homme*, 2, 5–21.

LEACH, E. R. (1961), 'Lévi-Strauss in the Garden of Eden: an examination of some recent developments in the analysis of myth', *Transactions of the New York Academy of Sciences*, series 2, 386–96.

LEACH, E. R. (1962), 'Genesis as myth', *Discovery*, May, 30–5.

LEACH, E. R. (1966), 'The legitimacy of Solomon: some structural aspects of Old Testament history', *European Journal of Sociology* 7, 58–101.

LÉVI-STRAUSS, C. (1955), 'The structural study of myth', *Journal of American Folklore*, 28, 428–44. Reprinted with modifications in Lévi-Strauss (1963a).

LÉVI-STRAUSS, C. (1956), 'Structure et dialectique' in *For Roman Jakobson on the Occasion of his Sixtieth Birthday*, The Hague, Mouton. Reprinted in Lévi-Strauss (1963a).

LÉVI-STRAUSS, C. (1957), 'Le symbolisme cosmique dans la structure sociale et l'organisation cérémonielle des tribus americaines', *Serie Orientale Roma*, XIV, Institut pour l'Étude de l'Orient et de l'Extrême-Orient, Rome, pp. 47–56.

LÉVI-STRAUSS, C. (1958a), 'La Geste d'Asdiwal', *École Pratique des Sciences Religieuses*. Extr. Annuaire 1958–9: 3–43. Reprinted in *Les Temps modernes*, March 1961.

LÉVI-STRAUSS, C. (1958b), *Anthropologie structurale*, Paris, Plon. (English translation, 1963a. *Structural Anthropology*. New York: Basic Books.)

LÉVI-STRAUSS, C. (1962), *La Pensée sauvage*, Paris, Plon.

LÉVI-STRAUSS, C. (1963a), *Structural Anthropology*, New York: Basic Books.

LÉVI-STRAUSS, C. (1963b), 'The bear and the barber', *Journal of the Royal Anthropological Institute*, 93, part I: 1–11.

NEEDHAM, R. (1962), *Structure and Sentiment*, University of Chicago Press.

RICOEUR, P. (1963), 'Structure et herméneutique', *Esprit*, November: 598–625.

WEIL, SIMONE (1950), *Attente de Dieu*, Paris, La Colombe.

11

Humans Speak

Every spoken sentence rests on unspoken knowledge for some of
its meaning. Some speech contains most of its meaning in verbal
form. Some carries very little. This is the essence of the distinction Professor Bernstein makes between two speech codes: the
one attempts to elaborate all its meanings verbally, the other
relies heavily on context. As I understand it, he is interested in
the dark side of the moon, in the meanings that are conveyed
without being spoken. He is concerned with the implicit in
human relations. The implicit is whatever is taken for granted. It
need not be put into words because it seems obvious. It represents
a community of shared assumptions.

In some guises Basil Bernstein is a pilgrim, seeking out these
holy secret places in human discourse, and honouring them.
When he describes the restricted speech code which is the
language of intimacy, a sense of loneliness and nostalgia
descends on the audience. Each person listening wishes to have
more of those silent friendships in which nothing needs to be
said, because everything is understood. Then they shake themselves free of the spell and remember that they are teachers and
that the whole educational project is for more explicitness and
for the inquiring frame of mind that takes nothing for granted.
In another guise, the same spell-binder is a breaker of sacred
images; this is when he reveals that what is hidden and implicit
is not necessarily nice.

The best reason for dimming any aura of sanctity is to get at
some reality which the dazzle obscures. Basil Bernstein is an
inveterate critic of sanctuaries in sociology and in education. For

173

this reason his work is disturbing and uncomfortable. No one likes to be told that his halo is slipping. Perhaps fortunately, the thrusts are wrapped in a complicated style. Anyone who doesn't want to hear can give a shrug, and the halo is back in place again, undimmed. There are other reasons why he is a controversial and enigmatic figure. For one thing, to be working on sociolinguistics with an ear cocked for what is not being said is eccentric from the linguists' point of view. For another, to treat speech as something emanating from and shaped by social relations seems to belittle the grand independence of language. However, in practice, the linguists seem to have been generous and welcoming. Through this approach a promising approach to the much neglected field of semantics can be glimpsed. Whereas the sociologists have found it much harder to adapt to the work of a highly original thinker. Sociology tends to be divided between armchair speculators whose library gives them their problems and solutions, and the empirical investigators. These last are restricted by what can be put through the mesh of field research and statistical inquiry. Many of the important speculations about man in society do not come ready made for testing. Therefore there is this gulf between two kinds of sociology, a gulf that everyone accepts. But here is Professor Bernstein, taking the most delicate, imaginatively stirring problems about how the social bond is constituted. There he is, not in his armchair at all, but absorbed in working out research techniques for refining and testing his ideas. Neither fish, flesh nor fowl – some tribes reject and fear anomalous beasts, some revere them. In sociology Professor Bernstein is to some a fearsome scaly monster, cutting across all the tidy categories. The light he sheds on thoughts we would prefer to keep veiled is often cruel. No wonder he holds an anomalous place in his profession.

Whatever he does, whether analysing how a mother controls her child, how a teacher teaches, how a patient confronts a psychoanalyst, how the curriculum is worked out in a school or college – he looks at four elements in the social process. First the system of control, second the boundaries it sets up, third the justification or ideology which sanctifies the boundaries, and fourth he looks at the power itself which is hidden by the rest. The analysis always ends by revealing the distribution of power. This is the trick of demystification. The discomfiture is for those who pretend there is no power, that institutions just happen to hold together by spontaneous loving bonds. As he pulls aside the curtain, the whip in their hand is revealed, while murmurings about love and spontaneity are still on their lips.

Professor Bernstein started by pointing out that humans speak, and that it is high time to note that speech is patterned in different ways according to the pattern of social relations. He likened the control of speech by social factors to a coding system. The difference between fully explicit speech, the elaborated code, and the context-dependent restricted code was obviously going to be crucial to education. For the child of middle-class family is introduced to a set of roles and speech forms which is geared to success in school and the outside world where verbal explicitness counts. The child who can only handle the restricted code and who only knows social roles which are given implicitly, not defined verbally, is at a disadvantage in education. If educationalists can't understand this, their tests and grading and remedial measures can go by the board. So much else goes with this difference that the implications of psychology are enormous. Whether words are used or not for relating to other people and for grasping one's own identity, the quality of the relations and the nature of the identity will be different. Hence the vast programme of research which English and American sources have financed over the last eight years and which makes Basil Bernstein's speculations the most rigorously tested body of new hypotheses in contemporary British sociology.

The papers published here record the growth of his work from early beginnings. It is very good to have them at last between hard covers and on sale. So much of the development is embedded in the empirical findings that his introduction leads continually to the companion volumes which will give the results of his research team's work. This is another reason why the impact on the wider sociological scene is only about to begin. Another reason again lies in his personal history.

In London University in the 1950s it is hard to think where a sociology graduate who wanted to study the transmission of culture could have had any support, even if his studies had been brilliantly successful. But Basil Bernstein says that he always had agonising difficulties in saying clearly what he himself was trying still to grasp. After such an undistinguished first degree, no grant for research into making the implicit explicit was forthcoming. He seems never to have thought of trying anthropology. Eventually, after six years of teaching at the City Day College, he was taken on as research assistant in the phonetics department of University College, London. This was the break-through that gave him his chance. But it meant that he was never ritually initiated, either as a sociology researcher or as a linguist. Betwixt and between he is still the threatening outsider, attacking sacred boundaries, introducing profound insights in a bizarre language. His personal biographical note looks benignly back on the history of struggle and exclusion. The same experience is recast as a theoretical proposition in the last chapter of the book, on classification and framing of educational knowledge. This chapter is a disturbing analysis of the exclusions and struggles for control implicit in the structure of the curriculum. I will come to that very disquieting piece later, for it is the crux of the whole matter. First for the ground work that leads to it.

Linguists and philosophers have long been saying that language limits the possibilities of thought. But language is not an independent variable, nor is thought controlled and formed by it. For both speech and thought are dependent parts of human communication. The control is not in the speech form but in the set of human relations which generate thought and speech. Basil Bernstein has focused upon this angle of the ancient problem. He asks what are the main kinds of social relations – what structuring in society itself calls for its own appropriate structures of speech. It is easy to create false problems by concentrating on speech apart from the people speaking. It is extremely difficult to hold in steady focus both the speech forms and the social forms and to ask how they are connected. No wonder he found it difficult, in his intellectual isolation, to grasp the problems he was trying to solve. No wonder he was not taken seriously in England where neither linguistics nor sociology were in an advanced state. Between 1958 and 1964, as he published the early papers, a flood of inquiries began to build up. Requests to speak or to reprint proved that an international forum was attentive. Basil Bernstein's approach to speech has its parallel and forerunner in Karl Marx's approach to money. For Marxist philosophy money is a symbolic system in which a particular pattern of power is realised. Marxist materialism allows no social relations to be seen as disembodied spiritual things. All relations are mediated through things which symbolise the power base. Therefore the burning question is who controls the symbolic system which does this mediation. Similarly for speech: I think that Professor Bernstein's work is the first to argue that the distribution of speech forms is equally a realisation of the distribution of power. There is an unfair scope for pulling carpets from under feet in this proposition. The exponents of culture who generously want everyone to speak like themselves in the top income and educational brackets may well be conniving at the present distribution, so fortunate for themselves. At a more theoretical and less political level, this work has much to say about the collective consciousness that constitutes the social bond. A common speech form transmits much more than words: it transmits a hidden baggage of shared assumptions. If this is so, and intuitively it would seem to be likely, then the research into speech codes is vitally important to sociology, and to understanding other media.

Several old misconceptions about Basil Bernstein's concept of the restricted code are still worth nailing. The educational system and the whole structure of industrial society sucks individuals out of their intimate corners and requires them to be conversant with the elaborated speech code. Abstract reflection upon meanings is what education is about and it fits the subject for high office, power and influence. Social inequality results from unequal ability to acquire fluency in this, the elaborated code. Consequently, in the schools, the person with the restricted code is seen to be impoverished. Basil Bernstein recognises that it is less adapted to exploring theoretical issues. But he values it for itself, and would pity a person who could not use it. Contempt for the restricted code would be equivalent to contempt for intimacy. Indeed he tries to make this point clear in a later essay on the idea of compensatory education. This he finds a particularly flat-footed way of blaming the home and the family for the educational difficulties of the child and distracting attention from the inadequacies of the school.

Another misconception is to suppose that the difference between the restricted and elaborate code rests on a difference between taciturn and garrulous speech habits. The restricted code can pour out an equal or greater flow of words per minute.

Loquacity can go either way, for the elaborated code requires more careful programming and its users under certain conditions can tolerate more hesitation and less fluency than users of the restricted code. Another mistake is to assume that the restricted code has little scope. On the contrary, its basis in metaphor makes it a good narrative form because it is richly allusive, highly condensed, and can dispense with slow and complex syntactic forms. But these are not linguistic criteria.

This volume shows the frustrating struggle that the sociological research unit at the Institute of Education suffered in trying to pin-point speech differences which linguists could recognise. 'Short, grammatically simple, syntactically poor sentences' was not acceptable as a description in linguistics. But finally, in the last few years, thanks to the collaboration of Professor Halliday and Dr Hasan, distinguished linguists, the original intuitions are finding their full theoretical expression and the research is sharpening its focus.

The early testing turned to class differences as the easiest material available and the whole issue became part of applied educational research. But the richest implications are more fundamental. At the end of this book, in the part headed 'Explorations', two types of family are contrasted. In the one the children are controlled by reference to positions in a pattern. They must do what they are told because they are children, older or younger, or boy or girl: no other reason than the pattern they belong in is offered as explanation. For example, a little boy playing with dolls, is told: 'Little boys don't play with dolls.' Gradually his sex role is made apparent to him in rules and categories. If he goes on playing with dolls, his mother ends up by saying: 'Here, play with this', and gives him a drum. In the other type of family the logical and emotional possibilities are explored verbally so that the child gets an idea of his unique self but no pattern in which he fits. Basil Bernstein does not say so, but biographies from such families suggest that this very personal mode of upbringing can be worrying for the child. Sartre describes his own doubts, as an only child of seven, about how he could possibly be loved at home for his unique personal qualities, beauty and brilliant intelligence of which his mirror and school friends showed no sign.

We are now two hundred years after Rousseau, his 'Emile' and the move to soft educational methods. Teaching is not authoritarian. We must first rouse curiosity and permit the child to internalise his own rules, himself spurring his own efforts. Summerhill, Dartington, Bedales, they are old history, part of the educational background. The middle-class parent takes it for granted that it is better to hide power, better to hide rules, better to answer verbally at great length. Professor Bernstein's analysis cuts us, the middle-class parents, down to size. Our verbosity and insincerity and fundamental uncertainty are revealed. Our service to an educational ideal that splendidly sustains the industrial system is stripped of its sweeter pretensions. The elaborated code is far from glorious when the hidden implications of the control system that generates it are laid bare.

As far as the family is concerned, Basil Bernstein betrays a preference for 'positional' control rather than for 'personal' appeals. In the last essay in the book he moves from family systems to educational ones. Here the contrast is between two kinds of curriculum, one he calls integrated, the other collection. But the contrast of educational theories is more deeply disturbing than that between families. One type corresponds to the middle-class 'personal' family system: no rules, no boundaries, no subjects, projects with no exams, apparently maximum choice, no hierarchy, a pretence of no power. This system advocates an integrated curriculum. The other type corresponds to the 'positional' family. Teachers like African chiefs in their autonomous chiefdoms rule over well-defined territories. Geography is geography, not history, archaeology or music. Graded examination results control entry from one year to the next; all the boundaries are clear. The student passes through degrees of initiation. At the end, clutching his certificate, the lucky few graduate with an educational identity. Such a one has also learnt that knowledge is a system of private property which controls distribution of social significance. Each system has its own mode of socialisation, its own characteristic distribution of power and techniques of control. In the 'collection' system power is manifest obliquely. It sparks out from the locked doors, 'keep out' signs and certificates. Under integration power is hidden. Anyone who follows that theory of education will never know what reef struck his boat. As far as education is concerned, Basil Bernstein remains enigmatic. He does not judge. On one side is the hidden cruelty, constraint and frustration of the old educational theory; on the other side, the same again for the new educational theory. The ledge between holds the drop-outs, kick-outs, escapees, those who don't hold with education at all, and those who missed it unintentionally. The frustration, cruelty and constraint they have to suffer is merely not hidden by mystification or pretence. Power is always power. The original oddball, inarticulate little man bursting with big ideas will get no more generous shrift from the one system or the other. As Donald Macrae's foreword says, when we see reality it is not consoling. But it is invigorating to have the veil drawn aside. It is consoling to know that this doughty original, armed with a sociological critique of great strength and subtlety can turn from speech forms and their underlying social patterns to educational theories and from those to any other systems of boundaries and their underlying distribution of power. Humans speak and a lot of what they say is cant, innocent enough unless it pretends that the dilemma is not tragic.

12

Louis Dumont's Structural Analysis

A challenge from across the Channel is issued to contemporary thought. This has been a regularly recurring event. Usually the English-speaking people ignore it for the first twenty years. The problems as initially posed in Europe seem either too metaphysical, too local, too remote from our professional concerns, or, if relevant, too lax in the manner of their posing. It takes time to anglicize the basic ideas. As they are often subversive, either of government or of religion, it also takes time to neutralize their explosive power. So we might easily have been tempted to shrug off Professor Dumont's *Homo Hierarchicus* as just another French gauntlet flung down. But this particular challenge cannot be dismissed.

For one thing the book is about India, whose history has been entwined with our own for so long. Then, at a time in Europe when both Christian and rationalist values are under attack, Professor Dumont writes of the relation between religion and society. Much as our aristocratic youth in the eighteenth century used to make the grand tour of Europe, our young people now troop off to India to learn the secrets of civilization. So the challenge is well-placed and well-timed. Furthermore, the manner of delivery is punctiliously correct. Here is the magisterial survey of what has been said, fully documented. Sometimes the outsider to Indian culture feels the demands of honour are met with an almost niggling nicety, when one opponent after another, rebuffed in the main text, is delicately slain in a footnote. No important contributor to Indian research has been ignored and the controversy disclosed is very much alive. With all the etiquette of scholarship correctly observed, we are forced to recognize that the author's thesis has an even stronger claim on our attention.

Professor Dumont presents India as a mirror image to ourselves: a society founded on principles exactly antithetical to those we honour. Our civilization is based on the premise of equality. The claims we make against one another are made in its name. Against this theory of what our basic human rights require, the realities of power continually create inequality. The idiom of our political life is the struggle to make good the principle of individual equality against all the pressures and contingencies that tend to invalidate it. So deeply imprisoned is our thought within this idiom that the sociological imagination itself is curbed. Even those scholars who specialize in considering the nature of justice cannot envisage a kind of social reality other than the one which their own society is striving to create. But in India the principle of inequality is formally recognized as governing all social relations. The scale of hierarchy is set up on well-known rules. Contingent pressures from the actual distribution of wealth and power tend inevitably to distort their application. Our social pattern is reversed by their taking for principle what we take for contingency, and vice versa. The full implications of the model he sets up are difficult for us to absorb.

The whole plane of Indian sociology might seem a broad enough field. But this study is pitched at a more general level of interest. India is only the ground, the experimental range, for an ambitious exercise in the sociology of knowledge. The central problem is the old, familiar one of objectivity. Since Marx put the matter in its most uncomfortable political form, sociologists have recognized that perception is in some large part controlled by social factors. To what extent it is controlled, whether there could be any knowledge not mediated by social institutions, whether knowledge of physical nature could be exempt from the taint of subjectivity – these questions are mulled over, softened and made safe to contemplate. Part of the process of defusing the dangerous potential of these ideas is to insulate the sociology of knowledge from sociology proper. The subjects are distinguished and separated. The student can choose which field he studies. He can concentrate on economic and political analysis or he can concentrate on the philosophy, history and sociology of knowledge. He is free to hive off one part from the other – but not if he wants to understand India, and not if he wants to know himself. The central message of this book is that such intellectual boundaries are only practical tools of knowledge; to treat them as sacred, God-given or in the nature of things is anathema. Professor Dumont assumes that the sociologist is lit by the passion to know. For him, the first step to knowledge is to recognize the individual consciousness as a social creation. Some of the limitations on knowledge may be necessary to our human condition. But it is self-defeating to restrict sociological inquiry to modern industrial societies and so to restrict the very idea of what forms man in society can take. If we seek objectivity, we must recognize our own fundamental assumptions for what they are: the creation of our place and time. If we mistake our current idea of the nature of man for the eternal laws of nature, we are blinkered by cultural restraints on perception. Hence the importance of India, a society based on contrary assumptions.

Like many a good historian, admittedly, but unlike the common run of anthropologists, the author starts by describing the structure of the classification within which conflicts are worked out and choices made. Understanding Indian society begins with the concept of hierarchy and the theory of the 'Varna'. He finds it impossible to make sense of his material other than through the religious ideas. To hail this as a bold procedure may seem curious to anyone who is not used to a quarter of a century of anthropological monographs which start with ecology, economy, politics and treat of religion only in the final chapter. The same order is frequently followed in the teaching of the subject. Anthropologists are unanimous in conceding just such a close relationship between religion and society, but their mode of presentation belies the precept. A technical difficulty may explain their bias. The anthropologist often has a peculiar problem in validating his research in the eyes of his colleagues. He is describing a hitherto unknown social system. His subjects will probably never read his books. His colleagues will probably never set foot in the place. Somehow he has to prove that he has done more than accept the most superficial local view of how the system works. The people may say that camels need to be watered every three days or every three weeks and that this fact of nature determines the organization of their tasks; or they may say that their land is fertile or infertile and that their villages are sited accordingly. Unless he gets zoological data and uses soil analysis, maps and historical records, his analysis will be convicted of staying within the categories of thought of the people he describes. Therefore the customary order of presentation meets some of the demands of professional integrity. But this scholar, who has the hardihood to present an overall view of the Indian caste system, is in a different predicament. He has to convince the millions who know India at first hand and the other millions who do not know India but recognize themselves in the European culture which balances his comparison.

Many a novelist and traveller has taken on such a programme and, claiming no special authority, expected his readers to take or leave his findings as they like. But Professor Dumont speaks with authority, using the conceptual tools derived from modern linguistics and communication theory. Indeed, a good part of the book is devoted to a summary of the underlying method. When the words 'complementarity and balanced opposition' are used in the Indian context, the reader is prepared beforehand to look for a polarization of categories of thought, for an idea to be defined by its contrary, for each part of the system of ideas to find its meaning, not in itself but in relation to a whole.

If we ask who are the adversaries whose views are contested here we find that there should be no major dispute. Scholars are entitled to follow the bent of their curiosity. Many sociologists are concerned with the concentration of power and its effects, and on the need for a clear set of conceptual tools for analysing forms of stratification. These in their quest for general concepts would include Indian caste within the set of known stratification systems. Professor Dumont is concerned with understanding the uniqueness of the caste system, expecting thereby to reveal something about the behaviour of man in society. Not wishing to abstract from it for the sake of composing a classification, he sees it in its entirety, and from this vantage point sets up new kinds of sociological comparison. The dispute (which obtrudes tiresomely from time to time) is like one between pilgrims travelling to quite different shrines who yet try to persuade each other to take the same route. This book is only concerned indirectly with the gravitational field of power and authority. More directly it is to do with finding the general structures underlying human society. When it was first published in French it was the first serious structural analysis of a particular society.

After the collapse of the Roman Empire, when Europe withdrew from its African and Far Eastern concerns to develop the distinctive culture of medieval Christendom, it came to see itself contrasted with its encroaching rival, Islam. The opposition no doubt strengthened its self-awareness. But the contrast was not so profound as the one which Professor Dumont draws between Europe and India. Indeed, India is still playing out that same opposition to Islam and it is relevant to note that precisely in the north, where Islamic influence is most felt, the principles of the Hindu hierarchy are weakest. For Europe, India, not Islam, affords the true mirror image where left and right are transposed with perfect regularity. Or it could be as true to say that India, revealed under this lens, can fulfil today for us the mirroring function which Judaism was always available to afford in Europe if it had not been thrust out of sight, background to the duelling figures of politically organized giants.

There are two essential characteristics of Hindu society: first, status is determined by principles independent of the distribution of authority; and second, the idiom in which higher or lower status is expressed is the idiom of purity. The first is the most fundamental and gives the author the most difficulty in developing and maintaining. To present his analysis he has to discriminate terms and restore the old definition of hierarchy as 'a principle of ranking elements of a whole'. So involved are we with the assumptions of our own culture that it has become impossible for us to understand the term hierarchy except as implying political and economic superiority. But this very assimilation of ideas which are distinct in India has distorted, so Professor Dumont contends, much modern research. The whole which gives the hierarchy its meaning is a religious whole. The system of ideas can be bent whenever the distribution of power allows authority to overwhelm the precepts of hierarchy. This happens when there are rajahs to dominate a state, or landowners to dominate a village. When the Brahmans are the landowners, hierarchy and authority temporarily coalesce. Weakness and fluctuations of authority have always characterized Indian political life. Only by taking the long view over time, or by taking an overall spatial view of India, do we see religious hierarchy asserting itself powerfully in the language of ritual purity.

The hierarchy is based on the scheme of the traditional Varnas, the highest, the Brahmans, or priests, below them the Kshatriyas, or rulers, then the Vaishyas, cultivators and later merchants, and then the Shudras, or servants. Finally, the unclassified, the untouchables, would be the fifth estate if they were in the classification at all. Like any language, the idiom of purity allows an infinite multiplication of criteria. The caste system, in which it works, allows for an infinitely subtle shadowing of status between subcastes, splitting into new subcastes, or merging with old ones.

My task in this introduction is not to explain the system but to show its relevance to ourselves. For me its most disturbing impact is in the thought that the idiom of purity is only too well known to us. It is liable to dominate our transactions with one another whenever other kinds of social distinction, based on authority and wealth, are not clear. Purity and impurity are principles of evaluation and separation. The purer must be kept uncontaminated by the less pure. In India the idiom of purity is used whenever the organic erupts into the social domain and particularly when ingestion of food is concerned. Demarcation, ranking and the separation of organic life from the social, that is enough to give a complete system of occupational ranking. Any occupation which deals more directly with organic processes is ranked lower than one which deals with them less directly, and all are lower than priesthood which by definition is concerned with the spiritual. The priestly role is to perform ceremonies which set boundaries around the organic processes which any live individual must undergo. He provides the ritual framing off by which intellectual categories are imposed on physiological experience. Eating is such a case, marriage another, childbirth another when physiological and social processes need to be coordinated. In Hinduism the various purity rules are systematized into one intelligible set. Enormous pains are taken to control who eats what and who is served food by whom. The foods also are subject to the same principles of evaluation as occupations. Some are more grossly organic than others: the juice of vegetables does not contaminate as does the blood of animals; the veneration of the cow means that its products are pure, but anyone who eats beef is impure. The food rules are such a prominent part of the culture that anthropologists have studied it more carefully and understood it better than we understand the working of the same principle among ourselves. We do well to pause and imagine an Indian anthropologist, notebook in hand, observing the rules which we do not admit but which we adopt in the transmission of food, drink and tobacco. Who eats with whom? Who smokes with whom, drinks what, with whom? Who jokes with whom and how near to the physiological knuckle can a joke be permitted to go when difference of status is desired? Over here the rules of purity (which we recognize whenever we apologize for a hiccough or other involuntary eruption of the organic into the social domain) are dominated by the principles of social stratification. Where these latter give no guidance, we are thrown back on freewheeling purity concepts as the always self-evident reason for exclusiveness and ranking.

Professor Dumont will forgive a trivial example if it brings home our own readiness to adopt rules of purity in precisely the small-scale miniature of the case which his canvas depicts in grandeur. He describes a village in central India studied by Professor Adrian Mayer, where twenty-three castes distinguish themselves from each other according to their readiness to smoke with the same pipe or to accept different categories of food from one another. For political and economic concerns the village is focused on a royal caste of Rajputs and their allies (including servants) in the command system. These are meat-eating castes and, naturally enough, being in command, they are very liberal in their attitudes to sharing pipes and food. Below them in power but above the servant castes in ritual status are the farmers. These are the people who observe purity rules with such strictness that they outdo the Brahmans themselves. They are very careful whom they invite to their feasts, and when invited to celebrate with the other castes, they ostentatiously avoid the risk of contamination with lower orders by asking for raw food to take and cook in the purity of their own hearths. The comparison that comes to mind is Pooter's lifelong struggle, set down in the *Diary of a Nobody*, to prove to the surrounding tradesmen that a city clerk can also be a gentleman. In the office Pooter knows his place and has no boundary problems. Power and authority make the social categories perfectly clear. But when he is invited to the

Mansion House Ball and finds there Farmerson, the ironmonger, ready to slap him on the shoulder, he reproves him for familiarity. The party is already spoilt for him by the improper social mixture and when Farmerson is hailed by one of the sheriffs as an old friend and asked to dine at the Lodge, his distress is deepened: 'To think that a man who mends our scraper should know any member of the aristocracy!' Two days later his wife comes out of her sulks:

> She said: 'Don't be so theatrical; it has no effect on me. Preserve that tone for your new friend *Mister* Farmerson, the ironmonger.' I was about to speak when Carrie, in a temper such as I have never seen her in before, told me to hold my tongue. She said: 'Now *I'm* going to say something! After professing to snub Mr Farmerson, you permit him to snub *you*, in my presence, and then accept his invitation to take a glass of champagne with you, and you don't limit yourself to one glass. You then offer this vulgar man, who made a bungle of repairing our scraper, a seat in our cab on the way home! . . .'

and so on. Yes, we certainly understand how rules of purity can spontaneously develop to control what is eaten, with whom and how much, where and when, and we can feel compassion for the unrealizable and restricting ideals of the lower orders of our own class system as well as for the puritanical farmers of the central Indian village. What is different here from the case of India is that our rules of purity, when they depart from the tramlines set up by power, are partial, and relate to no known whole. They do not belong to any hierarchy.

Currently our principles catch us in a dilemma which the Hindu system avoids. The caste system can absorb any alien element, simply by applying the universal ranking rule of the purity code and separating off. Anyone who wishes to enter the system of hierarchy can follow the rules and choose where he can expect to be ranked. Thus Christian missionaries find themselves being treated as new subcastes and even find themselves multiplying their own caste divisions and so being embraced in the system they seek to overcome. But at home we have no such universal ranking principle, and we disapprove of inequality. In dealing with alien immigrants our only solution is to assimilate, separating them from their cultural heritage and treating them as equals in a system that claims and aims to make no differentiation before the law.

It is difficult to argue that stratification according to wealth and authority is less or more ruthless as a way of exploiting human beings than is stratification by scale-ranking according to purity rules. Rather the sheer political ineffectualness of the system in which purity rules dominate guarantees that those at the bottom end of the scale will be short of material things and insecure of life and limb, as well as short of dignity. Being systematized, within a vision of the whole society hardly makes purity less pernicious a principle of separation than when it appears unsystematized, controlled by other principles. However, Professor Dumont is not concerned to judge but to reveal. He seeks to show that contrary to the explicit assumption of equality that our society makes, man is essentially hierarchical and that whenever some liberation is achieved in the name of equality, hierarchy will sooner or later raise itself over the rubble of the system that has been thrown down. Unless we take account of the hierarchical nature of man in society, we are limited to thinking of our own species as something that came into being with the Declaration of Human Rights. So we limit our vision – not arbitrarily, but predictably – if we take seriously the central problem to which the book is addressed. For according to the author's premise, the intellectual classifications on which a society rests are its most enduring part.

Two examples justify his view. Anthropologists will be interested to see here repeated his earlier account of Professor Evans-Pritchard's 1940 analysis in the sociological domain. This original and most important aspect of the Nuer study was missed by the contemporary school of British social anthropologists whose classifications were focused elsewhere upon power and authority. Likewise, more pertinently, he points to the permanence of the Indian Caste system and its power to resist change in spite of energetic political endeavour.

A few more points should be made to signal the general interest of this book. For the comparative study of religion, the 'holier-than-thou' competitive dialogue between Brahmans and renouncing sects has strong explanatory power. And again, to describe the renouncing sects primarily as systems which set themselves outside the society regulated on the purity scale challenges a European sociology of religion that tends to assume that religious sects arise among those who are socially deprived. The very rigidity of the caste system throws out renouncers from the highest and most privileged castes as well as from the others.

His own subsequent publications on comparative political theory point the way to the next developments. In this book, Professor Dumont's contrast is drawn between Hindu social thought and contemporary society starting with Hobbes and Rousseau. Consequently, he is comparing a society based on religious hierarchy with others where such hierarchy has been demolished. What is needed now is to develop these insights so that the contrast can be understood between the Hindu caste system and Christendom when its hierarchy was similarly intact. Both Christianity and Islam were equally committed to the project of making religion inform the institutions of command. Hinduism stands aside from power and hallows another hierarchy which is only accidentally affected by the growth and wane of kingdoms. Consequently there should be relevant differences to be traced in doctrines, differences in the way the common idiom of purity is used, and a different dialogue between the renouncers and the sacralizers of society. For Europe clear historical analyses already exist to show how the contrapuntal roles of priest and prince worked out their theme. The next steps in understanding should come from two kinds of research. One will trade the historical comparison between the Indian and European concepts of *Sacerdotium* and *Regnum* and the kinds of social environment where they flourished – a library task. The other should take to fieldwork in India the doctrinal issues that have divided Christendom over and over again. When the Brahman is ensconced as a rich and powerful hereditary land-owner, presumably a shift in doctrinal bias allows him to make the spiritual and temporal spheres less independent of each other. For him, a positive sacramental power might be seen, in a closer focus, to complement the negative bias of purification rites. When the head of the Christian Church himself claimed to be a great prince we had the parallel case, drawn large, of the Brahman landowner. Here is our chance to observe again social situations which correspond to the differences in theology which now strike us as so inert, and which we once so passionately defended.

So far I have confined my introduction to meanings of which the text treats explicitly. It is tempting to conclude with a point of which the writer may not be fully aware. He remarks in straightforward fashion that the Indian experiences of past time, mediated by the caste system, have their special quality. Indeed, for any societies, by reason of their structuring through unique cultural categories, the past is always and necessarily different in quality. This restoring of common sense makes absurd a number of popular mystifying statements about the experience of time in primitive societies and our own (such as that it may be static, or cyclic, or linear, hot or cold). Add to it the central theme that certain cultural categories are hardy and resistant to change. Then a link is made between the past and the future. Instead of a moving point between something vanished and something yet to be, the present moment for any society provides through its steady categories a fixed centre which holds the past and draws the future to itself. It could be very important to know what are these steady categories and the conditions in which they remain fixed. I recall E. A. Burtt's contrast between the medieval conception of time and our own philosophical puzzles on that score. In *The Metaphysical Foundations of Modern Science* he described the medieval philosopher's view:

> To put it in modern terms, the present exists unmoved and continually draws into itself the future. That this sounds absurd to our ears is because we have followed Galileo and banished man, with his memory and purpose, out of the real world. Consequently time seems to us nothing but a measurable continuum, the present moment alone exists, and that moment itself is no temporal quantity, but merely a dividing line between the infinite stretch of a vanished past and the equally infinite expanse of the untrodden future. To such a view it is impossible to regard the temporal movement as the absorption of the future into the actual or present, for there really is nothing actual. All is becoming. We are forced to view the movement of time as passing *from* the past *into* the future, the present being merely that moving limit between the two. Time as something *lived* we have banished from our metaphysics, hence it constitutes for modern philosophy an unsolved problem. . . . We forget that we are no longer part of the real world of modern metaphysics and that time as a measure-

able continuum – the dividing line of the present moving in regular and solemn silence from the dead past into the unborn future – is a notion whose ultimate metaphysical validity is conditioned upon making our own exclusion permanent.

Burtt, writing in 1924, hoped that once the load of uncriticized metaphysical assumptions carried under the cloak of Newton's authority had been exposed, the philosophy of science would reach some more mature self-awareness and even a more coherent cosmology to replace the medieval scheme. Many like him have looked to the social sciences to end an inherited dualism which separates a mindless external world from the universes organized by the activity of mind. But so far the social sciences have tended to accept whatever categories the natural sciences have created for them. Therefore they have been unable to contribute an independent vision. A number of studies of small, obscure tribal peoples are focused implicitly on this problem. But the present work is a more generally accessible contribution to understanding the relation of individual mind to socially generated intellectual processes. From the Indian system of pure and impure, above and below, order and disorder, social and organic, part and whole, a grim insight into our condition is obtained. These categories absorb and contain the past, and all the more effectively draw future choices into their pattern because of the intellectually convincing whole which they form.

To what extent do the socially sustained and therefore steady categories control individual perception and inhibit social experiment? How many such steady categories can there be and, if few, what various patterns can they combine to make? This particular system could only flourish where political authority is expected to be weak. What is the trade-off between the permanence of the category system and that of the social system? How vulnerable is the purity-scale to blasts from the command system? In pondering these old questions in this perspective we are led to very general problems about the similarities and differences between human and animal perception, and the kind of transactions with the environment which concern the philosophy of mind.

13

The Authenticity of Castaneda

If ever there was a writer tuned to his age or work likely to attract success, it must be Carlos Castaneda and his account of his apprentice years with a Mexican Indian sorcerer. There can be few who have never dreamed of such an adventure. Here is a young college student, who makes friends with a magician, no less, and persuades him to reveal his secrets.

The style is the adventure story of *Boy's Own* of eighty years ago. The hero's blood runs cold, his heart pounds, his throat parches, his pulse races, temperature soars or drops, his lungs burst, he faints, he recovers and is sick, he falls or faints again. He weeps with remorse or happiness. He can hardly ever believe his eyes, nor his ears. The pains he endures are excruciating, the hungers and long marches nigh impossible.

His Indian mentors are Olympic athletes, and disarmingly light-hearted. The training is long. He interrupts it frequently, sometimes because of university requirements, sometimes from sheer terror. After ten years he is told that the apprenticeship is over, he is fully trained, the rest is up to him.

Much has been said as to whether this is real anthropology or whether the pseudonym, Don Juan, hides any one real person, or where precisely the elements of fiction and truth are found. The purpose of this article is to consider whether the latest campus cult deserves serious attention from anthropologists. The answer is obviously, Yes.

In itself the philosophy of ascetic mysticism, so gradually pieced together, is enough evidence of truth in the tale. It would be flippant to dismiss it. But to take it seriously is to challenge most of what anthropologists tend to assume about the subject. The adage about primitive religions being this-worldly and world religions other-worldly can never again carry the same conviction.

The order of publication needs to be related to the order of events. The first book, *The Teachings of Don Juan* published in 1968, describes how an anthropology student from the University of California at Los Angeles, seeks an Indian to help him with his thesis on ethno-botany. He wants to classify and study the hallucinogenic plants, particularly peyote. In this book Don Juan introduces him to three such plants and their use: peyote (*Lophophora williamsii*), Jimson weed (*Datura inoxia syn. D. meteloides*) and a mushroom (possibly *Psilocybe mexicana*).

Under supervision he experiences extraordinary visions. But it is clear from the start that the controlled use of drugs is only the tip of the iceberg, much more importance is attached to learning how to interpret their effects.

Our vicarious apprentice, Mr Everyman, is as obtuse as we would be; he pesters Don Juan to tell him about the plants and feels he is being put off when instead of a lecture he is treated to a show or involved in a dramatic experience. Part of the extraordinary skill of the writing is the way that the reader is led to identify both with the student, doggedly asking questions and with the enigmatic teacher the meaning of whose riddling answers are clearer to us, thanks to the writer's hindsight, than they were to the student at the time of asking.

The first book brings the story to September 1965, with Castaneda terrified nearly to death, his mind rocking, vowing never again to ingest the hallucinogenic plants. The appendix gives a so-called structural scheme, written in a totally different style. Let us hope his university teachers were satisfied with what they must be presumed to have drafted: a careful précis of the teachings to date and a distinction between three kinds of reality.

The first, ordinary reality, achieved by everyday consensus; the second, a non-ordinary reality achieved by special consensus; and the third, special states of ordinary reality through cueing. The ethnomethodologists' programme is laid out in classic simplicity in this appendix.

One of the intriguing aspects of the series for the anthropologist is to read it as a struggle between two sets of teachers.

UCLA versus the old Indian sorcerers. In this first book, the anthropologists have won. Their cut-and dried analysis prevails over the sorcerers' insistence that the world is more marvellous than anything that human reason can comprehend.

The second book, *A Separate Reality*, takes up the story from 1968 when the writer returns with his note pad and certain questions he has formulated about how the special consensus or non-ordinary reality is achieved. He has a theory that at every peyote meeting there is a *de facto* leader who lays the interpretative cues for the others.

No sooner does he state his tidy little question than the battle is on again. Don Juan launches fairly and honestly into the problem of how consensus is achieved by taking it at its most general level. This book is about what he calls 'seeing', the faculty of initiates to discern a realm of being which other men miss by applying too ploddingly the criteria from their ordinary life.

Just as we would in his place, the student is slow to realize that his question is being answered and slow to realize that 'seeing' is not a matter of vision, but also of hearing and feeling in a special way. It involves a commitment to hold in suspense the judgments from the ordinary world, to switch off one set of responses and to be entirely open to anything that the senses may suggest.

But not entirely open, it soon becomes clear, for the apprentices are pushed to interpret their hallucinations in a stable way. They cannot report that they 'see' until they recognize each man as a luminous egg from whose abdominal region powerful threads of light flicker out, sustaining and informing him.

Very delicate is the line which appears between the alleged freedom of each apprentice to interpret a world for himself and the actual monitoring of their efforts which results in a consensus over certain broad principles of the common universe in which their experiences unfold. Ultimately the only reality taught for sure is that men are luminous beings who will one day die. The rest of their learning is about the arbitrary, factitious character of all knowledge.

This book is incomplete without the third, since the latter contains the conversations about death and reality which were verbal background to the astonishing conjuring tricks, hypnotic or trance-induced effects which again drive the student to the edge of reason and send him away in despair in 1970.

At this stage one might judge the contest between UCLA anthropology and the teachings of Don Juan to have resulted in a draw. The Indian tutor shows he knows the questions and delivers his answers with dazzling virtuosity. But the pupil cannot understand nor relay the message back home. He is beset with anxiety about his attempt to live in two worlds of reality, a problem whose validity is utterly denied by Don Juan.

The third book, *Journey to Ixtlan,* goes over all the ground again from the beginning in 1961. All the conversations with Don Juan which the university requirements for a doctoral disser- tation had previously screened out as irrelevant are put back into context. The whole experience takes on a very different tone as the full moral stature of Don Juan is revealed.

Now we discover that from their first encounters he has squarely established that the project of knowledge is a project in asceticism and non-attachment. He has quickly punctured the pupil's pretensions and exposed his personal weakness and vanity. To seek knowledge for the sake of a thesis is to be a pimp. The only valid seeking is for one's own life project. Knowledge is not to be divorced from living. To learn, the pupil must change his life, accept the thought of his own death, control all his own thought and action within that perspective.

When these pressures are revealed one can understand how the apprenticeship goes more quickly for some Indian boys and how they can learn to 'see' and move in the other world with creative confidence. Our representative, trying desperately to satisfy two schools, cannot give his heartfelt allegiance to his teacher's dis- cipline. He is literally torn between two worlds of reality. To his effort to control his vision in both, we owe this report.

The dialogue with Don Juan was originally conducted in Spanish. The translation reeks with clichés of spiritual writing in all the traditions which have flowed into our language. To be impeccable is only slightly different from 'Be ye perfect'. Change your life, leave your friends, drop your personal history, stop the world, learn the techniques of not-doing, the injunctions have familiar echoes. No wonder the books have sometimes been dis- missed as imaginative fiction.

When the third book is added to the first two, however, it is necessary to accept them as a serious challenge. The naiveties of expression can be taken as evidence of authenticity. The philosophy thus revealed is startlingly contemporary. Admittedly, the conscious concern with processes of validation, which preoccupies both phenomenologists and Yaqui Indian shamans, can make the suspicious-minded reviewer smell more fiction. But take the lessons, go along with the teachings, and quite a lot appears that is totally unexpected, new and provocative.

First for the common ground, whether set there by the writer, wittingly or unwittingly: since he cannot escape the structures of his own cognitive tradition and nor can we, it is worth enumerating how much philosophical overlap his material was made to bear.

The other world of non-ordinary reality was known to a number of other so-called sorcerers who were on their way to becoming men of knowledge. They each had their own way of achieving extraordinary effects, by hypnosis, sleight-of-hand and any of a hard-to-catalogue range of stage-setting, clueing procedures.

They seemed to hold each other in high esteem, even fear. Each was reckoned to be a master, in his own way, of dangerous powers in the universe. One was a master of equilibrium, he could vanish, cross a waterfall, appear ten miles away, before and behind, and create impressions of thunderous noise. Another's predilection was dancing, another was a herbalist. Don Juan was aiming to become a man of knowledge.

There were four enemies to be overcome by anyone who took his path. The seeker could first be stopped by fear. That overcome, he risked being seduced by his own clarity of mind. That temptation subdued, he could be seduced by the power he could now exert. After that the only enemy was old age which would sap his will to know.

The first book ends when the apprentice admits he has been defeated by fear; the second when he decides to protect the threatened clarity of his mind. The third ends ambiguously. He is tempted by power, but not yet past the hurdles of clarity or fear.

Throughout the trilogy tricks and horseplay interweave with themes of spirituality. The former recall the miracles of the early Judaeo-Christian tradition: the widow's curse; St Dorcas outsmarting the devil; St Jerome cherished by wild beasts; St Gregory by birds. The usual anthropological treatment of such stories is the full myth analysis. But perhaps we should now reverse the procedure and ask whether the tales of our own early religion do not bear witness to an ancient corpus of shamanistic skills. For these old men are just as witty in their pranks and as effective in controlling the winds or vanishing in smoke as any of our ancient saints.

We can ask whether the sorcerers' cosmology is more dominated by fear or love. All the apprentices when they meet, and most of the sorcerers, show touching affection for each other. One exception is an evil witch who takes the form of a blackbird and is allegedly out to kill Don Juan and his apprentice. Since fear is explicitly one of the techniques of training, the question of whether Don Juan really believes in her malice is left uncertain.

He certainly believes the world to be full of dangers and inimical powers. But once he has confessed that his pupil cannot learn for lack of sufficient motive and that the fear of a worthy opponent is necessary to force him to use his new found faculties, we cannot be sure how much the sorcerer's universe is dominated really by fear.

After the first book there is less said about joy and love. But a synoptic reading shows that the place of Mescalito needs to be restored to the later narratives. He is the being in the first book who guides and protects and who induces ecstatic joy in his elect. Once they have learnt to meet him in a peyote session, his reappearance can be triggered by various means, producing intense ecstasy and ruthless self-examination in his devotees.

The other world of reality seems to belong specially to Mescalito, so the accounts which exclude him are likely to be misleading. With Mescalito reinstalled at the centre, the attitude of the sorcerers to each other becomes very much like that recorded of mystics and wonderworkers in our history: self-deprecating and insisting on the spiritual heights reached by their fellows. Teresa of Avila speaking of John of the Cross might have exclaimed something equivalent to Vicente.

'You may say that I am only a man of lyric knowledge', he said. 'I'm not like Don Juan, my Indian brother.' Don Vicente was silent for another moment. His eyes were glassy and were staring at the floor by my left side. Then he turned to me and said, almost in a whisper, 'Oh, how high soars my Indian brother!'

Don Juan, on hearing of this tribute, gruffly rebuts it – 'lyric knowledge, my eye! Don Vicente is a sorcerer.' So much for the crude divisions between religion and sorcery used in anthropological typologies.

It may be difficult to judge the spirituality of the religion revealed in this series because of the deafening clichés in which it is perforce rendered. But it would be more difficult to defend formally the view that their echoing of contemporary philosophical concerns is proof of their bogus character. For they are consistently knitted into an attitude towards life and death and human rationality whose very coherence is alien to our own contemporary thought.

In the Hegelian aftermath, when Cowper Powys gave a character in *Maiden Castle* a remark about Being and Nonbeing, it was a wry and fanciful aside; when Kierkegaard or Husserl contrasted thought and existence, they conveyed a yearning sense of problem and insoluble dilemma; when Don Juan teaches the difference between doing and not-doing he is entirely matter of fact.

But in one context after another he demonstrates that focusing thought or intention or appetite or sensory responses creates one kind of intelligibility. Unfocusing is a technique for ridding the mind of its preconceptions of the everyday world and opening it to the inexplicable mysteries unleashed in hallucinations.

He teaches his novice to stare at foliage, focusing on the dark space between the leaves; he must stare at a bank of cloud until his eyes see it as a dazzling pattern of light; then he must deliberately undo that pattern by focusing on the dark holes between the lines of light until the pattern reverses. He must do the same with hearing until he can shut out the sounds he normally selects and listen to silence. Harder still, he must learn to control his dreams; the most not-doing of all not-doing is to control sleeping experience, but abandon the will to impose any pattern on waking experience.

Somehow, this balance between strict control and strict readiness to take on any vision that is offered and sustain it as long as possible is the condition of 'seeing'.

The last book ends with two old sorcerer-saints recalling their lives. They have been splitting their sides with laughter at elaborate jokes at the expense of their pupil. Then, replying to his questions, they look back on a long tale of withdrawal from worldly delights and sadness overwhelms them. One by one they have rejected the comforts of friendship for the sake of holding to their hard-won knowledge. They know that all doings are unreal: 'to hinge yourself on to either one is a waste of time because the only thing that is real is the being in you that is going to die. To arrive at that being is the not-doing of the self.'

Somewhere between the words of surrealists, phenomenologists and ethnomethodologists, somewhere between secular modern Zen and John Cage's not-music and saying nothing, this philosophy makes a split-level version of what everyone is currently hearing. The young apprentice may have imposed more than he realized of our own culture upon the non-doing of 'seeing'. But, even so, this remarkable document throws a big spanner in the works of anthropologists who have put much more doing than he has into the recording of primitive religions.

The temporary discomfiture of a few professionals is not the important issue. Much more interesting are the suggestions about how different forms of visual experience are induced, by squinting, focusing and unfocusing and rapid sideway scanning. Most interesting of all are the ways in which a spatial metaphor is used for pegging the otherworldly experiences, rather in the style of the Renaissance memory theatre.

From these ideas we are likely to get advances in anthropology.

Bibliography

CASTANEDA, C., *The Teachings of Don Juan*, Harmondsworth, Penguin, 1970.
CASTANEDA, C., *A Separate Reality*, London, Bodley Head, 1971.
CASTANEDA, C., *Journey to Ixtlan*, London, Bodley Head, 1973.

Part 3

The *a priori* in Nature

Introduction

It is a privilege for a researcher's work to be taken up by another. The neophyte who has spotted a technique or a useful piece of information is lucky if someone more experienced absorbs the initial research and solves the main questions as a footnote to his own work. My experience was the other way round. In Congolese fieldwork among the Lele I observed some material relevant to then current anthropological concerns, and published it summarily in 1955 and 1957 (chapters 1 and 2 of this book). The material explained some of the assumptions about animals and humans that operated as hidden categories through which the Lele organised their experience. The categories came to the surface as explicit rules of diet, hygiene and etiquette. Though fragmentary they were remarkably consistent. Clearly, further research into the rules for everyday dealing with animate and inanimate things would reveal a more coherent ordering of the universe and reveal more and more clearly the social imprint it received through their system of classification. In its broad outline this was not specially new to British social anthropology or to any anthropologists trained in the traditions of *L'Année sociologique*. Durkheim and Mauss had dealt in Australian, Eskimo, Chinese and American ethnography, and had gained access to the category system through the grand principles actualised in moiety, phratry or marriage class organisation. My material was African and access to it was gained through staying with the women as they cooked, divided food, talked about illness, babies and proper care of the body. I had added a geographical region to the existing literature on the subject of implicit categories, and also a different social dimension, more intimate than those already studied. In this sense, the reporting was normal science: it extended the application of principles already understood. But the fact that the Lele cults could better be interpreted through knowing their principles of personal hygiene and diet, and that these turned out to be consistent with the principles for classifying animal kinds, could be of more than regional interest. It suggested an even stronger channelling of experience through socially significant categories than was already assumed. This in turn would suggest that a much closer fit between religious and other forms of organisation could be revealed through studying higher level classification systems. At the time of research I had had the good fortune to attend lectures in Oxford on Nuer sacrifice and on Tallensi ancestral cults. It was impressive to learn how the specialised religious institutions gathered up the varied strands of social and psychological experience and affirmed the normative values in dramatic rituals. The tribal religions were saying something, expressing something, if you must, that was happening independently at a secular level, in clan and lineage organisation. In spite of assertions to the contrary (Evans-Pritchard, 1956:313) the approach was strongly Durkheimian: religion crystallised the great moments, the deepest emotions, it focused for the individual his relation to society. Lele had no lineages, did not perform sacrifice or venerate ancestors. Most of their cultic energies were devoted to warding off sorcery. Since for them specialised religious institutions were not so apparent as for those other tribal societies, they promised a fertile ground for interpreting ritual more broadly. The Lele case should have been able to show the link between the great moments and the minor ones, the structuring of thought and response in every aspect of lived experience. The principles of classification, when their burden of social concern had all been revealed, would show how culture is created. Obviously, if such a programme lay ahead, it would not do to leave the analysis of animal classification where I put it down in 1957. That article concludes tamely that once the implicit framework of Lele metaphysical ideas had been uncovered, the 'different cult groups no longer seemed to be disconnected and overlapping, but rather appeared as complementary developments of the same basic theme.' Left out of this conclusion was practically everything that really preoccupied the Lele. One gets the impression of a lot of squeamish, hypochondriac old maids, worried about absurdly elaborate etiquette and superstitious hygiene. No sign of their truculence, their raiding and abductions of women, their harping on violent revenge and sexual virility. These values come to the fore in the book on their social organisation (1963). But their principles of classification merely relate their cult groups to their assertion of male dominance over females, human dominance over animals, both given in terms of finer discrimination of food and table manners. And on that platitude the matter rested.

At that time it was likely that each year would see a new batch of anthropologists in Central Africa. Inevitably some of them would be confronted by similar problems. It was reasonable to hope that my analysis would be superseded by more complete recordings of animal taxonomy in other tribes and the rules of behaviour by which they were known. As a result of concerted research on principles of belief in that region, it could be expected that one day the implications for the theory of knowledge, which I could vaguely indicate, would be expounded for wider understanding. At that time, moreover, it did not seem necessary to highlight as a discovery the advantages this kind of data holds over mythology for revealing the basis of culture. The difficulty of controlling a given interpretation of mythology is that there are no criteria of relative importance for the different elements identified. By contrast, beliefs which are pegged by rules of behaviour and underwritten by beliefs in automatic sanctions have some guarantee of the weight that is attached to them. The anthropologist's subjective bias is brought under control. But the development of anthropology has gone in other directions so that my friend David Schneider has lately rediscovered for himself a procedure that my generation of fieldworkers took to be traditional in anthropology (Schneider, 1972 : 37):

> The second major aspect of the strategy I have used follows directly from, and is required by, the third, which is the use of a different, narrower, and I think sharper and more powerful concept of culture than has been traditional in anthropology. Briefly, I start with concrete, observable patterns of behaviour and abstract from it a level of material which has usually been

called 'norms.' The normative system consists in the rules and regulations which an actor should follow if his behaviour is to be accepted by his community or his society as proper. These are the 'how-to-do-it' rules, as Goodenough has recently put it (1970). They should on no account be confused with the patterns of behaviour which people actually perform. It is the rule 'thou shalt not steal' that is the norm, not the fact that many people do not steal; it is the rule that a middle class father should earn the money to support his family, not the fact that many actually do.

Not only did anthropology eventually change its focus, with the happy result that my original assumptions are in favour again, but, less happily, the region I worked in suffered great change. Congo Independence in 1961 was followed by civil war. The dispersal of my Belgian colleagues led to some drying up of research in that region. That is why I can enjoy the rare privilege of cashing my own cheques, postdated as they seem to have been. Twenty years later I can chide myself for negligence, and get to work afresh by contemplating the relation of my own with colleagues' subsequent work.

The earliest paper (1955; chapter 1 of this book) records some Lele ideas about cleanliness and propriety. It shows that they reach forth from water-gourd and cooking-pot to the sphere of religion. Filth here is clearly associated with sexual shame and improper sex. Rules of avoidance of all kinds, whether for showing respect between sons and fathers, seniors and juniors or in-laws, is always referred explicitly to the dominant idea of in-law avoidance. Therefore, if I found that animals were said to be lacking shame and without respect, the connotations of sex and marriage could not be ignored – surely not. However, in the 1957 paper (chapter 2 of this book), dealing directly with animal categories and cults, this connection is completely overlooked. The pangolin is on record there as an animal which, unlike all other beasts, shows shame and practises respect avoidance. If it ever occurred to me that the dominant metaphor of sex was dominant here too, I simply did not know how to interpret the connection. I merely concluded from the superficial meaning of Lele remarks about the pangolin's human-like characteristics that its politeness made it a fit mediator between the species whose defining boundaries its physical existence transcended. I was uncomfortably aware that this was a pretty thin explanation of its awesome power. But it was a private discomfort. No one else I ever consulted disagreed with that particular analysis. I was sometimes asked when I would write a book on Lele religion, but confessed that I had recorded all I knew.

When I came back from the first stint of fieldwork, my supervisor, Professor Evans-Pritchard, looking sympathetically through my sketchy reports, told me that I had plenty of information – what was wanting was understanding: this would come with empathy and work, one's own and other people's. I now see that the problem of understanding foreign beliefs is distorted by the concentration on great moments dramatically enacted. The very category of religion, focusing, as Victor Turner puts it so well, on rites of life crisis and of affliction (see chapter 9 of this book) would be a distraction to the task I should have had in hand. It implies that a scanning of the grand affirmatory points in social experience will always turn up the corresponding catalogue of rituals of affirmation, separation and healing, and thus map in advance that part of the culture which corresponds to religion the world over. But the problem of relating Lele classification of animals to their on-going male competition for women did not open to that approach. It could not be solved until posed in a different comparative framework. It involved a conversion to a form of alliance theory, as the last paper here, 'Self-evidence', shows. It involved clarifying the untidy language of magic and religion, the work which was begun in *Purity and Danger* and continued in these essays. To have shown some of the ways in which each tribal universe is constructed out of the mutual coercion of social life did not bring me anywhere near solving the problem of the pangolin's extraordinary power as a sign to the Lele. I was stuck. Stimulus had to come from other research. It was given in handsome endowments from Ralph Bulmer and S. Tambiah.

In *Purity and Danger* I paralleled the Lele classification of animals with that in Leviticus 11. Ralph Bulmer was the only person to protest that in writing on Hebrew cosmology I had done the very thing that the rest of the book was written to stop. It was an analysis of a system of ideas with no demonstration of its connection with the dominant concerns of the people who used it for thinking with. Both Bulmer's and Tambiah's animal classifications brilliantly avoided this defect. In each case a concern about wrong sexual partners came through to the animal classification in the form of concern about uncontrolled boundary-crossing animals. The systems of marriage rules made themselves felt in the systems of rules about touching and eating animals. Full of admiration, my first thought was that it would be impossible to push the Hebrew and Lele analyses to parallel conclusions, for lack of good ethnography. Then I re-read E. R. Leach's *Legitimacy of Solomon*, which brought home to the anthropologist with a resounding thud something which Old Testament scholarship has been agreed upon for a very long time. This was that the Pentateuch was full of concern for the evils that flowed from marriages with foreigners. Israelite marriage laws were not based upon a rule of lineage or tribal exogamy, rather the contrary. Therefore it was reasonable that the Israelites would not manifest the same concerns about wrong sexual partners as tribes whose whole social organisation was based on a rule of exogamic exchange. And if the Israelites were significantly different in their marriage laws, what about the Lele? Here again a more reflective study might show up important differences in their attitude to the son-in-law and his provenance.

The last two papers supplement one another closely. The new approach to animal classification could not proceed without extending the analysis of Hebrew rules of purity. I chose the rules governing the Jewish meal (chapter 16 of this book) so as to reach beyond the classification of animal kinds to the social and political preoccupations of the Jewish people themselves. This exercise seemed to illustrate well the thesis that a social preoccupation with boundaries will be reflected in the treatment of boundaries in general and therefore that classification systems may be compared according to the way their boundaries are arranged. Having demonstrated the connection between Leviticus 11 on the Mosaic dietary laws and the dominant concerns of the ancient Hebrews, I was ready to compare the four classification systems, Thai, Karam, Lele and Hebrew, from this very abstract point of view. Their different patterns of insulation and overlap finally provided the context in which I solved the puzzle about the pangolin's power (chapter 17). A more sophisticated logical exposition is very desirable. The essence of the argument is that the logical patterning in which social relations are ordered affords a bias in the classification of nature, and that in this bias is to be found the confident intuition of self-evident truth. And here, in this intuition, is the most hidden and inaccessible implicit assumption on which all other knowledge is grounded. It is the ultimate instrument of domination, protected from inspection by every warm emotion that commits the knower to the social system in which his knowledge is guaranteed. Only one who feels coolly towards that society can question its self-evident propositions.

The path for this next state of inquiry is sign-posted by the lecture, 'In the Nature of Things' (chapter 14). It seeks to clarify the relation between classification and social concerns which Durkheim saw so clearly for primitive classification but from whose action he somehow exempted ourselves.

Bibliography

EVANS-PRITCHARD, E. E. (1956), *Nuer Religion,* Oxford, Clarendon Press.

DOUGLAS, M. M. (1963), *The Lele of the Kasai,* London, Oxford University Press for the International African Institute.

GOODENOUGH, W. H. (1970), *Description and Comparison in Cultural Authority,* Chicago, Aldine.

SCHNEIDER, D. (1972), 'What is kinship all about?' in *Kinship Studies in the Morgan Centennial Year,* ed. P. Reining, Anthropological Society of Washington, D.C.

14

In the Nature of Things

It seems right to choose for this lecture the distinction between humans and animals. Our department has two entrances: one is headed Anatomy, the other Biological Sciences. Its work was begun by the great anatomist, Professor Eliot-Smith. The first chair was held by Professor Daryll Forde. During the twenty years I had the privilege of being on his staff, he required that the standard of research be no less strict into 'man-as-a-social-being' than that applied in the other half of the department by the physical anthropologists. Cautiously, therefore, I broach the question of why it is so exceedingly difficult to see ourselves as objects among other objects. Whenever we consider the nature of things, there is this tendency to exempt ourselves. Thus appears a boundary between us and animal creation, a boundary between spirit and matter. Every great revolution of thought has touched that boundary. Defenders of the Bible against Darwin's biology fought upon it. Marxists would demolish the line between spirit and matter as a shoddy excuse to assert the superiority of rulers over ruled, of mental over manual work. Christians who usually defend it, for different reasons, should likewise be ready to demolish that sharp line. The doctrines of Easter are already hard enough to common sense. To diminish that boundary between spirit and matter would make them more plausible. And certainly, it seems most unlikely that a really big discontinuity in nature should happen to crop up just here. The other breaks in the nature of things have turned out, one by one, to be optical illusions, or fences put there by ourselves for our own purposes: why not this one too?

Furthermore, the wish to protect that boundary is itself rooted in physical nature. Marx traced it to political and economic concerns. But it goes much deeper: in any living organism, as Merleau-Ponty pointed out, (1965) an observer's bias creates a distinction; even the chimpanzee behaves as if he was the only mobile thing in a universe of static objects. He apparently can't see his own body as an object among others. He does not see other objects endowed with the same freedom that he enjoys. Place a piece of fruit on the other side of a barrier. The animal can get it all right if he only has to bestir himself and walk round for it. Arrange the experiment so that staying put himself he must push the fruit away and round the barrier, and he is defeated. He cannot imagine the object moving away and coming back. Far easier to move himself than get the object to move. We can be so tired that we prefer to do a thing ourselves rather than explain to another how to do it; or we find it easier to explain with gestures than verbally. The motor system can take over and work out cognitive functions which it normally sustains; yet its own processes are hidden to the organism. What Merleau-Ponty (1965) called 'the privilege of the organism' causes the perceiving subject to exempt itself and to credit itself with more autonomy than other objects and species. Whether this is really true of chimpanzees, I don't know. But certainly the empiricist himself tends to have the same illusion; otherwise, he could not credit the individual of his own species with such freedom. To avoid knowing what kind of brainwashing or control society imposes on individual perception is to indulge the privilege of the organism. Merleau-Ponty supposed that the symbolic order makes men free of the constraints which apply to lower forms of life. It is a flattering refrain: each animal species is limited by its proper mode of being; its goals are set; its capacity to learn is limited; not so ours. Thanks to our unspecialised skills and thanks to our control of symbols, especially language, we can choose freely from an infinite range of goals. There is no proper mode of being which is specifically our own. The human mind, playing freely in symbolic worlds which it creates itself, must bear the weight of its freedom. Smugly tragic, the favourite theme goes on: free to be noble, free to embrace error, free to poison ourselves, free to extinguish our species. This familiar chant nowhere admits that the symbolic life is not entirely free. It works through a medium of expression. The peculiar limitations set by the medium are worth examining. For this inspection, we must lower the fence between us, ourselves, and them, the primitive tribes, and between us, humanity, and them, the animals.

When I first read Durkheim his sociological determinism affronted me. His main propositions run as follows: God is society; society is God; the idea of class is derived from society; classification depends on social experience. But outrage or no outrage, Professor Evans-Pritchard in the chair of anthropology at Oxford made it very clear that our subject stood in direct line of descent from Durkheim. The central task of anthropology was to explore the effects of the social dimension on behaviour. The task was grand, but the methods humble. We were taught to work in very small areas of the total field. We had to stay with a remote tribe, patiently let events unfold and let people reveal the categories of their thought. Irresistibly the scrutiny would strip human thought of its claims to independence. Following on Professor Evans-Pritchard's analysis of Azande metaphysics, several key works appeared, or rather key tribes – the Tallensi, the Bemba, the Nuer, Yako, Barotse, then Dinka and others, mostly African. In these far-off fields we could see that the main structures of thought are generated in the hurly-burly of political life and draw their stability from the institutions they underwrite. In this way, the wild claims that Durkheim and his followers had made were pinned down in distant areas, then tamed and groomed for showing in anthropological seminars.

This work made clear a sense in which society is worshipped as God and in which God appears mediated by the social dimension. Equally clearly the social categories influence those of the intellect. But tribal society is a long way away. We could agree that the primitive mind worships and thinks in categories generated in social action, and still nourish the belief that *we* are different. What holds for them does not hold for us. This way we could leave the boundary between mind and society uncriticised, because of the boundary, tall and thick, between 'us' and 'them'. We exempted ourselves. On their side of the boundary, individual thought is socially controlled. On our side, by the privilege of the organism, it is free.

Of the two obvious things we have, and which the primitives

lack, one is industrialisation (and the technology and science that uphold it). Max Weber addressed himself to the problem of understanding why *we* are different from the civilisations that have gone before. He and Marx together dominated sociology with analyses focused on the grand differences. Now is the time to turn the telescope the other way. If we wish seriously to see all humanity in one continuous perspective, some device is needed for cutting out the glare and dazzle from the effects of industrial development. The other obvious difference between us, and (some of) them, the primitives, is the extreme confusion and complexity of our beliefs. From this difference some anthropologists conclude that *their* cosmologies are socially determined, while *we* enjoy freedom within a range of options. They are brainwashed by their cultures; we need not be.

Any gadget we devise for seeing ourselves as things in nature would have to cut through the disorderly riot of modern belief systems and discover some regular relations between the social structure and the structure of beliefs. I shall try to provide such a device. First I will show how the way we express ourselves is constrained by rules, moreover by rules of communication which import judgments of their own about the relation of nature to culture. Try shouting at someone and they tend to shout back, try whispering – recently I lost my voice; a conversation started in a normal tone soon became an exchange of whispers. But on that more intimate channel, the content changed too. Mimetically the style controls the message, and the style itself is an automatic social response. There is a range between intimacy and social distance which is expressed according to what I can call the purity rule. It is essential to appreciate what the purity rule does to support a division between nature and culture.

To domesticate an animal means to teach it to bring organic processes under control. To socialise a child means the same thing. There is a universal code for grading expressive forms. Living organisms shed their own used products. Excretion, urination, vomiting, spitting, nail-paring, hair-losing, these are the processes which rank lowest. Other physiological processes which are not part of discourse *should* be controlled: sneezing, hiccups. As for giggling and yawning, an apology frames them off. The more important the social event, the greater the demand for bodily control, and the lower the threshold of tolerance of bodily processes. The more hierarchised the social system, the stronger the control demanded. Social distance measures itself by distance from organic process. In Hinduism, as Professor L. Dumont puts it, wherever the organic erupts into the social, there is impurity; birth, death, sex, eating and defecation incur impurity and so are hedged with rituals. But we understand the code as well as any Hindu. It is as if each person were expected to segment his social universe into control levels more and more remote from physiological functions and physical comfort. All the other media express the purity rule. In space, for instance, the design of architecture allows for the fact that proximity means direct face-to-face relations, the watery eye, the breath upon the face. Distance transforms the living body into a cardboard dummy with none of these unwanted effects. Social distance is simple to express spatially but it is a mistake to suppose that there is more room at the top. Rather the top needs to be less crowded so as to express differentiation spatially. Turning to music, we understand the contrast of complex long rhythms in funeral marches with quick jolly jogs. More spacing means more solemnity. The same again applies to food. Being a medium, food, like the other media, must be able to show the gamut from intimacy to distance. Raw meats are trimmed to geometric shapes by convention, which is also the gamut from nature to culture.

Above all, consider language. There are graded linguistic registers radiating out from the most private, physical experiences, to the most heavily laden with social meaning. The forceful four-letter words with their straight physiological reference are the right channel for blasphemy, intimacy, insult. Another linguistic channel is selected perforce for more formal events. Its very restricted usage divorces it from the physiological level, and so on for the next, and the next. Conceptual categories develop a range of reference by more and more general terms. If the legs of the opposite sex really ever had to be referred to in polite English by a circumlocution, and if it was ever rude in Victorian England to mention the legs of a piano, the rules were at work. Perhaps it has been developed most systematically in Dyirbal, a language in North Queensland studied by Robert Dixon (1968). Here, out of respect for the wife's mother, a special mother-in-law language was used. It substituted a more general term for groups of specific nouns and verbs (such as 'nether bifurcation' instead of 'leg'). The linguist expected to spend months on the componential analysis of the language. Suddenly he realised that the aborigines had done it for him. All that he had to do was ask for the equivalent word in mother-in-law language and then record all the specific words for which the more general term was substituted. There is the perfect example of the purity rule expressing respect by avoiding physiological processes.

These rules of analogy, purity and distance, may seem to form a thoroughly invidious, élitist, class-conscious mode of communication. Though I am presenting it as a natural code, it sounds already as factive in its conventions and as difficult to learn and to use as any verbal language. And I have not even described half of the complex procedures of scanning and adaptation required. One has to watch all the different channels; they must match and reinforce each other. No good signalling intimacy today and distance tomorrow. Everyone around is trying to assess stability and consistency of meaning from the signals. If one of the different channels does not match the intimacy level shown in the others, its messages will be ignored. According to research in California, when white middle-class mothers go on smiling, whether their verbal comments are friendly or not, their children just ignore the smile channel. They consider male smiles to be more friendly than female ones. (Bugenthall, Love and Gianetto 1971 : 572).

Several branches of the social sciences are trying now to interpret human and animal facial expression, gestures, etc. Earlier W. H. Sheldon tried to work out the connection between personality and physical type. I maintain that these avenues of research are doomed unless they take into account the demand of the social system as such to be expressed. For it is the social system which allows smacking of the lips, belching and second helpings, or the social system which forbids signs of bodily enjoyment. By processes of adaptation and selection physical types must end by corresponding to the local system of permissions and restraints. In an old film, the hero repulsed a woman's advances, saying: 'Lady, if you think every time a man says "Good morning", he is making a pass at you, then you have led a very sheltered life.' Like the lady, ethologists need a formula for assessing the strength of signals whose meaning would vary according to the social load the system of coding is set to carry (see chapter 6, 'Do Dogs laugh?').

We assume that, compared with speech, non-verbal communication ought to be simple. It turns out to be highly complex. Would it not be better to cut through the tangle of signals and restore the simplicity of animals? Social animals seem to gain comfort and reassurance from physical contact with one another. We are sometimes admonished to overcome our inhibitions in this respect. We are told it would do us all good to touch each other more. Take care. Uncontrolled, such a practice would rip up any system of communication. Supposing everyone you have contacted in a crowded day of touching comes back offering you more and more intimate exchanges – will you necessarily want them all? It would be the same as if a religion with an elaborate vocabulary of grace, sin and salvation were reformed and left with one word, glory, glory, glory. Many human experiences would be left unshared. The same applies with appropriate changes to public obscenity. These moves which are intended to make more rational and to simplify, ultimately defeat communication.

The purity rule is a control system to which communicating humans all submit. It imposes a scale of values which esteem formal relations more than intimate ones. The more the society is vested with power, the more it despises the organic processes on which it rests. At this point the very distinction which we set out to query, between humanity and animals, turns out itself to be conditioned by fixed rules common to all human intercourse. We started by suspecting that it is part of animal nature to suppose ourselves endowed with greater freedom than other species. We now find it is an apparently necessary part of our common system of communication to distance our social life from animal origins. Some scholars would glorify speech so much above the mute channels of communication that they even locate the source of our intellectual freedom in the power of abstract verbal symbols. Any piece of living matter functions and renews itself by abstracting complex information. It cannot be the capacity to abstract that distinguishes us and gives us the sense of a difference between spirit and matter. To me it is more convincing to argue that the experience of an organism shedding its own used cells is enough of a direct analogy for knowing the difference between living and dead matter. But consciousness of the knowledge we owe to our animal being is veiled by the purity rule. The first step in achieving objectivity is to discount messages about ourselves that are carried in the purity rule. It is the nub of our difficulty in judging ourselves as things in nature.

The next stage in trying to see ourselves plainly is to separate out the individual from the social environment he is in. We can start to characterise the environment by distinguishing two experiences of social pressure: personal pressure or pressure by classification (Bernstein 1971). Everyone knows the pressure people put on one another as persons: 'You can't do that to me!' or 'Please, just because I ask...' Or else they put pressure through systems of classification. This perhaps needs more explanation. The inner-directed person is supposed to carry his system of classification inside him, regardless of external support. But no system of classification commands wide acceptance without some supporting social pressure. Even the distinction of sex is sustained by the interest in property transferred at marriage. Mr Justice Ormrod once declared that in law sex is a matter of biology, not of gender. He would never have been asked to rule on an alleged change of sex if no property had been at stake (1971). The more coherent and all-embracing the classification, the more the pressure needed to sustain its general credibility against rival schemes.

We can try to characterise the individual's environment in two social dimensions: order and pressure. Order stands for classification, the symbolic system. This dimension can vary in coherence and scope. Classifications can be shown in taxonomic flow charts, but usually these show no costs or social value. When the station-master rules that a tortoise is not to be classed with dogs, he is making a generous interpretation of the case. To charge nothing for conveying a tortoise will ruin no one. But other grades and classifications are under more pressure. In the heart of Bordeaux region, the right to bear the label St Emilion is very valuable and entry to all the grades from *grand cru classé* to plain Bordeaux jealously guarded. Plainly social and economic pressures keep those four rows of bottles displayed in the municipal headquarters firmly in their rank order. Moreover, the classification of wines and vineyards in St Emilion may coincide with many of the other social classifications, wealth, local influ-

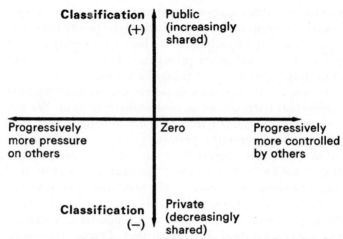

Figure 14.1 Classification and control (adapted from Professor Basil Bernstein's discussion of the classification and framing of educational knowledge, 1971)

ence, education – but not all. So the extent to which the environment is strongly classified depends on the intermeshing of various criteria. Competing systems which order different fields of experience may not mesh together well. In such a case, the individual experiences less coherence in his environment. Our gadget for seeing ourselves in nature will represent order in the environment on a vertical axis; the more coherent system would come higher, the less coherent one lower. In the middle is zero (Figure 14.1). Here all possible classifications are in abeyance. It is a blank with no meaning whatever. It could be anomie, the suicide's doubt. It could be the ineffable moment of the mystic. Moving upwards from this most interesting point of all, we can mark the increasing coherence and scope of classifications accepted by other people. This is the way for communication. Moving downward is towards the private philosophy or the jarring choice between a hundred partial and conflicting philosophies. The mere fact of choice means that the environment leaves the individual free. Further down the route of originality is madness.

Continuing to develop the device for objectively seeing ourselves, I will draw pressure on a horizontal line. The middle is zero pressure, no demands are made on the individual. He is alone. Zero is complete freedom. Moving to the right, ego is increasingly bonded by others. When the pressures and counter-pressures are summed, if the outcome is that he puts others under his bonding, we mark him to the left of zero. In fact at any point in time, an individual's network of social relations is spread across the square. Say his wife puts heavy pressure on him for some cash; say his office puts on another set of pressures for more work; say his old friends leave him alone or pursue him for their purposes; say the only people he can dominate are his children and when he is alone he escapes into a private, Walter Mitty world. We will need to talk in more general terms about the weight of these specific pressures and the reference to classification that they involve. For the most effective way to bind other people is by appeal to classification.

Let me illustrate this first by going round the diagram, taking the mid-point in the two right-hand quadrants, looking at the family. First, for strong order and strong bonding, when minimum options are open, a child's parents use classifications for controlling him. Second, for a strong bonding without classification: the child finds himself controlled by person-to-person appeals to respond to his mother's migraine or his father's tiredness. The child is meant to be building up his own set of classifications (Bernstein, 1971).

Most tribal societies have developed systems of public knowledge in which the physical and social categories are analogies of one another. Any meaning available at one level of classification is also realised at others. A breach of a social rule is seen as equivalent to a damage against physical nature – and sanctioned according to gravity. But tribal societies are not alone in the top right-hand quadrant. Most of us are there too. It is the most crowded spot on the diagram. Why we herd together there, what forces push us there, is the problem of freedom and the subject of this lecture. Like the tribal peoples, we have internalised the classifications of our social group; we see no other kinds of reality. Timid and gregarious, we accept more pressure than we exert. We rush to protect the insulation of the system, whether we like it or not. Breakdown of insulation covers all social change, technology, war, invasion. Don't expect too much of this diagram. It is not concerned with power except in so far as power can weaken insulation. Another dimension would be needed to show whether a given person consented fully to the

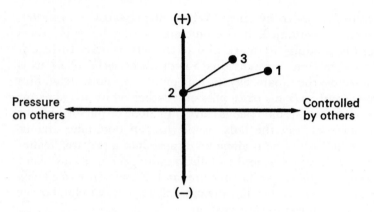

Figure 14.2   Young Rousseau's temporary conversion

classifications and pressures he responds to. It does not show whether a person finds himself where he is by accident or choice, whether there is hardship there for him or joy. The diagram is meant simply to show the individual in two dimensions of his social field. These two dimensions are enough to open up ways of charting conversions and shifts of intellectual allegiance.

The use of the diagram can be illustrated from famous life histories. Take for a first example the early life of Jean Jacques Rousseau, apprenticed at seventeen to a cruel master. He decided to run away. His childhood had been organised within the Calvinist cosmology. From Geneva there was a regular mode of escape for criminals, victims of oppression and drop-outs of all kinds. This was to seek conversion to Catholicism. Another system of classification was nearby, at Annecy, with people only too ready to incorporate immigrants into a new system of control. For a few days after his escape he vagabonded freely, then he accepted the other faith, and with it a lighter yoke, which in its turn he later dispensed with.

Somewhere mid-way between strong bond and no classification provided by society, the individual is free to make up his own rules and to classify the universe as he pleases. The only requirement is to accept the personal pressures of his fellows. In this range the religious sects are founded whose only rule is 'love ye one another'. But this second right hand quadrant is thinly popu-

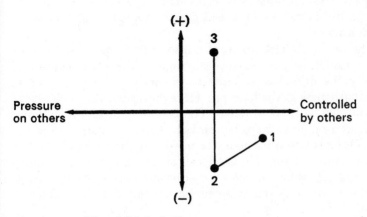

Figure 14.3 The child Strindberg

lated because the position is inherently unstable. Sooner or later some hard lines and boundaries are drawn, starting with the line between saints and sinners. Even the Surréalist movement, founded as a reproach to all classification and ordering, came to concentrate violent pressure on its own external boundary. The Plymouth Brethren, originally resolved to have no rules, for the sake of order at the common meal, decided that the eldest brother should always break the bread and distribute it. The thought of zero point, of perfect freedom in love, exerts an extraordinary seductive power. Caught by the dilemma of how to exist in community without rules, people resort to the paradox of legislating for rulelessness. The history of the sect normally starts low on the line and soon moves upwards. For different reasons Strindberg's childhood follows this pattern. Classified as an infant, there was nothing he could do but sit still. Move in any direction and he would be in trouble. This was maximum control by personal pressure and minimum classification. Nothing was explained to him except his static role. As he grew older his freedom was increased but no classification emanating from the others set up a rational universe around him. One of his brothers was his father's favourite and the other his mother's. He would be blamed for what his brothers had done and stereotyped as a sulky, thieving liar. Nothing he could find out about other people's classifications was consistent or acceptable. Once at school, however, he soon excelled and adopted a different set of classifications.

The next (top left) quadrant is also thinly populated. Now we are considering the person who makes the classifications of society his own, but submits to no one's pressures except to dominate them in the long run. He is the leader. But the move to the top left is hard to make. The counter-pull of his followers controls him: in so far as he thinks he needs them, they grip him fast. Or he is a frontier man, the missionary bringing civilisation to a cannibal island. He is on this side so long as he is telling everyone else what the rules are: they are following him and he thinks he is freely following no person but a traditional set of rules.

Now for the case when both kinds of options are open to the maximum degree. The individual is making up his own categories. He does not care who follows him. No one pushes him around. Such a person must be a recluse, or an artist, or both. John Cage writes as if he meant to stay like this. He works in the medium of sound so as to maximise the unexpected and minimise the filters and controls which separate 'music' from noise. He is against the governing theme on which traditional music is based. He is against control of all kinds. He exalts silence and tries to listen to the natural procession of sounds, his heartbeat and the rhythms of the nervous system, without imposing any pre-ordained framework. Francis of Assisi tried to enshrine spontaneity and to hover all his life around the double zero of religious ecstasy. Cage makes his work on the same principle. His coin-tossing procedures are foreshadowed by Francis's equally simple oracular devices for making decisions without making rules. Whether Cage would care to stay at this point if he had gathered no disciples is another matter. But he can only stay there now by not caring. So long as he has no message or prophecy, no wish to convert and nothing to convert to, he can stay. 'I have nothing to say, and I am saying it.' (1971) (Compare another original, Francis Bacon is said to declare: 'I am not an Expressionist. I have nothing to express.') Clearly John Cage's programme is taxing, morally and intellectually. He must deploy unrelenting energy and continual inventiveness to cherish spontaneity, even for one brief day. No wonder that most people give up the attempt.

A distinctive view of nature belongs to each quarter of the diagram. The closer to zero the lower the barrier between men and nature descends.

Three quotations from John Constable's letters (*Constable and the Art of Nature*, Tate Gallery, 1971) describe the case of a person moving away from the pressure of others and rejecting their classifications. The first describes the emotion.

> Every tree seems full of blossom of some kind and the surface of the ground seems quite living. Every step I take and on whatever object I turn my eye that sublime expression in the Scripture 'I am the resurrection and the life' seems verified about me. (1819)

The next one describes his situation.

> though I am here in the midst of the world, I am out of it – and am happy – and endeavour to keep myself unspoiled. I have a kingdom of my own both fertile and populous – my landscape and my children. (1823)

The last describes his independence of the judgments of others.

> I now see that I shall never be able to paint down to ignorance. Almost all the world is ignorant and vulgar. (1836)

Listening to me you will be getting echoes of many sociological theories about religion and society. Let me restate some of them with the help of this device. The movement of the sects and communities away from their founder's ideal of love without rules is routinisation of charisma. The breakdown of classifications entails the shift towards more personal ways of dealing with one another. This way of describing how the Protestant ethic develops does not relate it uniquely to capitalist forms of enterprise. Max Weber is saved thereby from having to explain how early capitalism flourished without Protestant religious forms as in fourteenth-century Venice. The mesh he used was too gross. We would expect the shift to personal values and personal independence to accompany social change where classification is weakened. For the breakdown of classification gives tantalising glimpses of zero point, and whispers of unmediated, unstructured social relations, and union with nature.

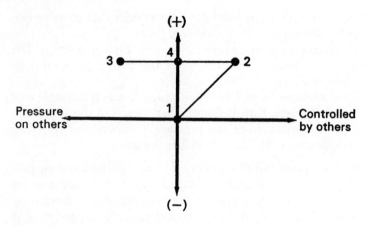

Figure 14.4 St Augustine

It is taken almost for a platitude in sociology that the movement of religious change is up and down on the right-hand side
of the diagram. First there is an institution set up in enthusiasm.
Then the disciples age and die. The next generation applies their
rules with less enthusiasm and finally a new generation wakes
up to find itself cramped by meaningless routines. The only way
to reform is to reject the rules, thus moving downwards on the
chart, and starting the process over again. But this says nothing
about the rebel ritualists, the Oxford Movement, for example,
who moved direct from one comprehensive system of classification, the Church of England, to another, yet more detailed and
exigent, Rome. As our diagram suggests, it is uncomfortable and
ineffective to take a stand high up on the vertical line, committed
to an elaborate cosmology which has no hold on anyone else. A
man who wishes to be a pastor of souls, such as W. G. Ward, finds
that his creed separates him from his fellow man. He can
strengthen its bite on his own life and that of his flock by turning
to a more sacramental form. First he moves to the right, for
example submitting to Rome, then he finds himself influencing
others and we locate him to the left, along with Newman and
other leaders of his day.

The loneliness of any point on the vertical line helps to answer
another question. Why do some people in old age mellow and
sweeten, while others grow sour and enraged? St Augustine's

theology shifted in this sense at the close of his life. Starting from his conversion to Christianity (down to zero) and his baptism, he moves first to the right, accepting the creed and, with his band of friends, adapting his life to it. Then as he becomes head of a monastery and later Bishop of Hippo, we locate him further and further to the left. It is he who is using the grid to constrain other people. He is confidently clarifying its categories to confound heretical Arians and Pelagians. He is judge and legislator and administrator all combined. But the Vandals land in Africa and sweep all before them. His people desert. Even his monks falter. He controls fewer and fewer people. We shift him back to the mid-point where the classifications are as strong as ever for him, but he has no influence on anyone or they on him. As he perceives this destiny he never chose, he begins to thunder hell-fire and brimstone. At the start God is likened to a kind mother, then to a wise physician; at the end God becomes cruel and vengeful; one who chooses his friends in advance and pre-destines the others to a terrible fate.

This is the device, and how to work it. If it showed up no regularities in people's cosmological ideas, I would throw it away and start again. But even on these broad and simple criteria, regularities appear. My examples happen to have been mostly in religious sociology, but I am claiming to uncover a set of general biases about how universes are construed. Shifting from left to right, the view of the universe becomes progressively less benign. The world is less friendly; a more punishing, difficult place to survive in. Here are located the political advocates of legislation for hanging and flogging, to the middle of the top right quadrant.

From top to bottom, false appearances begin to emerge as we move down. Diverse classifications compete. There is less coherence. A gap between reality and formal appearance is observed. In tribal society, a man will worry whether his neigh-bours are what they seem, honest humans, or man-eating witches in disguise. Among ourselves, philosophers become dubious about the possibility of knowledge of the external world. Artists lose their simplicity and start to ask questions about form and content. The conspiracy theory of history flourishes. One don suspects another of being not a 'real scholar': or of uttering hidden dangers. The footnotes are there; it looks like scholarship

Figure 14.5 Railway Porter (to Old Lady travelling with a Menagerie of Pets). 'Station Master say, Mum, as Cats is "Dogs", and Rabbits is "Dogs", and so's Parrots; but this 'ere "Tortis" is a Insect, so there ain't no charge for it!'

on the outside; inside it stinks. In such an environment it would be hard for a person with paranoiac tendencies to keep his sanity, for everyone (low on the right-hand side) connives with his belief that society is constituted by insincere maskers. On the left, where human presence is sparser, though false appearances equally abound, the masquerade is thought to be more foolish than sinister.

So there we are: deceived by the purity rule, our minds structured by the cosmologies which are generated by the ways we deal with one another, our categories reinforcing our social choices. The problem of freedom is the problem of how to divest our categories of their halo of eternal truth. Here there is a chink of hope. For, mercifully, the system of classification never fits. When there is non-fit, there is choice. The classification can either be clamped down more firmly, and the misfit removed in the name of purity, or the classification can be softened. The interesting question in social anthropology used to be to know how we fabricate the categories we use. Now it is important to ask how we deal with anomaly, strictly or generously. How many station-masters have we met who applied the book of rules as sacred and unstretchable. In Charles Keene's picture the station-master could have refused to allow the tortoise to travel, he could have charged it as livestock, he could have charged it as a pet. But the porter reports: 'Station Master say, Mum, as Cats is "Dogs" and Rabbits is "Dogs", and so's Parrots; but this 'ere "Tortis" is a Insect, so there ain't no charge for it!' Some social structures can tolerate anomaly and deal with it constructively, while others are rigid in their classifications. This difference is probably the most important subject on which sociological research can focus.

We have tried to demystify all cosmologies to peer past the purity filter and see ourselves as things in nature. The exercise ought to give an exhilarating sense of freedom. But instead we are faced with dilemmas.

Where most of us are crowded together, with restricted options and heavy social pressure, we can be higher or lower along the vertical line of classification. The higher on the line we are, the more scope for communication, the greater the intellectual and emotional range, the more meanings can be realised. But there are costs. One is to swallow for God's truth all the implications of the purity rule; another is to see the categories of man and beast, spirit and matter, black and white, haloed as eternal verities, and to accept a punishing cosmos. The reinforcing pressures in the social system make it very hard for the person here to challenge the weight of the purity rule and suspect that his categories are man-made, provisional boundaries. There is a protected innocence about his assumptions. Even if he crosses the line to the left and is more a leader than led, the same applies. This innocence may be necessary for functioning. The lower down this line we travel, the less overall coherence and credibility. But this is not necessarily freedom. It is possible to be very tyrannously controlled by inescapable personal pressures. No one would wish for this, if there were an easier liberty. But the sect or commune is apt to concentrate its energies on protecting its external boundaries – another limitation. The eclectic who picks and chooses consciously, each position taken according to his judgment of the issue, shifts up and down the vertical line, crossing between private and public bits of philosophy. He is likely to be plagued with the sense of unreality and danger. The gap between sinister appearances and real existence absorbs his mind. Between sophistication and incoherence, he is almost unmanned.

If the exercise has been worthwhile it is because it includes zero in the general scheme. The tension between the possibility of zero and the maximum possible order and pressure which a society provides is the measure of possible joy and sorrow. Zero is the inexpressible, timeless, weightless unembodied experience. There is only a flash-point at zero-zero; it can never be fixed. The thought of zero, of love which has no rule but itself, nothingness instituted, is the magnet which pulls the sociological imagination off course. Its vision haunts us with false cosmologies whose social conditions can never be met. That is the first freedom to be gained from this demystifying exercise: to recognise impossibility. Another is to recognise as mere practical lenses the classifications we habitually use. Another is to appreciate clowns. From our most crowded common stance, clowning is difficult. There is not much time for it. We take ourselves seriously. Moreover, clowns tend to break the purity rules. But the clown gyrates around zero, where meanings are destructible and interchangeable. The clown can lift the weight of the system of categories and show its provisional, makeshift character. He can teach us to respect the person who moves out alone to the far left-hand bottom corner of the diagram. Here the solitary mystic, without legislating for others, tries to live with his own heart set to zero, where no boundaries or pressures pull God and the self apart. Such a person finds it especially absurd to draw a line between man and nature. Here is a remark: It could come from Zen or Assisi. The writer is determining not to follow any deliberate programme; he is a musician; for him it is a hard turning-point; sacrifice is involved. He says it 'seems at first to be a giving up of music ... gradually or suddenly one sees that humanity and nature, not separate, are in this world together; that nothing was lost when everything was given away. In fact everything is gained' (Cage, 1971:8). Evidently, we have located the vantage point where the distinction between man and beast is easiest to dismantle.

Bibliography

BERNSTEIN, B. (1971), *Class, Codes and Control, Vol. 1*, London, Routledge & Kegan Paul.

BUGENTHALL, D. E., LOVE, L. R. and GIANETTO, R. M. (1971), *Journal of Personality and Social Psychology*, vol. 17, 3: 314 (cited in *New Society*, 23 September 1971: 572).

CAGE, JOHN (1971), *Silence*, London, Calder & Boyars.

DIXON, R. M. W. (1968), 'Noun Classes', *Lingua*, 21: 104–25.

MERLEAU-PONTY, M. (1965), *The Structure of Behaviour*, translated by Alden Fisher. London, Methuen (originally published in 1942 as *La Structure du comportement*).

ORMROD, R. (1971), summing up the case Corbett v. Corbett (otherwise Ashley), *The Law Reports*, Part 5, May 1971, Probate Division.

15

Environments at Risk

When the scientist has a very serious message to convey he faces a problem of disbelief. How to be credible? This perennial problem of religious creed is now a worry for ecology. Roughly the same conditions that effect belief in a denominational god affect belief in any particular environment. Therefore, in a series of lectures on ecology, it is right for the social anthropologist to address this particular question. We should be concerned to know how beliefs arise and how they gain support. Tribal views of the environment hold up a mirror to ourselves. Putting ourselves in line with tribal societies, we can try to imagine the figure we would cut in the eyes of an anthropologist from Mars. From our own point of view he would take an agnostic stand. But today, to do justice to this lecture's subject, we should ourselves attempt the difficult trick of letting go of what we know about our environment – not forgetting it, but treating it as so much science fiction. Like the alien anthropologist, let us suspend belief for a little while, so as to confront a fundamental question about credibility.

We are far from being the first civilisation to realise that our environment is at risk. Most tribal environments are held to be in danger in much the same way as ours. The dangers are naturally not identical. Here and now we are concerned with overpopulation. Often they are worried by underpopulation. But we pin the responsibility in quite the same way as they do. Always and everywhere it is human folly, hate and greed which puts the human environment at risk. Unlike tribal society, we have the chance of self-awareness. Because we can set our own view in a

general phenomenological perspective, just because we can compare our beliefs with theirs, we have an extra dimension of
responsibility. Self-knowledge is a great burden. I shall be arguing that part of our current anxiety flows from loss of those very
blinkering or filtering mechanisms which restrict perception of
the sources of knowledge.

First, let us compare the ecology movement with others of
historical times. An example that springs to mind is the movement for the abolition of slavery of a century ago. The abolitionists succeeded in revolutionising the image of man. In the same
way, the ecology movement will succeed in changing the idea of
nature. It will succeed in raising a tide of opinion that will put
abuses of the environment under close surveillance. Strong
sanctions against particular pollutions will come into force. It will
succeed in these necessary changes for the same reason as the
slavery abolition movement, partly because of its dedication and
mostly because the time is ripe. In many countries in the nineteenth century slavery was becoming more costly than wage
labour.[1] If this had not been the case, I doubt if that campaign
would ever have got off the ground. Where locally it was not the
case, all the arguments about brotherly love, Christianity and
common humanity were of no avail. The Clapham Sect, I believe,
abstained from sugar as a protest against plantation slavery. In
the same spirit some of my friends have abstained from South
African sherry. This is a less impressive sacrifice since there are
other better sherries. But those of us who do not own a car will
not end exhaust fume pollution any more than the Clapham Sect
diminished by one whit the place of sugar in the native diet. The
tide of opinion against slavery was not against industrial
development. And the tide of opinion which will reduce the
worst pollution effects will not stem industrialisation. Here is the
crunch of the environmental problem that leads it far beyond the
nuisance of water and air pollution and increasing noise. The
ecologists have had to raise their sights to the global level. Their
gloomy forecasts for the imminent end of our planet put us, the
laymen, in the role of the helpless hero of a thriller. Several nasty
deaths are in store for us. Time will reveal whether the earth will
be burnt up by the unbalancing of its radiation budget, or
whether a film of dust will blank out the sun's rays, or whether it
will explode in an atomic war. Over-population and over-

industrialisation are the twin causes. But herein lies the dilemma. The obviously overpopulated and starving masses are in the non-industrial regions. Their hope of food lies in new technological developments. But these come from the already industrial countries. Must we stop the growth of science which may one day feed the existing hungry? How do we control population any-way? And which ones should we start with? On a giant hoarding over the Chicago Expressway is a notice which says: 'Think before you litter.' A rather coarse expression, I thought, when I first assumed it to be family planning advice. But if I understand Dr Paul Ehrlich aright the anti-litter campaign could do well to take on the double objective, especially in Chicago. The starving millions of Asia are not the ones who own two cars, whose factories discharge effluent into lakes, or whose aeroplanes give off loud bangs. Ehrlich says: 'The birth of every American child is fifty times more of a disaster for the world than the birth of each Indian child. If you take consumption of steel as a measure of overall consumption, you find that the birth of each American child is 300 times more of a disaster for the world than the birth of each Indonesian child.'[2]

At the top global level the scientists speak with different voices, and none a clear solution. This is the level at which we are free to believe or disbelieve. The scientists would not wish to be treated as so many old sandwich-men bearing placards which say: 'The end is near.' Our disbelief is just as much a problem for them as our gullibility. Therefore, whether their message is true or false, we are forced to study the basis of plausibility.

Another movement of ideas which this current ecology question recalls is the growth of classical economics. A realisation which transfixed thoughtful minds in the eighteenth century and onwards was that the market is a system with its own immutable laws. How can we appreciate the boldness of the illumination with which Ricardo discerned that system and its homeostatic tendencies? In our day and for this audience I can only hope to give an idea of the thrill of analysing its complexity, and the power and even sheer beauty of the system as it revealed itself, by reminding you of the excitement engendered in linguistics by Chomsky's revelation of the structural properties of language. But that is a very pale analogy. Consider how few political decisions are affected by linguistics compared with the implications of economic science. For the sake of that system and its unalterable laws, many good men have had to harden their hearts to the plight of paupers and unemployed. They were deeply convinced that much greater misery would befall if the system was not allowed to work out its due processes. In the same way, the ecologists have perceived system. In fact, their whole science consists in assuming system, reckoning inputs and outputs and assessing the factors making for equilibrium. The pitch of excitement in the ecological movement rises when the analysis is lifted to the level of whole continents and even to the level of this planet as a whole. In exactly the same way as the old economists, the ecologists find themselves demanding a certain toll of human suffering in the name of the system which, if disturbed, will loose unimaginable misery on the human race. Sometimes there is a question of bringing water a thousand miles to irrigate a desert. The ecologists know how to do it. They can easily make a desert blossom and so bring food and life to starving people. They hesitate to answer for the consequences in the area from which the water has been diverted. Their professional conscience bids them consider the system as a whole. In the same spirit as Ricardo deploring the effects of the Poor Laws, ecologists find themselves unwillingly drawn into negative, even reactionary positions.

These digressions into economics and slavery suggest a way of restricting somewhat the problem of credibility which is altogether too wide. It will be rewarding to watch how belief is committed along the bias towards or away from restriction. For ultimately this is it – restriction or controlled expansion? Which of us tend to believe the experts who warn that our system of resources is limited? And which of us optimistically follow those who teach that they cannot possibly tell yet what resources may lie unknown beneath the soil or in the sea or even in the air? And the same question about our own bias may be raised for the bias of the experts themselves.

Phenomenology, as I understand it, is concerned with what it is we believe we know about reality and with how we come to believe it. An anthropologist's survey of tribal environments is different from the ecologist's survey. Ecology imports objective measures from a scientific standpoint and describes in those terms the effect of the system of cultivation on the soil and of the

233

soil on the crop yield, etc. It is concerned with interacting systems of physical realities. The anthropologist, if he is not lucky enough to have access to an ecological survey in his research area, has to make a rough dab at this kind of assessment and then use it to check with the tribe's own view of their environment. In this sense an anthropologist's survey of tribal environments is an exercise in phenomenology. Each tribe is found to inhabit a universe of its own, with its own laws and its own distinctive set of dangers which can be triggered off by incautious humans. It is almost as if there were no limit on the amount of variation two tribes can incorporate into their view of the same environment. Some objective limits must apply. Nevertheless, if we were to rely entirely on tribal assessments, we would get wildly incongruous views of what physical possibilities and constraints are in force.

For example, I worked in the Congo on the left bank of the Kasai river, among the Lele. On the other bank of the same river lived the Bushong, where my friend Jan Vansina worked a little later on. Here were two tribes, next-door neighbours, who celebrated their cold and hot seasons at opposite points in the calendar. When I first arrived, green to Africa, the Belgians said how wise I had been to arrive in the cold season: a newcomer, they said, would find the hot rainy season unbearable. In fact it was not a good time to arrive, because all the Lele were working flat out to clear the forest and fire the dead wood, and then to plant maize in the ash. No one but the very aged and the sick had time to talk to me and teach me the language, until the rains arrived and ended their period of heavy work. When I knew the language better, I learnt of a total discrepancy between the European and native assessment of the weather. The Lele regarded the short dry season as unbearably hot. They had their sayings and rules about how to endure its heat. 'Never strike a woman in the dry season', for example, 'or she will crumple up and die, because of the heat.' They longed for the first rains as relief from the heat. On the other bank of the Kasai, the Bushong agreed with the Belgians that the dry season was pleasantly cool and they dreaded the onset of the first rains. Fortunately the Belgians had made excellent meteorological records, and I found that in terms of solar radiation, diurnal and nocturnal temperatures, cloud cover, etc, there was very little objective difference that

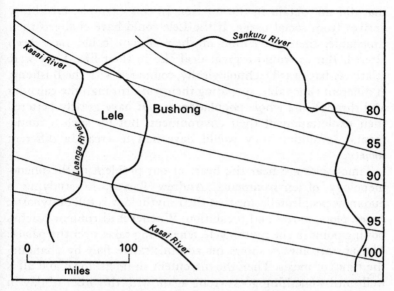

Figure 15.1 Average length of dry season expressed in days (form F. Buetot, *Saisons et Périodes Sèches et Pluvieuses au Congo Belge*, Brussels, 1954)

could entitle one season to be called strictly hotter than the other.[3] What the Europeans objected to, apparently, was the humidity of the wet season and the absence of cloud which exposed them directly to the rays of the sun. What the Lele suffered from in the dry season was the increased radiant heat which resulted from the heavy screen of clouds. They recognised and hated the famous glass-house effect that we are told will result from an excessive carbon dioxide screen for ourselves. But above all, the Lele time-table required them to do all their agricultural work in one short, sharp burst, in the dry season. The Bushong, across the river, with a more complex agricultural system, worked away steadily the whole year round. They also distinguished wet and dry seasons, but they concurred with the Europeans about the relative coolness of the dry period. How did the Europeans arrive at their assessment, since objectively there was so little to choose? No doubt because the seasons were named and their attributes set at Leopoldville, the capital, where temperature readings showed a difference between the seasons that did not obtain in the interior. In this example, credibility derives from social usage. If the Lele could have changed their time-table, their perception of their climate could have been altered. But so would a great deal else in their life. They were relatively backward technologically, compared with the Bushong. A different time-table, spreading their work through the calendar and through the whole population, would have greatly bettered their exploitation of their environment. But for such a fundamental revolution they would have had to create a different society.

Time-tables are near the heart of our problem in the phenomenology of environments. Andrew Baring, in studying a Sudanese people, tells one that their mythology is full of dynastic crises, plots, unrest and revolution. Whenever discontent reaches boiling-point in the myth cycle, a new king takes over the palace. The upstart always shows his administrative flair by changing the times of meals. Then the discontent simmers down and all is well until something goes wrong again with the order of day in the royal household. Then the stage is set for a new dynastic upheaval and a new king to settle the time-table problem afresh. Largely, the doom ecologists are trying to convince us about a kind of time-bomb. Time is running out they say. Whenever I suggested to the Lele small capital-intensive projects that would improve their hunting or the comfort of their houses, they would answer 'No time'. The allocation of time is a vital determinant of how a given environment is managed. It is also true that time perspective held by an expert determines what answer he will give to a technical problem. Therefore, we should start our discussion of how credibility is engendered by considering the time-dimension.

Among verbal weapons of control, time is one of the four final arbiters. Time, money, God, and nature, usually in that order, are universal trump cards plunked down to win an argument. I have no doubt that our earliest cave ancestress heard the same, when she wanted a new skirt or breakfast in bed. First 'There wouldn't be time', and then, 'We couldn't afford it anyway'. If she still seemed to hanker: 'God doesn't like that sort of thing'. Finally, if she were even prepared to snap her fingers at God, the ace card: 'It's against nature, and what is more, your children will suffer'. It is a strong hand when the same player, by holding all these cards, can represent God and nature, as well as control the time-table and the bank account. Then the time-scale, as presented by that player in control, is entirely credible.

It is only just beginning to be appreciated how much the perception of time-scale is the result of bargaining about goals and procedures. For a touching insight, read Julius A. Roth's little book *Timetables, Structuring the Passage of Time in Hospital Treatment and Other Careers*.[4] Here he describes the attempts of long-term patients in a TB hospital to get some satisfactory response out of their doctors. Spontaneously and inevitably the clash of interests expressed itself in a battle about the time-tabling of diagnosis and treatment. For the patient, his whole life is held in suspense, no plans can be made, no sense of progress enjoyed until he knows when he can go home. His anxiety concentrates in a passionate study of the time-scaling of the disease and its treatment. With no means of extracting from them any clue to his central preoccupations, and no sanctions to employ to enforce their collaboration, the patient would try to impose on the medical staff a kind of natural time-table. 'I've been here six months now, doctor, by this time you ought to have decided whether I need surgery.' 'Massey got a pass after only three months here – why can't I?' 'Hayton got discharged three months after surgery – why should I have to wait four months?' The doctors' strategy is evasive. They consistently reject the very idea of a rigid time-table, and struggle to refute the culture of the ward where patients go on working out a clear set of phases by which they judge the competence of the doctors and the course of their illness. Sometimes if the doctor does not seem to accept these spontaneously emerging laws of disease and treatment, the patient discharges himself, feeling that the basis of mutual understanding has failed.

The Lele afford another example of how time-tabling is used as a weapon of control. They think that they can do something to bring on the rains. This technique of weather control was not a rain-dance, or a magic spell. It was something which any individual might do, with the effect of hastening the onset of the rainy season. The belief in its effectiveness became an instrument for mutual coercion. Laggard farmers would beg others to wait until they had had time to clear their fields and burn the wood. The punctual ones would warn them to hurry up, lest the rain be provoked by action in the north. It seemed to me, sceptical as I was of the value of their technique, exactly like the departmental head who creates artificial deadlines to hasten decisions or otherwise keep his staff on their toes. 'I can only vouch for the students' reaction if we get our policy settled by the next meeting.' Much later I learnt that the Lele techniques of seeding the clouds by the smoke of their burning forests might indeed be effective. Air pollution can increase condensation and precipitation of moisture. It seems that a district in Indiana, thirty miles downwind of South Chicago's smoky steelworks, tends to have 31 per cent more rain than other communities where the air is clearer.[5] The joke was on me that the Lele weather control turned out to be scientifically respectable. For the purpose of my present argument, its efficacy is irrelevant. All that matters is that time is a set of manipulable boundaries. Time is like all the other doom points in the universe. One and all are social weapons of control. Reference to their power sustains a view of the social system. Their influence is thoroughly conservative. For no one can wield the doom points credibly in an argument who is not backed by the majority view of how the society should be run. Credibility depends so much on the consensus of a moral community that it is hardly an exaggeration to say that a given community lays on for itself the sum of the physical conditions which it experiences. I give two well-known examples.

In many tribal societies it is widely agreed that wives should be faithful to their husbands. Women probably concur in that ideal, and they would perhaps like to add to it that husbands should be equally faithful to their wives. However, the latter view does not obtain whole-hearted male support. Therefore, since the men are the dominant sex, to sustain their view of sexual morality they need to find in nature a sanction which will enforce the chastity of wives without involving male infidelity. The solution has been to fasten on a natural danger to which only female physiology is exposed. Hence we find very commonly the idea that miscarriage is due to adultery. What a weapon that provides: the woman tempted to adultery knows that her unborn baby is at risk, and her own life too. Sometimes she is taught that the health of her older children will also suffer.[6] What a paraphernalia of confession and cleansing and compensation attends the guilty mother in her labour. What she has done is against nature and nature will retaliate.

For a different example – a warlike tribe of Plains Indians, the Cheyenne, believes that murder of a fellow tribesman is the ultimate wickedness. The tribe used to depend on wandering herds of bison for its food. The bison, it was thought, did not react to the murder of men of other tribes. The bison were not affected by ordinary homicide as such. But a fratricide emitted a putrid stink which frightened off the herd and so put the vital resources of the tribe at risk. This danger from the environment justified special sanctions to outlaw the murderer.[7]

When homicide and adultery are seen to be triggering agents for danger points in a physical environment, the tribal view of nature begins to emerge as a coherent principle of social control. Red in tooth and claw, perhaps, but nature responds in a highly moral and avenging form of aggression. It is on the side of the constitution, motherhood, brotherly love, and it is against human wickedness.

When I first wrote *Purity and Danger* about this moral power in the tribal environment, I thought our own knowledge of the physical environment was different.[8] I now believe this to have been mistaken. If only because they disagree, we are free to select which of our scientists we will harken to, and our selection is subject to the same sociological analysis as that of any tribe.

We find that in tribal society certain classes of people are liable to be classed as polluters. These classes are not the same for all tribes. In some social structures the polluters will be one type, in others another. Imagine a tribal insurance company which set out to cover people against the risk of being accused of causing pollution. Their market researchers and surveyors should be able to work out where they should charge the highest premiums in any particular social system. In some societies the elite possessors of esoteric knowledge are certain to be charged with owning too much science and misapplying it to selfish ends. Sorcery charges against big operators in New Guinea or against cunning old polygamists among the Lele can be paralleled by our own charges against big business polluting lakes and rivers and poisoning the children's food and air for their commercial profit. The Lele shared with other Congolese tribes an acute anxiety about their population. They believed themselves to be dying out because of malicious attacks by sorcerers against the fertility of women and on their lack of babies. They continually said that their numbers had declined because of jealousy. 'Look around you,' a man said to me on this theme, 'do you see any people? Do you see children?' I looked about. A handful of children played at our feet and a few people sat around. 'Yes,' I said, 'I see people and children.' 'Look again', he said, disgusted with my missing the cue. 'There are no people here, no children.' His question had been couched in the rhetorical style expecting the answer 'No'. It took me a long time to learn the tonal pattern which should have led our dialogue to run in this way.[9]

'Look around you! Do you see any people? Tell me – do you?'
Emphatic answer: 'No!'

'Do you see any children? Tell me, do you?'

Emphatic answer: 'No!' Then his answer would come: 'See how we have been finished off. No one is left now, we are destroyed utterly. It's jealousy that destroys us.' For him, the sorcerer's sinful lore was as destructive as for us the science that serves military and business interests with chemical weapons and pesticides.

In another type of society the probability of being accused of pollution will fall on paupers and second-class citizens of various types. Paupers I define as those who, by falling below a required level of achievement, are not able to enter into exchanges of gifts, services and hospitality. They find themselves not only excluded from the main responsibilities and pleasures of citizenship but a charge upon the community. They are a source of embarrassment to their more prosperous fellows and a living contradiction to any current theories about the equality of man. In tribal societies, wherever such a possibility exists, these unfortunates are likely to be credited with warped emotions. By and large they may be called witches, and risk being accused of causing the natural disasters which other people suffer. Somehow they must be eliminated, controlled and stopped from multiplying. If you want to intuit from our own culture how such accusations of witchcraft gain plausibility I recommend you to attend a conference of professional social workers. Over and over again you will hear the objects of the social workers' concern being described as 'non-coping'. The explanation given for their non-coping is widely attributed to their having 'inadequate personalities'. In something of this way, landless clients in the Mandari tribe are said by their patrons to have a hereditary witchcraft streak which makes them vicious and jealous.[10] The fact that they are emotionally warped justifies their fellow-men in withholding the liberties and protections of citizenship.

As for females, in all these societies and anywhere that male dominance is an important value, women are likely to be accused of causing dangerous pollution by their very presence when they invade the men's sphere. I have written enough about female pollution in *Purity and Danger*.

It should be clear now that credibility for any view of how the environment will react is secured by the moral commitment of a community to a particular set of institutions. Nothing will overthrow their beliefs if the institutions which the beliefs support command their loyalty. Nothing is easier than to change the beliefs (overnight!) if the institutions have lost support. If we could finish classifying the kinds of people and kinds of behaviour which pollute the tribal universes we would have performed an ecological exercise. For it would become clear that the view of the universe and a particular kind of society holding this view are closely interdependent. They are a single system. Neither can exist without the other. Tribal peoples who worship their dead ancestors often explicitly recognise that each ancestor only exists in so far as cult is paid to him. When the cult stops, the ancestor has no more credibility. He fades away, unable to intervene, either to punish angrily, or to reward kindly. We should entertain the same insight about any given environment we know. It exists as a structure of meaningful distinctions. In so far as it is only knowable by the powers attributed to it and the practical action taken in its regard, and in so far as its powers are evoked as techniques of mutual control, a known environment is as fragile as any ancestor. While a limited social reality and a local physical environment are meshed together in a single experience, there is perfect credibility for both. But if the society falls apart, and separate voices claim to know about different environmental constraints, then do credibility problems arise.

At this point I should correct some possible false impressions. I have tried to avoid examples which lend themselves to a skullduggery, conspiracy theory of how the environment is constructed in people's minds. There is no possibility of one group conning another about what nature will stand for, and what is against nature. I certainly would not imply that fears of world overpopulation are spread by frustrated car-owners in the commuter belt who would like a clear run from Surrey to the City. I would not imply that residents on the south coast press for legislation to control population because they know there is no hope of legislating specifically to ban summer crowds from the seaside. But personal experience could make them lend a friendlier ear to those demographers who are most gloomy about population increase, and ignore the optimistic ones. It obviously suits Lele men and Cheyenne men to teach that the physiology of childbirth and the physiology of the wild bison respond to moral situations. But no one can impose a moral view of physical nature on another person who does not share the same moral assumptions. If Lele wives did not believe in married fidelity as a part of the social order they might be more sceptical about an idea which suits husbands extremely well. Because all Cheyenne endorse the idea that murder in the tribe is disastrous they can believe that bison are sensitive to its smell. The common commitment to a set of social meanings makes inferences about the response of nature plausible.

Another misunderstanding concerns the distinction between true and false ideas about the environment. I repeat the invitation to approach this subject in a spirit of science fiction. The scientists find out true, objective things about physical nature. The human society invests these findings with social meaning and constructs a systematic time-tabled view of the way that human behaviour and physical nature interact. But I fear that it is an illusion if scientists hope one day to set out a true, systematic, objective view of that interaction. And so it is also illusory to hope for a society whose fears of pollution rest entirely on the scientists' teaching and carry no load of social and moral persuasion. We cannot hope to develop an idea of our environment which has pollution ideas only in the scientists' sense, and none which, in that strict sense, are false. Pollution ideas, however they arise, are the necessary support for a social system. How else can people induce each other to cooperate and behave if they cannot threaten with time, money, God and nature? These moral imperatives arise from social intercourse. They draw on a view of the environment to support a social order. As normative principles they have an adaptive function. Each society adapts itself to its habitat by precisely these means. Telling each other that there is no time, that we can't afford it, that God wouldn't like it and that it is against nature and our children will suffer, these are the means by which we adapt our society to our environment, and it to ourselves. In the process our physical possibilities are limited and extended in this way and that, so that there is a real ecological interaction. The concepts of time, money, God and nature do for human society the adaptive work which is done non-verbally (but otherwise probably by very similar means) in animal society.

I have spoken of pollution ideas which are used by people as controls on themselves and on each other. In this light they seem to be weapons or instruments. However, there is another fundamental aspect of the subject. Pollution ideas draw their power from our own intellectual constitution. Impossible here to describe the learning process by which each individual works out a set of expectations, and derives rules which guide him in his behaviour. The beliefs that there are rules and that future experience is expected to conform to them underlies social intercourse. There is some fascinating experimental work on this aspect of behaviour by American sociologists. However faulty our probings and conclusions may be, we assume a rule-obeying, stable environment. We expect, as we learn a fairly satisfactory set of rules, that the *et cetera* principle can be left to look after the known. The *et cetera* principle is like the automatic pilot which, once the controls are fixed, will keep the plane on course. *Etcetera, etcetera.* Finding rules that work is satisfying as it allows us to suppose that more of the machine can be turned over to the automatic pilot to look after. Discovering a whole system that works is exciting because it suggests an even greater saving of *ad hoc* painful blundering. Hence the emotional response to discovering that market prices work as a system, or that language or mythology has a systematic element.

The deepest emotional investment of all is in the assumption that there is a rule-obeying universe, and that its rules are objective, independent of social validation. Hence the most odious pollutions are those which threaten to attack a system at its intellectual base. The system itself rests on a number of unchallengeable classifications. One of the well-known examples in anthropology is that of the Eskimo girl in Labrador who would persistently eat caribou meat after winter had begun.[11] A trivial breach of an abstinence rule, it seems to us. But by a unanimous verdict, she was banished in midwinter for committing what was judged to be a capital offence. These Eskimo have constructed a society whose fundamental category is the distinction of the two seasons. People born in winter are distinguished from those born in summer. Each of the two seasons has a special kind of domestic arrangement, a special seasonal economy, a separate legal practice, almost a distinct religion. The regularity of Eskimo life depends upon the observances connected with each season. Winter hunting equipment is kept apart from summer equipment, summer tents are hidden in winter. No one should touch the skins of animals classed as summer game in winter. As Marcel Mauss put it, 'even in the stomachs of the faithful' salmon, a summer fish, should have no contact with the sea animals of the winter.[12] By disregarding these distinctive categories the girl was committing a wrong against the social system in its fundamental form. A lack of seriousness about the categories of thought was not the reason given for why she was condemned to die by freezing. She had to die because she had committed a dangerous pollution which set everyone's livelihood at risk. Contrast this sharp categorisation and this cruel punishment for contempt with the Eskimo experience of the last millennium. Here is a civilisation which has seen precisely what may well be in store for us, a slow but steady worsening of the environment. Are we going to react, as doom draws near, with rigid applications of the principles out of which our intellectual system has been spun? It is horribly likely that, along with the Eskimo, we will concentrate on eliminating and controlling the polluters. It might be a more worthwhile recourse to think afresh about our environment in a way which was not possible for the Eskimo level of scientific advance. Nor is it only scientific advance which lies in our grasp. We have the chance of understanding our own behaviour.

If the study of pollution ideas teaches us anything it is that, taken too much at face value, such fears tend to mask other wrongs and dangers. For example, take the population problem. A straight response to pollution fears suggests we should urgently try to control population. The question is treated in an unimaginative and mechanical way. It is made a matter of spreading information and making available contraceptive devices. At first, people's eagerness to use them is taken for granted, but soon the clinics report apathy, carelessness, lack of determination, lack of agreement between husbands and wives. Then the question moves from voluntary to automatic methods such as sterilisation or compulsion by law. We are almost back to 'Think before you litter' and forcible control of animal populations. But if we were to learn from biologists, Wynne-Edwards' work on animal populations has many a moral for the demographer.[13] In some human societies social factors encourage the voluntary control of family size. Not all tribes tolerate unlimited expansion of their numbers. It cannot be ignored that the world demographic problem is an Us/Them situation. Even in Ricardo's day it was They, the labourers, whose improvident fecundity created the pressure on resources, while We, the rich, could be relied on to procreate more cautiously. And today it is We, the rich nations, who wag our fingers at Them, the poor ones, with their astronomical annual increase. Somewhere a social problem about the distribution of prestige and power underlies the stark demographic facts. Let us not miss the lessons of this confrontation with biology and anthropology.

In essence, pollution ideas are adaptive and protective. They protect a social system from unpalatable knowledge. They protect a system of ideas from challenge. The ideas rest on classification. Ultimately any forms of knowledge depend on principles of classification. But these principles arise out of social experience, sustain a given social pattern and themselves are sustained by it. If this guideline and base is grossly disturbed, knowledge itself is at risk.

In a sense the obvious risk to the environment is a distraction. The ecologists are indeed looking into an abyss. But on the other side another abyss yawns as frighteningly. This is the terror of intellectual chaos and blind panic. Pollution is the black side of Plato's good lie[14] on which society must rest: it is the other half of the necessary confidence trick. We should be able to see that we can never ask for a future society in which we can only believe in real, scientifically proved pollution dangers. We *must* talk threateningly about time, money, God and nature if we hope to get anything done. We must believe in the limitations and boundaries of nature which our community projects.

Here we return to the comparison with the classical economists and the slavery abolitionists. It would be good to know which of our experts is likely to take a restrictive view of the environment, certain that time, money, God and nature are against change, and which of them is likely to favour expansionary policies. It is easy to see why the laymen can't lift their noses above the immediate horizon. The layman tends to assimilate the total planetary environmental problems to his own immediate ones. His horizon is his back yard. For the scientists, as well as this same tendency, there is another source of bias. To understand a system – any system – is a joy in itself. The more that is known about it the more the specialist is aware of its intricacies, and the more wary he is of the complex disturbances which can result from ignorance. The specialist thus has an emotional investment in his own system. As Professor Kuhn has said, in his *The Structure of Scientific Revolutions*,[15] scientists rarely change their views, they merely retire or die away. If there are to be solutions to a grave problem, they will come from the fringes of the profession, from the amateur even, or from those areas of knowledge in which two or three specialisms meet. This is comforting. In the long run, if there is a long run, unless the man in the street specially wants to choose the pessimistic restrictionist view on any ecological problem, he can wait and see. The scientific establishment has its own structure of stability and challenge. Our responsibility as laymen and as social scientists is to probe deeper into the sources of our own bias. Suppose we are really set for the worst terrors that the ecologists can predict. How shall we comport ourselves?

Our worst problem is the lack of moral consensus which gives credibility to warnings of danger. This partly explains why we fail so often to give proper heed to the ecologists. At the same time, for lack of a discriminating principle, we easily become overwhelmed by our pollution fears. Community endows its environment with credibility. Without community, unclassified rubbish mounts up, poisons fill the air and water, food is contaminated, eyesores block the skyline. Flooding in through all our senses, pollution destroys our well-being. Witches and devils ensnare us. Any tribal culture selects this and that danger to fear and sets up demarcation lines to control it. It allows people to live contentedly with a hundred other dangers which ought to terrify them out of their wits. The discriminating principles come from social structure. An unstructured society leaves us prey to every dread. As all the veils are successively ripped away, there is no right or wrong. Relativism is the order of the day. I myself have tried to join the work of taking down some of the veils. We have adopted first this standpoint, then that, seen tribal society from within and from without, seen ourselves as the scientists see us or from the stance of the anthropologist from Mars. This is the invitation to full self-consciousness that is offered in our time. We must accept it. But we should do so knowing that the price is William Burroughs' *Naked Lunch*.[16] The day when everyone can see exactly what it is on the end of everyone's fork, on that day there is no pollution and no purity and nothing edible or inedible, credible or incredible, because the classifications of social life are gone. There is no more meaning. Neither melancholic madness nor mystic ecstasy, the two modes in which boundaries are dispensed, can accept the other invitation of our time. The other task is to recognise each environment as a mask and support for a certain kind of society. It is the value of this social form which demands our scrutiny just as clearly as the purity of milk and air and water.

Notes

1 John Hicks, *A Theory of Economic History*, London, 1969, pp. 122–40.
2 Paul Ehrlich, *Listener*, 30 August 1970, 215.
3 Mary Douglas, 'The Lele, Resistance to Change' in *Markets in Africa*, ed. Bohannan and Dalton, Evanston, Ill., 1962. The author is grateful to Northwestern University Press for permission to reproduce Fig. 15.1 from *Markets in Africa*.
4 Julius A. Roth, *Timetables, Structuring the Passage of Time in Hospital Treatment and other Careers*, New York, 1963.
5 Eric Aynsley, 'How air pollution alters weather', *New Scientist*, 9 October 1969, pp. 66–7.
6 Mary Douglas, *The Lele of the Kasai*, International African Institute, Oxford, 1963, p. 51.
7 E. A. Hoebel, *The Cheyénnes, Indians of the Great Plains*, New York, 1960, p. 51.

8 Mary Douglas, *Purity and Danger, An Analysis of Concepts of Pollution and Taboo*, London, 1966.
9 Mary Douglas,'Elicited responses in Lele language', *Kongo-Overzee*, 1950, xvi, 4, 224–7.
10 Jean Buxton, 'Mandari Witchcraft', in *Witchcraft and Sorcery in East Africa*, ed., John Middleton and Edward Winter, London, 1963.
11 E. A. Hoebel, *The Law of Primitive Man: A Study in Comparative Legal Dynamics*, Harvard, 1954.
12 Marcel Mauss and M. H. Beuchat, 'Essai sur les variations saisonnières des sociétés Eskimos', *L'Année Sociologique*, 9 (1904–5), 39–132.
13 V. C. Wynne-Edwards, *Animal Dispersion in Relation to Social Behaviour*, Edinburgh and New York, 1962.
14 Plato, *The Republic,* paras 376–92 Lindsay translation, Everyman.
15 T. S. Kuhn, *The Structure of Scientific Revolutions*, Chicago, 1962.
16 William Burroughs, *The Naked Lunch*, New York, 1962; London, 1965.

16

Deciphering a Meal

If language is a code, where is the precoded message? The question is phrased to expect the answer: nowhere. In these words a linguist is questioning a popular analogy.[1] But try it this way: if food is a code, where is the precoded message? Here, on the anthropologist's home ground, we are able to improve the posing of the question. A code affords a general set of possibilities for sending particular messages. If food is treated as a code, the messages it encodes will be found in the pattern of social relations being expressed. The message is about different degrees of hierarchy, inclusion and exclusion, boundaries and transactions across the boundaries. Like sex, the taking of food has a social component, as well as a biological one.[2] Food categories therefore encode social events. To say this is to echo Roland Barthes[3] on the sartorial encoding of social events. His book, *Système de la mode,* is primarily about methodology, about code-breaking and code-making taken as a subject in itself. The next step for the development of this conceptual tool is to take up a particular series of social events and see how they are coded. This will involve a close understanding of a microscale social system: I shall therefore start the exercise by analyzing the main food categories used at a particular point in time in a particular social system, our home. The humble and trivial case will open the discussion of more exalted examples.

Sometimes at home, hoping to simplify the cooking, I ask, 'Would you like to have just soup for supper tonight? I mean a good thick soup – instead of supper. It's late and you must be hungry. It won't take a minute to serve.' Then an argument starts: 'Let's have soup now, and supper when you are ready.' 'No no, to serve two meals would be more work. But if you like, why not start with the soup and fill up with pudding?' 'Good heavens! What sort of a meal is that? A beginning and an end and no middle.' 'Oh, all right then, have the soup as it's there, and I'll do a Welsh rarebit as well.' When they have eaten soup, Welsh rarebit, pudding, and cheese: 'What a lot of plates. Why do you make such elaborate suppers?' They proceed to argue that by taking thought I could satisfy the full requirements of a meal with a single, copious dish. Several rounds of this conversation have given me a practical interest in the categories and meaning of food. I needed to know what defines the category of a meal in our home.

The first source for enlightenment will obviously be Claude Lévi-Strauss's *The Raw and the Cooked* and the other volumes of his *Mythologiques*[4] which discuss food categories and table manners. But this is only a beginning. He fails us in two major respects. First, he takes leave of the small-scale social relations which generate the codification and are sustained by it. Here and there his feet touch solid ground, but mostly he is orbiting in rarefied space where he expects to find universal food meanings common to all mankind. He is looking for a precoded, panhuman message in the language of food, and thus exposing himself to the criticism implicit in the quoted linguist's question. Second, he relies entirely on the resources of binary analysis. Therefore he affords no technique for assessing the relative value of the binary pairs that emerge in a local set of expressions. Worse than clumsy, his technical apparatus produces meanings which cannot be validated. Yea, or nay, he and Roman Jakobson may be right on the meanings in a sonnet of Baudelaire's.[5] But even if the poet himself had been able to judge between theirs and Riffaterre's alternative interpretation of the same work[6] and to say that one was closer to his thought than the other, he would be more likely to agree that all these meanings are there. This is fair for literary criticism, but when we are talking of grammar, coding, and the 'science of the concrete,'[7] it is not enough.

For analyzing the food categories used in a particular family the analysis must start with why those particular categories and not others are employed. We will discover the social boundaries which the food meanings encode by an approach which values the binary pairs according to their position in a series. Between breakfast and the last nightcap, the food of the day comes in an ordered pattern. Between Monday and Sunday, the food of the week is patterned again. Then there is the sequence of holidays and fast days through the year, to say nothing of life cycle feasts, birthdays, and weddings. In other words, the binary or other contrasts must be seen in their syntagmatic relations. The chain which links them together gives each element some of its meaning. Lévi-Strauss discusses the syntagmatic relation in his earlier book, *The Savage Mind,* but uses it only for the static analysis of classification systems (particularly of proper names). It is capable of a much more dynamic application to food categories, as Michael Halliday has shown. On the two axes of syntagm and paradigm, chain and choice, sequence and set, call it what you will, he has shown how food elements can be ranged until they are all accounted for either in grammatical terms, or down to the last lexical item.[8]

Eating, like talking, is patterned activity, and the daily menu may be made to yield an analogy with linguistic form. Being an analogy, it is limited in relevance; its purpose is to throw light on, and suggest problems of, the categories of grammar by relating these to an activity which is familiar and for much of which a terminology is ready to hand.

The presentation of a framework of categories for the description of eating might proceed as follows:

Units: Daily menu
Meal
Course
Helping
Mouthful

Unit: Daily Menu	$\rightarrow$
Elements of primary structure	E, M, L, S ('early,' 'main,' 'light,' 'snack')
Primary structures	EML EMLS (conflated as EML(S))
Exponents of these elements (primary classes of unit 'meal')	E: 1 (breakfast)
	M: 2 (dinner)
	L: 3 ⎫ (no names available; see
	S: 4 ⎭ classes)

Secondary structures	EL_aS_aM EL_aM EML_bS_b EMS_aL_c
Exponents of secondary elements (systems of secondary classes of unit 'meal')	L_a: 3.1 (lunch)
	L_b: 3.2 (high tea)
	L_a: 3.3 (supper)
	S_a: 4.1 (afternoon tea)
	S_b: 4.2 (nightcap)
System of sub-classes of unit 'meal'	E: 1.1 (English breakfast)
	1.2 (continental breakfast)

Passing to the rank of the 'meal,' we will follow through the class 'dinner:'

Unit: Meal, Class: dinner $\rightarrow$

Elements of primary structure	F, S, M, W, Z ('first,' 'second,' 'main,' 'sweet,' 'savoury')
Primary structures	MW MWZ MZW FMW FMWZ FMZW FSMW FSMWZ FSMZW (conflated as (F(S)MW(Z))
Exponents of these elements (primary classes of unit 'course')	F: 1 (antipasta)
	S: 2 (fish)
	M: 3 (entrée)
	W: 4 (dessert)
	Z: 5 (cheese*)
Secondary structures	(various, involving secondary elements $F_{a..d}$, $M_{a.b}$, $W_{a.c}$)
Exponents of secondary elements (systems of secondary classes of unit 'course')	F_a: 1.1 (soup)
	F_b: 1.2 (hors d'oeuvres)
	F_c: 1.3 (fruit)
	F_d: 1.4 (fruit juice)
	M_a: 3.1 (meat dish)
	M_b: 3.2 (poultry dish)
	W_a: 4.1 (fruit*)
	W_b: 4.2 (pudding)
	W_c: 4.3 (ice cream*)
Systems of sub-classes of unit 'course'	F_a: 1.11 (clear soup*)
	1.12 (thick soup*)
	S: 2.01 (grilled fish*)
	2.02 (fried fish*)
	2.03 (poached fish*)
	W_b: 4.21 (steamed pudding*)
	4.22 (milk pudding*)
Exponential systems operating in meal structure	opera-F_c: grapefruit/melon
	F_d: grapefruit juice/pineapple

juice/tomato juice
Mₐ: beef/mutton/pork
Mᵦ: chicken/turkey/duck/
goose

At the rank of the 'course,' the primary class 'entrée' has secondary classes 'meat dish' and 'poultry dish.' Each of these two secondary classes carries a grammatical system whose terms are formal items. But this system accounts only for simple structures of the class 'entrée,' those made up of only one member of the unit 'helping.' The class 'entrée,' also displays compound structures, whose additional elements have as exponents the (various secondary classes of the) classes 'cereal' and 'vegetable.' We will glance briefly at these:

Unit: Course, Class: entrée

Elements of primary structure	J, T, A ('joint,' 'staple,' 'adjunct')
Primary structures	J JT JA JTA (conflated as J((T)(A)))
Exponents of these elements (primary classes of unit 'helping')	J: 1 (flesh) T: 2 (cereal) A: 3 (vegetable)
Secondary structures	(various, involving – among others – secondary elements Jₐ,ᵦ, Tₐ,ᵦ, Aₐ,ᵦ)
Exponents of secondary elements (systems of secondary classes of unit 'helping')	Jₐ: 1.1 (meat) ⎫ Jᵦ: 1.2 (poultry) ⎬ systems as at M in meal structure ⎭ Tₐ: 2.1 (potato) Tᵦ: 2.2 (rice) Aₐ: 3.1 (green vegetable*) Aᵦ: 3.2 (root vegetable*)

And so on, until everything is accounted for either in grammatical systems or in classes made up of lexical items (marked *). The presentation has proceeded down the rank scale, but shunting is presupposed throughout: there is mutual determination among all units, down to the gastronomic morpheme, the 'mouthful.'

This advances considerably the analysis of our family eating patterns. First, it shows how long and tedious the exhaustive analysis would be, even to read. It would be more taxing to observe and record. Our model of ethnographic thoroughness for a microscopic example should not be less exact than that practiced by anthropologists working in exotic lands. In India social distinctions are invariably accompanied by distinctions in commensality and categories of edible and inedible foods. Louis Dumont's important work on Indian culture, *Homo Hierarchicus*, discusses the purity of food as an index of hierarchy. He gives praise to Adrian Mayer's detailed study of the relation between food categories and social categories in a village in Central India.[9] Here twenty-three castes group themselves according to the use of the same pipe, the provision of ordinary food for common meals, and the provision of food for feasts. Higher castes share the pipe with almost all castes except four. Between twelve and sixteen castes smoke together, though in some cases a different cloth must be placed between the pipe and the lips of the smoker. When it comes to their food, a subtler analysis is required. Castes which enjoy power in the village are not fussy about what they eat or from whom they receive it. Middle range castes are extraordinarily restrictive, both as to whom they will accept food from and what they will eat. Invited to family ceremonies by the more powerful and more ritually relaxed castes they puritanically insist on being given their share of the food raw and retire to cook it themselves in their own homes.[10] If I were to follow this example and to include all transmission of food from our home my task would be greater. For certainly we too know situations in which drink is given to be consumed in the homes of the recipient. There are some kinds of service for which it seems that the only possible recognition is half or even a whole bottle of whiskey. With the high standards of the Indian research in mind, I try now to identify the relevant categories of food in our home.

The two major contrasted food categories are meals versus drinks. Both are social events. Outside these categories, of course, food can be taken for private nourishment. Then we speak only of the lexical item itself: 'Have an apple. Get a glass of milk. Are there any sweets?' If likely to interfere with the next meal, such eating is disapproved. But no negative attitude condemns eating before drinks. This and other indices suggest that meals rank higher.

Meals contrast with drinks in the relation between solids and liquids. Meals are a mixture of solid foods accompanied by liquids. With drinks the reverse holds. A complex series of syntagmatic associations governs the elements in a meal, and connects the meals through the day. One can say: 'It can't be lunchtime. I haven't had breakfast yet,' and at breakfast itself cereals come before bacon and eggs. Meals in their sequence tend to be named. Drinks sometimes have named categories: 'Come for cocktails, come for coffee, come for tea,' but many are not named events: 'What about a drink? What shall we have?' There is no structuring of drinks into early, main, light. They are not invested with any necessity in their ordering. Nor is the event called drinks internally structured into first, second, main, sweet. On the contrary, it is approved to stick with the same kind of drink, and to count drinks at all is impolite. The judgment 'It is too early for alcohol' would be both rare and likely to be contested. The same lack of structure is found in the solid foods accompanying drinks. They are usually cold, served in discrete units which can be eaten tidily with fingers. No order governs the choice of solids. When the children were small and tea was a meal, bread and butter preceded scones, scones preceded cake and biscuits. But now that the adult-child contrast no longer dominates in this family, tea has been demoted from a necessary place in the daily sequence of meals to an irregular appearance among weekend drinks and no rules govern the accompanying solids.

Meals properly require the use of at least one mouth-entering utensil per head, whereas drinks are limited to mouth-touching ones. A spoon on a saucer is for stirring, not sucking. Meals require a table, a seating order, restriction on movement and on alternative occupations. There is no question of knitting during a meal. Even at Sunday breakfast, reaching for the newspapers is a signal that the meal is over. The meal puts its frame on the gathering. The rules which hedge off and order one kind of social interaction are reflected in the rules which control the internal ordering of the meal itself. Drinks and their solids may all be sweet. But a meal is not a meal if it is all in the bland-sweet-sour dimensions. A meal incorporates a number of contrasts, hot and cold, bland and spiced, liquid and semi-liquid, and various textures. It also incorporates cereals, vegetables, and animal proteins. Criticism easily fastens on the ordering of these elements in a given case.

Obviously the meanings in our food system should be elucidated by much closer observation. I cut it short by drawing conclusions intuitively from the social categories which emerge. Drinks are for strangers, acquaintances, workmen, and family. Meals are for family, close friends, honored guests. The grand operator of the system is the line between intimacy and distance. Those we know at meals we also know at drinks. The meal expresses close friendship. Those we only know at drinks we know less intimately. So long as this boundary matters to us (and there is no reason to suppose it will always matter) the boundary between drinks and meals has meaning. There are smaller thresholds and half-way points. The entirely cold meal (since it

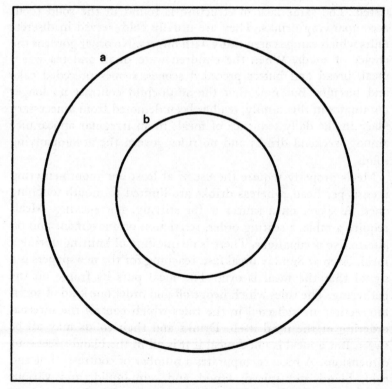

Figure 16.1 Social universe (a) share-drinks; (b) share-meals-too

omits a major contrast within a meal) would seem to be such a modifier. So those friends who have never had a hot meal in our home have presumably another threshold of intimacy to cross. The recent popularity of the barbecue and of more elaborately structured cocktail events which act as bridges between intimacy and distance suggests that our model of feeding categories is a common one. It can be drawn as in Figure 16.1. Thus far we can go on the basis of binary oppositions and the number of classes and subclasses. But we are left with the general question which must be raised whenever a correspondence is found between a given social structure and the structure of symbols by which it is expressed, that is, the question of consciousness. Those who vehemently reject the possibility of a meal's being constituted by soup and pudding, or cake and fruit, are certainly not conscious that they are thereby sustaining a boundary between share-drinks and share-meals-too. They would be shocked at the very idea. It would be simplistic to trace the food categories direct to the social categories they embrace and leave it at Figure 16.1. Evidently the external boundaries are only a small part of the meaning of the meal. Somewhere else in the family system some other cognitive activity is generating the internal structuring.

We can go much further toward discovering the intensity of meanings and their anchorage in social life by attending to the sequence of meals. For the week's menu has its climax at Sunday lunch. By contrasting the structure of Sunday lunch with week-day lunches a new principle emerges. Weekday lunches tend to have a tripartite structure, one element stressed accompanied by two or more unstressed elements, for example a main course and cold supporting dishes. But Sunday lunch has two main courses, each of which is patterned like the weekday lunch – say, first course, fish or meat (stressed) and two vegetables (unstressed), second course, pudding (stressed), cream and biscuits (unstressed). Christmas lunch has three courses, each on the same tripartite model. Here we stop and realize that the analogy may be read in the reverse sense. Meals are ordered in scale of importance and grandeur through the week and the year. The smallest, meanest meal metonymically figures the structure of the grandest, and each unit of the grand meal figures again the whole meal – or the meanest meal. The perspective created by these repetitive analogies invests the individual meal with additional meaning. Here we have the principle we were seeking, the intensifier of meaning, the selection principle. A meal stays in the category of meal only in so far as it carries this structure which allows the part to recall the whole. Hence the outcry against allowing the sequence of soup and pudding to be called a meal.

As to the social dimension, admission to even the simplest meal incorporates our guest unwittingly into the pattern of solid Sunday dinners, Christmases, and the gamut of life cycle celebrations. Whereas the sharing of drinks (note the fluidity of the central item, the lack of structuring, the small, unsticky accompanying solids) expresses by contrast only too clearly the detachment and impermanence of simpler and less intimate social bonds.

Summing up, syntagmatic relations between meals reveal a restrictive patterning by which the meal is identified as such, graded as a minor or major event of its class, and then judged as a good or bad specimen of its kind. A system of repeated analogies upholds the process of recognition and grading. Thus we can broach the question of interpretation which binary analysis by itself leaves untouched. The features which a single copious dish would need to display before qualifying as a meal in our home would be something like those of the famous chicken Marengo of Napoleon after his defeat of the Austrians.[11]

> Bonaparte, who, on the day of a battle, ate nothing until after it was over, had gone forward with his general staff and was a long way from his supply wagon. Seeing his enemies put to flight, he asked Dunand to prepare dinner for him. The master-chef at once sent men of the quartermaster's staff and ordnance in search of provisions. All they could find were three eggs, four tomatoes, six crayfish, a small hen, a little garlic, some oil and a saucepan ... the dish was served on a tin plate, the chicken surrounded by the fried eggs and crayfish, with the sauce poured over it.

There must have been many more excellent meals following similar scavenging after the many victories of those campaigns. But only this one has become famous. In my opinion the reason is that it combines the traditional soup, fish, egg, and meat courses of a French celebratory feast all in a *plat unique*.

If I wish to serve anything worthy of the name of supper in

one dish it must preserve the minimum structure of a meal. Vegetable soup so long as it had noodles and grated cheese would do, or poached eggs on toast with parsley. Now I know the formula. A proper meal is A (when A is the stressed main course) plus 2B (when B is an unstressed course). Both A and B contain each the same structure, in small, a + 2b, when a is the stressed item and b the unstressed item in a course. A weekday lunch is A; Sunday lunch is 2A; Christmas, Easter, and birthdays are A + 2B. Drinks by contrast are unstructured.

To understand the categories we have placed ourselves at the hub of a small world, a home and its neighborhood. The precoded message of the food categories is the boundary system of a series of social events. Our example made only oblique reference to costs in time and work to indicate the concerns involved. But unless the symbolic structure fits squarely to some demonstrable social consideration, the analysis has only begun. For the fit between the medium's symbolic boundaries and the boundaries between categories of people is its only possible validation. The fit may be at different levels; but without being able to show some such matching, the analysis of symbols remains arbitrary and subjective.

The question that now arises is the degree to which a family uses symbolic structures which are available from the wider social system. Obviously this example reeks of the culture of a certain segment of the middle classes of London. The family's idea of what a meal should be is influenced by the Steak House and by the French *cuisine bourgeoise*. Yet herein is implied a synthesis of different traditions. The French version of the grand meal is dominated by the sequence of wines. The cheese platter is the divide between a mounting crescendo of individual savory dishes and a descending scale of sweet ones ending with coffee. Individual dishes in the French sequence can stand alone. Compare the melon course in a London restaurant and a Bordeaux restaurant. In the first, the half slice is expected to be dusted with powdered ginger and castor sugar (a + 2b) or decorated with a wedge of orange and a crystallized cherry (a + 2b). In the second, half a melon is served with no embellishment but its own perfume and juices. A + 2B is obviously not a formula that our family invented, but one that is current in our social environment. It governs even the structure of the cocktail canapé. The latter, with its cereal base, its meat or cheese middle section, its sauce or pickle topping, and its mixture of colors, suggests a mock meal, a minute metonym of English middle-class meals in general. Whereas the French pattern is more like: $C^1 + B^1 + A^1/A^2 + B^2 + C^2$, when the cheese course divides A^1 (the main savory dish) from A^2 (the main sweet). It would be completely against the spirit of this essay to hazard a meaning for either structure in its quasi environmental form. French families reaching out to the meal structure of their cultural environment develop it and interact with it according to their intentions. English families reach out and find another which they adapt to their own social purposes. Americans, Chinese, and others do likewise. Since these cultural environments afford an ambient stream of symbols, capable of differentiating and intensifying, but not anchored to a stable social base, we cannot proceed further to interpret them. At this point the analysis stops. But the problems which cannot be answered here, where the cultural universe is unbounded, can usefully be referred to a more closed environment.

To sum up, the meaning of a meal is found in a system of repeated analogies. Each meal carries something of the meaning of the other meals; each meal is a structured social event which structures others in its own image. The upper limit of its meaning is set by the range incorporated in the most important member of its series. The recognition which allows each member to be classed and graded with the others depends upon the structure common to them all. The cognitive energy which demands that a meal look like a meal and not like a drink is performing in the culinary medium the same exercise that it performs in language. First, it distinguishes order, bounds it, and separates it from disorder. Second, it uses economy in the means of expression by allowing only a limited number of structures. Third, it imposes a rank scale upon the repetition of structures. Fourth, the repeated formal analogies multiply the meanings that are carried down any one of them by the power of the most weighty. By these four methods the meanings are enriched. There is no single point in the rank scale, high or low, which provides the basic meaning or real meaning. Each exemplar has the meaning of its structure realized in the examples at other levels.

From coding we are led to a more appropriate comparison for

the interpretation of a meal, that is, versification. To treat the meal as a poem requires a more serious example than I have used hitherto. I turn to the Jewish meal, governed by the Mosaic dietary rules. For Lu Chi, a third century Chinese poet, poetry traffics in some way between the world and mankind. The poet is one who 'traps Heaven and Earth in a cage of form.'[12] On these terms the common meal of the Israelites was a kind of classical poem. Of the Israelite table, too, it could be said that it enclosed boundless space. To quote Lu Chi again:[13]

> We enclose boundless space in a square-foot of paper;
> We pour out deluge from the inch-space of the heart.

But the analogy slows down at Lu Chi's last line. For at first glance it is not certain that the meal can be a tragic medium. The meal is a kind of poem, but by a very limited analogy. The cook may not be able to express the powerful things a poet can say.

In *Purity and Danger*[14] I suggested a rational pattern for the Mosaic rejection of certain animal kinds. Ralph Bulmer has very justly reproached me for offering an animal taxonomy for the explanation of the Hebrew dietary laws. The principles I claimed to discern must remain, he argued, at a subjective and arbitrary level, unless they could take account of the multiple dimensions of thought and activity of the Hebrews concerned.[15] S. J. Tambiah has made similarly effective criticisms of the same short-coming in my approach.[16] Both have provided from their own fieldwork distinguished examples of how the task should be conducted. In another publication I hope to pay tribute to the importance of their research. But for the present purpose, I am happy to admit the force of their reproach. It was even against the whole spirit of my book to offer an account of an ordered system of thought which did not show the context of social relations in which the categories had meaning. Ralph Bulmer let me down gently by supposing that the ethnographic evidence concerning the ancient Hebrews was too meager. However, reflection on this new research and methodology has led me to reject that suggestion out of hand. We know plenty about the ancient Hebrews. The problem is how to recognize and relate what we know.

New Guinea and Thailand are far apart, in geography, in history, and in civilization. Their local fauna are entirely different. Surprisingly, these two analyses of animal classification have one thing in common. Each society projects on to the animal kingdom categories and values which correspond to their categories of marriageable persons. The social categories of descent and affinity dominate their natural categories. The good Thailand son-in-law knows his place and keeps to it: disordered, displaced sex is reprobated and the odium transferred to the domestic dog, symbol of dirt and promiscuity. From the dog to the otter, the transfer of odium is doubled in strength. This amphibian they class as wild, counterpart-dog. But instead of keeping to the wild domain it is apt to leave its sphere at flood time and to paddle about in their watery fields. The ideas they attach to incest are carried forward from the dog to the otter, the image of the utterly wrong son-in-law. For the Karam the social focus is upon the strained relations between affines and cousins. A wide range of manmade rules sustain the categories of a natural world which mirrors these anxieties. In the Thailand and Karam studies, a strong analogy between bed and board lies unmistakably beneath the system of classifying animals. The patterns of rules which categorize animals correspond in form to the patterns of rules governing human relations. Sexual and gastronomic consummation are made equivalents of one another by reasons of analogous restrictions applied to each. Looking back from these examples to the classifications of Leviticus we seek in vain a statement, however oblique, of a similar association between eating and sex. Only a very strong analogy between table and altar stares us in the face. On reflection, why should the Israelites have had a similar concern to associate sex with food? Unlike the other two examples, they had no rule requiring them to exchange their womenfolk. On the contrary, they were allowed to marry their parallel paternal first cousins. E. R. Leach has reminded us how strongly exogamy was disapproved at the top political level,[17] and within each tribe of Israel endogamy was even enjoined (Numbers 36). We must seek elsewhere for their dominant preoccupations. At this point I turn to the rules governing the common meal as prescribed in the Jewish religion. It is particularly interesting that these rules have remained the same over centuries. Therefore, if these categories express a relevance to social concerns we must expect those concerns to have remained in some form alive. The three rules about meat are: (1)

the rejection of certain animal kinds as unfit for the table (Leviticus 11; Deuteronomy 14), (2) of those admitted as edible, the separation of the meat from blood before cooking (Leviticus 17:10; Deuteronomy 12:23–7), (3) the total separation of milk from meat, which involves the minute specialization of utensils (Exodus 23:19; 34:26; Deuteronomy 14:21).

I start with the classification of animals whose rationality I claim to have discerned. Diagrams will help to summarize the argument (first outlined in *Purity and Danger*, 1966). First, animals are classified according to degrees of holiness (see Figure 16.2). At the bottom end of the scale some animals are abominable, not to be touched or eaten. Others are fit for the table, but not for the altar. None that are fit for the altar are not edible and vice versa, none that are not edible are sacrificeable. The criteria for this grading are coordinated for the three spheres of land, air, and water. Starting with the simplest, we find the sets as in Figure 16.3.

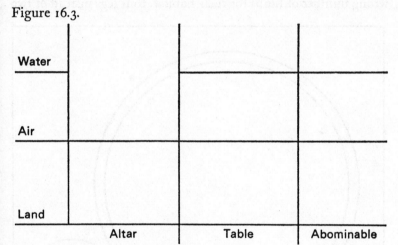

Figure 16.2 Degrees of holiness

Water creatures, to be fit for the table, must have fins and scales (Leviticus 13:9–12; Deuteronomy 14:19). Creeping swarming worms and snakes, if they go in the water or on the land, are not fit for the table (Deuteronomy 14:19; Leviticus 11:41–3). 'The term swarming creatures (*shéreç*) denotes living things which appear in swarms and is applied both to those which teem in the waters (Genesis 1:20; Leviticus 11:10) and to those which swarm on the ground, including the smaller land animals, reptiles and creeping insects.'[18] Nothing from this sphere is fit for the altar. The Hebrews only sanctified domesticated animals and these did not include fish. 'When any one of you brings an offering to Jehovah, it shall be a domestic animal, taken either from the herd or from the flock' (Leviticus 1 : 2). But, Assyrians and others sacrificed wild beasts, as S. R. Driver and H. A. White point out.

Air creatures (see Figure 16.4) are divided into more complex sets: set (a), those which fly and hop on the earth (Leviticus 11 : 12), having wings and two legs, contains two subsets, one of which contains the named birds, abominable and not fit for the table, and the rest of the birds (b), fit for the table. From this latter subset a sub-subset (c) is drawn, which is suitable for the altar – turtledove and pigeon (Leviticus 14; 5: 7–8) and the sparrow (Leviticus 14 : 49–53). Two separate sets of denizens of the air are abominable, untouchable creatures; (f), which have the wrong number of limbs for their habitat, four legs instead of two

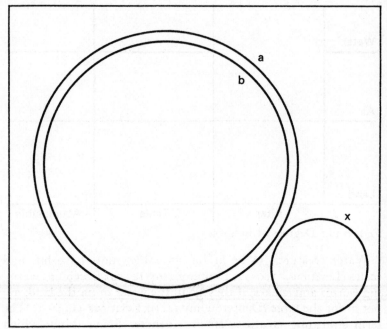

Figure 16.3 Denizens of the water (a) insufficient criteria for (b); (b) fit for table; (x) abominable: swarming

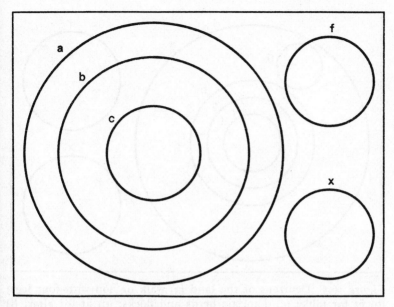

Figure 16.4 Denizens of the air (a) fly and hop: wings and two legs; (b) fit for table; (c) fit for altar; (f) abominable: insufficient criteria for (a); (x) abominable: swarming

(Leviticus 9:20), and (x), the swarming insects we have already noted in the water (Deuteronomy 14:19).

The largest class of land creatures (a) (see Figure 16.5) walk or hop on the land with four legs. From this set of quadrupeds, those with parted hoofs and which chew the cud (b) are distinguished as fit for the table (Leviticus 11:3; Deuteronomy 14:4–6) and of this set a subset consists of the domesticated herds and flocks (c). Of these the first born (d) are to be offered to the priests (Deuteronomy 24:33). Outside the set (b) which part the hoof and chew the cud are three sets of abominable beasts: (g) those which have either the one or the other but not both of the required physical features; (f) those with the wrong number of limbs, two hands instead of four legs (Leviticus 11:27 and 29:31; and see Proverbs 30:28); (x) those which crawl upon their bellies (Leviticus 11:41–4).

The isomorphism which thus appears between the different categories of animal classed as abominable helps us to interpret the meaning of abomination. Those creatures which inhabit a

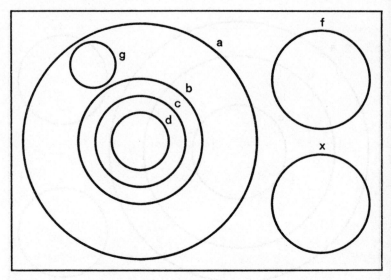

Figure 16.5 Denizens of the land (a) walk or hop with four legs; (b) fit for table; (c) domestic herds and flocks; (d) fit for altar; (f) abominable: insufficient criteria for (a); (g) abominable: insufficient criteria for (b); (x) abominable: swarming

given range, water, air, or land, but do not show all the criteria for (a) or (b) in that range are abominable. The creeping, crawling, teeming creatures do not show criteria for allocation to any class, but cut across them all.

Here we have a very rigid classification. It assigns living creatures to one of three spheres, on a behavioral basis, and selects certain morphological criteria that are found most commonly in the animals inhabiting each sphere. It rejects creatures which are anomalous, whether in living between two spheres, or having defining features of members of another sphere, or lacking defining features. Any living being which falls outside this classification is not to be touched or eaten. To touch it is to be defiled and defilement forbids entry to the temple. Thus it can be summed up fairly by saying that anomalous creatures are unfit for altar and table. This is a peculiarity of the Mosaic code. In other societies anomaly is not always so treated. Indeed, in some, the anomalous creature is treated as the source of blessing and is specially fit for the altar (as the Lele pangolin),

Under the Covenant

Human	Israelites	others
Nonhuman	their livestock	others

Figure 16.6 Analogy between humans and nonhumans

or as a noble beast, to be treated as an honorable adversary, as the Karam treat the cassowary. Since in the Mosaic code every degree of holiness in animals has implications one way or the other for edibility, we must follow further the other rules classifying humans and animals. Again I summarize a long argument with diagrams. First, note that a category which divides some humans from others, also divides their animals from others. Israelites descended from Abraham and bound to God by the Covenant between God and Abraham are distinguished from all other peoples and similarly the rules which Israelites obey as part of the Covenant apply to their animals (see Figure 16.6). The rule that the womb opener or first born is consecrated to divine service applies to firstlings of the flocks and herds (Exodus 22:29-30; Deuteronomy 24:23) and the rule of Sabbath observance is extended to work animals (Exodus 20:10). As human and animal firstlings are to God, so a man's own first born is unalterably his heir (Deuteronomy 21:15-17). The analogy by which Israelites are to other humans as their livestock are to other quadrupeds develops by indefinite stages the analogy between altar and table.

Since Levites who are consecrated to the temple service represent the first born of all Israel (Numbers 3:12 and 40) there is an analogy between the animal and human firstlings. Among the Israelites, all of whom prosper through the Covenant and observance of the Law, some are necessarily unclean at any given time. No man or woman with issue of seed or blood, or with forbidden contact with an animal classed as unclean, or who has shed blood or been involved in the unsacralized killing of an animal (Leviticus 18), or who has sinned morally (Leviticus 20), can enter the temple. Nor can one with a blemish (Deuteronomy 23) enter

267

the temple or eat the flesh of sacrifice or peace offerings (Leviticus 8:20). The Levites are selected by pure descent from all the Israelites. They represent the first born of Israel. They judge the cleanness and purify the uncleanness of Israelites (Leviticus 13, 14, 10:10; Deuteronomy 21:5). Only Levites who are without bodily blemish (Leviticus 21:17–23) and without contact with death can enter the Holy of Holies. Thus we can present these rules as sets in Figures 16.7 and 16.8. The analogy between humans and animals is very clear. So is the analogy created by these rules between the temple and the living body. Further analogies appear between the classification of animals according to holiness (Figure 16.2) and the rules which set up the analogy of the holy temple with its holier and holier inner sanctuaries, and on the other hand between the temple's holiness and the body's purity and the capacity of each to be defiled by the self-same forms of impurity. This analogy is a living part of the Judeo-Christian tradition which has been unfaltering in its interpretation of New Testament allusions. The words of the Last Supper have their meaning from looking backward over the centuries in which the analogy had held good and forward to the future celebrations of that meal. 'This is my body ... this is my blood' (Luke 22:19–20; Mark 14:22–4; Matthew 26:26–8). Here

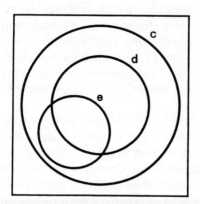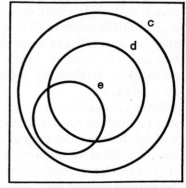

Figure 16.7   The Israelites (c) under the Covenant; (d) fit for temple sacrifice: no blemish; (e) consecrated to temple service, first born

Figure 16.8   Their livestock (c) under the Covenant; (d) fit for temple sacrifice: no blemish; (e) consecrated to temple service, first born

the meal and the sacrificial victim, the table and the altar are made explicitly to stand for one another.

Lay these rules and their patternings in a straight perspective, each one looking forward and backward to all the others, and we get the same repetition of metonyms that we found to be the key to the full meaning of the categories of food in the home. By itself the body and its rules can carry the whole load of meanings that the temple can carry by itself with its rules. The overlap and repetitions are entirely consistent. What then are these meanings? Between the temple and the body we are in a maze of religious thought. What is its social counterpart? Turning back to my original analysis (in 1966) of the forbidden meats we are now in a much better position to assess intensity and social relevance. For the metonymical patternings are too obvious to ignore. At every moment they are in chorus with a message about the value of purity and the rejection of impurity. At the level of a general taxonomy of living beings the purity in question is the purity of the categories. Creeping, swarming, teeming creatures abominably destroy the taxonomic boundaries. At the level of the individual living being impurity is the imperfect, broken, bleeding specimen. The sanctity of cognitive boundaries is made known by valuing the integrity of the physical forms. The perfect physical specimens point to the perfectly bounded temple, altar, and sanctuary. And these in their turn point to the hard-won and hard-to-defend territorial boundaries of the Promised Land. This is not reductionism. We are not here reducing the dietary rules to any political concern. But we are showing how they are consistently celebrating a theme that has been celebrated in the temple cult and in the whole history of Israel since the first Covenant with Abraham and the first sacrifice of Noah.

Edmund Leach, in his analysis of the genealogy of Solomon, has reminded us of the political problems besetting a people who claim by pure descent and pure religion to own a territory that others held and others continually encroached upon.[19] Israel is the boundary that all the other boundaries celebrate and that gives them their historic load of meaning. Remembering this, the orthodox meal is not difficult to interpret as a poem. The first rule, the rejection of certain animal kinds, we have mostly dealt with. But the identity of the list of named abominable birds is still a question. In the Mishnah it is written: 'The characteristics of birds are not stated, but the Sages have said, every bird that seizes its prey (to tread or attack with claws) is unclean.'[20] The idea that the unclean birds were predators, unclean because they were an image of human predation and homicide, so easily fits the later Hellenicizing interpretations that it has been suspect. According to the late Professor S. Hooke (in a personal communication), Professor R. S. Driver once tried out the idea that the Hebrew names were onomatopoeic of the screeches and calls of the birds. He diverted an assembly of learned divines with ingenious vocal exercises combining ornithology and Hebrew scholarship. I have not traced the record of this meeting. But following the method of analysis I have been using, it seems very likely that the traditional predatory idea is sufficient, considering its compatibility with the second rule governing the common meal.

According to the second rule, meat for the table must be drained of its blood. No man eats flesh with blood in it. Blood belongs to God alone, for life is in the blood.[21] This rule relates the meal systematically to all the rules which exclude from the temple on grounds of contact with or responsibility for bloodshed. Since the animal kinds which defy the perfect classification of nature are defiling both as food and for entry to the temple, it is a structural repetition of the general analogy between body and temple to rule that the eating of blood defiles. Thus the birds and beasts which eat carrion (undrained of blood) are likely by the same reasoning to be defiling. In my analysis, the Mishnah's identifying the unclean birds as predators is convincing.

Here we come to a watershed between two kinds of defilement. When the classifications of any metaphysical scheme are imposed on nature, there are several points where it does not fit. So long as the classifications remain in pure metaphysics and are not expected to bite into daily life in the form of rules of behavior, no problem arises. But if the unity of Godhead is to be related to the unity of Israel and made into a rule of life, the difficulties start. First, there are the creatures whose behavior defies the rigid classification. It is relatively easy to deal with them by rejection and avoidance. Second, there are the difficulties that arise from our biological condition. It is all very well to worship the holiness of God in the perfection of his creation. But the Israelites must be nourished and must reproduce. It is impossible for a pastoral people to eat their flocks and herds without damaging the bodily completeness they respect. It is impossible to renew Israel without emission of blood and sexual fluids. These problems are met sometimes by avoidance and sometimes by consecration to the temple. The draining of blood from meat is a ritual act which figures the bloody sacrifice at the altar. Meat is thus transformed from a living creature into a food item.

As to the third rule, the separation of meat and milk, it honors the procreative functions. The analogy between human and animal parturition is always implied, as the Mishnah shows in its comment on the edibility of the afterbirth found in the slaughtered dam: if the afterbirth had emerged in part, it is forbidden as food; 'it is a token of young in a woman and a token of young in a beast.'[22] Likewise this third rule honors the Hebrew mother and her initial unity with her offspring.

In conclusion I return to the researches of Tambiah and Bulmer. In each case a concern with sexual relations, approved or disapproved, is reflected on to the Thailand and Karam animal classifications. In the case of Israel the dominant concern would seem to be with the integrity of territorial boundaries. But Edmund Leach has pointed out how over and over again they were concerned with the threat to Israel's holy calling from marriages with outsiders. Foreign husbands and foreign wives led to false gods and political defections. So sex is not omitted from the meanings in the common meal. But the question is different. In the other cases the problems arose from rules about exchanging women. In this case the concern is to insist on not exchanging women.

Perhaps I can now suggest an answer to Ralph Bulmer's question about the abhorrence of the pig.

Dr Douglas tells us that the pig was an unclean beast to the Hebrew quite simply because it was a taxonomic anomaly, literally as the Old Testament says, because like the normal domestic animals it has a cloven hoof, whereas *un*like other cloven-footed beasts, it does not chew the cud. And she pours a certain amount of scorn on the commentators of the last 2,000 years who have taken alternative views and drawn attention to the creature's feeding habits, etc.

Dr Bulmer would be tempted to reverse the argument and to say that the other animals are prohibited as part of an elaborate exercise for rationalizing[22]

> the prohibition of a beast for which there were probably multiple reasons for avoiding. It would seem equally fair, on the limited evidence available, to argue that the pig was accorded anomalous taxonomic status because it was unclean as to argue that it was unclean because of its anomalous taxonomic status.

On more mature reflection, and with the help of his own research, I can now see that the pig to the Israelites could have had a special taxonomic status equivalent to that of the otter in Thailand. It carries the odium of multiple pollution. First, it pollutes because it defies the classification of ungulates. Second, it pollutes because it eats carrion. Third, it pollutes because it is reared as food (and presumably as prime pork) by non-Israelites. An Israelite who betrothed a foreigner might have been liable to be offered a feast of pork. By these stages it comes plausibly to represent the utterly disapproved form of sexual mating and to carry all the odium that this implies. We now can trace a general analogy between the food rules and the other rules against mixtures: 'Thou shalt not make thy cattle to gender with beasts of any other kind' (Leviticus 19:19). 'Thou shalt not copulate with any beast' (Leviticus 18:23). The common meal, decoded, as much as any poem, summarizes a stern, tragic religion.

We are left the question of why, when so much else had been forgotten[24] about the rules of purification and their meaning, the three rules governing the Jewish meal have persisted. What meanings do they still encode, unmoored as they partly are from their original social context? It would seem that whenever a people are aware of encroachment and danger, dietary rules controlling what goes into the body would serve as a vivid analogy of the corpus of their cultural categories at risk. But here I am, contrary to my own strictures, suggesting a universal meaning, free of particular social context, one which is likely to make sense whenever the same situation is perceived. We have come full-circle to Figure 16.1, with its two concentric circles. The outside boundary is weak, the inner one strong. Right through the diagrams summarizing the Mosaic dietary rules the focus was upon the integrity of the boundary at (b). Abominations of the water are those finless and scaleless creatures which lie outside that boundary. Abominations of the air appear less clearly in this light because the unidentified forbidden birds had to be shown as the widest circle from which the edible selection is drawn. If it be granted that they are predators, then they can be shown as a small subset in the unlisted set, that is as denizens of the air not fit for table because they eat blood. They would then be seen to threaten the boundary at (b) in the same explicit way as among the denizens of the land the circle (g) threatens it. We should therefore not conclude this essay without saying something more positive about what this boundary encloses. In the one case it divides edible from inedible. But it is more than a negative barrier of exclusion. In all the cases we have seen, it bounds the area of structured relations. Within that area rules apply. Outside it, anything goes. Following the argument we have established by which each level of meaning realizes the others which share a common structure, we can fairly say that the ordered system which is a meal represents all the ordered systems associated with it. Hence the strong arousal power of a threat to weaken or confuse that category. To take our analysis of the culinary medium further we should study what the poets say about the disciplines that they adopt. A passage from Roy Fuller's lectures helps to explain the flash of recognition and confidence which welcomes an ordered pattern. He is quoting Allen Tate, who said: 'Formal versification is the primary structure of poetic order, the assurance to the reader and to the poet himself that the poet is in control of the disorder both outside him and within his own mind.'[25]

The rules of the menu are not in themselves more or less trivial than the rules of verse to which a poet submits.

Note

I am grateful to Professor Basil Bernstein and to Professor M. A. K. Halliday for valuable suggestions and for criticisms, some of which I have not been able to meet. My thanks are due to my son James for working out the Venn diagrams used in this article.

Notes

1 Michael A. K. Halliday (1961), 'Categories of the theory of grammar,' *World, Journal of the Linguistic Circle of New York, 17,* 241–91.
2 The continuing discussion between anthropologists on the relation between biological and social facts in the understanding of kinship categories is fully relevant to the understanding of food categories.
3 Roland Barthes (1967), *Système de la mode,* Paris Editions Seuil.
4 Claude Lévi-Strauss (1970), *The Raw and the Cooked: Introduction to a Science of Mythology,* I, London, Jonathan Cape. The whole series in French is *Mythologiques: I. Le Cru et le cuit, II. Du Miel aux cendres, III. L'Origine des manières de table* (Paris, Plon, 1964–8).
5 Roman Jakobson and Claude Lévi-Strauss (1962), 'Les Chats de Charles Baudelaire,' *L'Homme, 2,* 5–21.
6 Michael Riffaterre (1967), 'Describing poetic structures: two approaches to Baudelaire's *Les Chats,*' *Structuralism,* Yale French Studies 36 and 37.
7 Claude Lévi-Strauss, *The Savage Mind* (London, Weidenfeld & Nicolson, 1966; University of Chicago Press, 1962, 1966).
8 Halliday, 'Categories of the theory of grammar,' pp. 277–9.
9 Adrian C. Mayer (1960), *Caste and Kinship in Central India: a Village and its Region,* London, Routledge.
10 Louis Dumont, *Homo Hierarchicus: the Caste System and its Implications,* trans. M. Sainsbury (London, Weidenfeld & Nicolson, 1970; French ed., Gallimard, 1966), pp. 86–9.
11 See under 'Marengo,' *Larousse Gastronomique* (Hamlyn, 1961).
12 A. MacLeish (1960), *Poetry and Experience,* London, Bodley Head, p. 4.
13 *Ibid.*
14 Mary Douglas (1966), *Purity and Danger: an Analysis of Concepts of Pollution and Taboo,* London, Routledge.
15 Ralph Bulmer (1967), 'Why is the cassowary not a bird? A problem of zoological taxonomy among the Karam of the New Guinea Highlands,' *Man,* new ser., 2, 5–25.
16 S. J. Tambiah (1969), 'Animals are good to think and good to prohibit,' *Ethnology,* 7, 423–59.
17 E. R. Leach (1969), 'The Legitimacy of Solomon,' *Genesis as Myth and Other Essays,* London, Jonathan Cape.
18 S. R. Driver and H. A. White, *The Polychrome Bible, Leviticus,* v.l.fn. 13.
19 Leach, 'Legitimacy of Solomon.'

20 H. Danby, trans. (1933), *The Mishnah*, London, Oxford University Press, p. 324.
21 See Jacob Milgrom (1971), 'A prolegomena to Leviticus 17:17', *Journal of Biblical Literature*, 90, II: 149–56. This contains a textual analysis of the rules forbidding eating flesh with the blood in it which is compatible with the position herein advocated.
22 *Ibid.*, p. 520.
23 Bulmer, 'Why is the cassowary not a bird?', p. 21.
24 Moses Maimonides (1904), *Guide for the Perplexed*, trans. M. Friedlander, London, Routledge, first ed., 1881.
25 Roy Fuller (1971), *Owls and Artificers: Oxford Lectures on Poetry*, London, Deutsch, p. 64.

K*

17

Self-evidence

Over two hundred years ago David Hume declared that there is no necessity in Nature: 'Necessity is something that exists in the mind, not in objects.' In other words, he insisted that knowledge of causality is of the intuitional kind, guts knowledge; causality is no more than a 'construction upon past experience'; it is due to 'force of habit', a part of human nature whose study, he averred, is too much neglected. As anthropologists our work has been precisely to study this habit which constructs for each society its special universe of efficacious principles. This very habit peoples each world with humans, alive and dead, animal bodies and animal spirits, half-humans, half-animals, and divinities mixed with each. From the sheer variety of these constructed worlds, the anthropologist is led to agree, but only guardedly, with Hume. Other people's causal theories are put into two sets: those which accord with our own and need no special explanation, and those which are magical and based on subjective associations as Frazer believed, or on affective rather than cognitive facilities, as Lévy-Bruhl said (see Cazeneuve, 1972: 44, 68, 70) when he tried to distinguish the mystical from the scientific mind. But Hume claimed that all causal theories whatever and without exception arise from what he called the sensitive rather than the cognitive part of our nature. Whenever we reserve our own causal theories from sceptical philosophy, our gut response proves him utterly right. But it is almost impossible not to make this reservation. One of the objects of this paper is to propose a more formal mode of discussion in which we can hope to compare causal systems, including our own. Without that shift our only recourse

276

as anthropologists is to translate from other cultures into our own. The better the translation, the more successfully has our provincial logic been imposed on the native thought. So the consequence of good translation is to prevent any confrontation between alien thought systems. We are left as we were at the outset, with our own familiar world divided by its established categories and activated by the principles we know. This world remains our stable point of reference for judging all other worlds as peculiar and other knowledge as faulty. Translation flourishes where experience overlaps. But where there is no overlap, the attempt to translate fails. The challenge of a new meaning by which to test our own ideas is turned into a challenge to find a new expression for our old meanings. The only confrontation takes place when the lack of overlap between our culture and others suggests a few academic puzzles about the peculiarities of native thought. This is the failing I wish to remedy in this essay. Puzzles about native thought are puzzles about thought in general and so puzzles about our own thought. We anthropologists tend to discuss problems of meaning in a too segregated framework. We have to see that the categories and actual principles which we find in our own world present the same problems of rational justification that baffle us in the exotic worlds of foreigners. Just where there is no cultural overlap the effort to interpret should be driven to ascend from the particular puzzling statement to higher and higher levels of generalisation until finally the conflict of opinion is uncovered at its source. Two different sets of hypotheses about the nature of reality and how it is divided up are exposed, each carrying the ring of self-evident truth so clearly that its fundamental assumptions are implicit and considered to need no justification.

By this route we are already in the middle of the question of self-evidence. A self-evident statement is one which carries its evidence within itself. It is true by virtue of the meaning of the words, 'All bachelors are unmarried men'; '$2+2=4$'. Quoting Professor Quine, on whose work this discussion draws heavily, a self-evident or analytic statement can be defined 'as any statement which, by putting synonyms for synonyms, is convertible into an instance of a logical form all of whose instances are true' (1943: 120). But what is synonymity? It is 'the relation between expressions that have the same meaning'. And what is the mean-

ing of an expression? It is 'the class of all expressions synonymous with it'. So we are in a circle out of which anthropology can
hardly hope to show the way. But our material might explain
better how the relation of synonymity is recognised and con-
firmed. The strategy of this paper is to start with Quine's description of how intuitions of sameness are established, and to
improve it by inserting a fuller account of the sociological
dimension. As it stands, his account has certain limitations. For
one, it leaves the intuition of sameness on the wrong side of
rationality: guts are guts and reason is reason, there is still a gap
in the account of how the two relate. For another, it leaves us
with an empty cultural relativism: each universe is divided up
differently, period. From here there is nothing more to say about
the comparison of universes, since we are always forced to speak
within the categories of our own language. But I dare to hope
that I can show a path which will lead out of that particular
circle, towards generalisation about kinds of universes. As a by-
product of the discussion there is a contribution to comparative
religion, because theodicy provides one of the most comprehensive explanatory systems and the argument will therefore be
most easily demonstrated by comparing religious doctrines.

Quine is a philosopher who has taken the anthropologist's
problems and materials very seriously. His *Word and Object*
(1960) is directed straight to the matter in hand and I cannot do
justice to the breadth of view and clarity with which it is discussed. His arguments are directed against many of our time-
honoured and favourite fallacies, from pre-logical mentality to
the idea that meaning is an independent, free floating entity,
which words try to capture more or less completely (1960:76).
Here I only need to summarise the argument that relates to
synonymy. The recognition of sameness is firmly anchored in
social experience: an individual in the community experiences
stimulus-synonymy, which approximates to sameness of confirm-
ing experiences and disconfirming experiences. Sameness of
meaning is traced to verbal habits which are determined by
community-wide collateral information. Thus we are given an
outline for the psychological and sociological basis for producing
words to which the same meanings are allocated. We are also
directed away from worrying about short synonyms towards the
longer and more complex ones. This is a relief. The most baffling

translations of foreign ideas are the shortest ones, presented out of context, as parts away from their wholes. The Bororo told von den Steinen in 1894 that they were parrots (Lévy-Bruhl, 1910). The Nuer say human twins are birds (Evans-Pritchard, 1956: 128–34). The Karam say that the cassowary is their sister's child (Bulmer, 1967). In certain specifiable contexts the animal or the human member of the class could be substituted, the one for the other, without affecting the meaning. But in the short synonym the translation of the copula 'is' has almost certainly been badly rendered. Edmund Leach has discussed Malinowski's refusal to recognise synonyms where the sameness escaped his own understanding. Each time the word *tabu* appeared as a kinship term Malinowski claimed that it was a homonym modified by context so that differences of meaning were conveyed.

> Malinowski (1935: p. 66ff.) spared his islanders the imputation of prelogicality by so varying his translations of terms, from occurrence to occurrence, as to side-step contradiction. Leach (p. 130) protested, but no clear criterion emerged. It is understandable that the further alternatives of blaming the translation of conjunctions, copulas or other logical particles is nowhere considered; for any considerable complexity on the part of the English correlates of such words would, of course, present the working translator with forbidding practical difficulties (Quine 1960: 58f.n.).

And so we are absolved. As it happens, Edmund Leach has successfully interpreted the sameness in the kinship relationships of the Trobrianders conveyed by the word *tabu* (1958: 120–45). So anthropology may have reached a stage at which the generous absolution for our neglect of logical particles may be less necessary. I certainly would prefer to discuss longer synonyms which would approximate 'to what it might mean "to speak of two statements as standing in the same germaneness, relating to the same particular experience"' (Quine, 1960, quoting Grice and Strawson 1956: 156). For example, 'in villages in Ceylon the fact that a woman cooks food for a man is a public statement of a conjugal relationship' (Tambiah, 1969). To cook for him is the same as cohabiting with him, 'she is his cook'='she is his wife'. This synonym, in any form, is not a puzzling one for us because of the overlap between our customs and theirs. The dividing line between cooks and wives is an unimportant one. The big mysteries arise when an important dividing line of meaning is ignored; when certain human categories, for example, are made synonymous with animal species. Then the short form has to be expanded into its longer form and the logical particles carefully examined. Surely there can be no recognition of sameness without a grasp of the logical relations which hold the class of things with the same meaning to the same particular experiences in the same way. For an account of recognising sameness I turn to Quine (1960:66–7):

> By an intuitive account I mean one in which terms are used in habitual ways without reflecting how they might be defined or what presuppositions they might conceal [Quine, 1960, note to p. 36]. Intuition figures in the case of analyticity despite the technical sound of the word; sentences like 'No unmarried man is married', 'No bachelor is married'. and '2 + 2 = 4' have a feel that everyone appreciates . . . one's reaction to denials of sentences typically felt as analytic has more in it of one's reaction to ungrasped foreign sentences. Where the sentence concerned is a law of logic, something of this reaction is discerned . . . dropping a logical law disrupts a pattern on which the communicative use of a logical particle heavily depends. . . .
>
> If the mechanism of analyticity intuitions is substantially as I have vaguely suggested, they will in general tend to set in where bewilderment sets in as to what the man who denies the sentence can be talking about. This effect can be gradual and also cumulative.

Avoiding bewilderment and experiencing bewilderment are the two extremes at which it is easy to see how logic bites into the emotional life. In between the extremes, the emotions are channelled down the familiar grooves cut by social relations and their requirements of consistency, clarity and reliability of expectations. I feel we should try to insert between the psychology of the individual and the public use of language, a dimension of social behaviour. In this dimension logical relations also apply. This is the nub of my contribution to how intuitions of self-evidence are formed. Persons are included in or excluded from a given class, classes are ranked, parts are related to wholes. It is argued here that the intuition of the logic of these social experiences is the basis for finding the *a priori* in nature. The pattern of social relations is fraught with emotional power; great stakes are invested in their permanence by some, in their overthrow by others. This is the level of experience at which the guts reaction of bewilderment at an unintelligible sentence is strengthened by potential fury, shock and loathing. Apprehending a general pattern of what is right and necessary in social relations is the basis of society: this apprehension generates whatever *a priori* or set of necessary causes is going to be found in nature. This 'pure, unreconstructed Durkheimianism', as a friend has called it, develops naturally from my earlier work on the idea of pollution (1966). There I tried to show how the world of nature is dragged into the arguments about society, and how it benefits each protagonist in the dialogue to refer to dangers from the allegedly objective system of causes out there. The issue now is to rescue the notion of intuition or guts reaction from any contrast with rationality by anchoring it in the experience the individual has of the logical properties of social forms.

Each universe is to be seen as a whole, generated with a particular kind of social experience. It may be objected that such an infinite number of possible classifications of nature operating for such a variety of social relations can be imagined that there is no sense in talking of universes as wholes. But the wholeness that concerns us lies in the finite range of favoured patternings of reality. I shall develop this argument with special reference to the treatment meted to borderline cases. The idea is that a continuum of social systems could be constructed in which, at one end, outsiders would be excluded completely and irrevocably, and working through various modifications, at the other extreme outsiders would be admitted to full membership of the community. Each point on the continuum would have its corresponding world of nature, with a characteristic way of dealing with hybrids and anomalous beings. Judgments that such and such creatures because they escape through the meshes of the local system of classification are contrary to nature, tend to evoke a further judgment. The monster in question may indeed be ignored. But equally it may be regarded as a vehicle of prosperity or of disaster. The judgment is made evident to the observer by rules about how it is to be treated when encountered. By this route we can rise to a higher level of formal comparison. Instead of talking about particular beliefs, say in unicorns or wombats, and instead of talking about causal systems or synonymy in general, we can identify distinctive predilections for agreeing certain kinds of self-evident propositions, each anchored in its correlated social environment.

By focusing on how anomalous beings may be treated in different systems of classification, we make a frontal attack on the question of how thought, words and the real world are related. Granted that the known world is socially constructed, no matter how flexible and subtle the principles of classification used, there will be some living beings which fit badly in the local taxonomic scheme. Bulmer and Tambiah give many different examples in their important essays on Karam and Thai classifications of animals, stressing the social nature of the taxonomic system. Creatures that emerge as anomalous on one could be perfectly acceptable on another. For example, Thai villages count domestic land animals as distinct from birds. As if they had no niche for domestic birds, ducks and chickens are counted land animals, their birdlike features notwithstanding. Land animals with wings suggest an anomaly to us, but they do not perceive it. On the other hand, the otter, like voles and seals, has no connotation of monstrosity for us: for the Thai it is a revolting hybrid, a fish as it were, with a head like a dog, a wild beast which invades their domestic fields in flood time. There are obviously as many kinds of anomaly as there are criteria for classifying. For the purpose in hand, it is enough to speak of creatures which in their morphology show criteria of more than one major class, or not enough criteria to enable them to be assigned to any one class, and of creatures which in themselves belong clearly enough to a recognised class but which have either the habits or which stray into the habitat of another class. An example of the first will be the pangolin or scaly ant-eater, honoured by the Lele as a tree-dwelling mammal with scales like a fish; of the second, the cassowary which Karam reckon has neither the feathers nor the brains of a bird; of the third, nocturnal antelopes distinguished by the Lele on account of this habit from other antelopes; of the fourth, the Thai view of the otter and the Nile monitor and other invasive creatures which stray out of the habitat to which they could be assigned on other criteria.

Any universe is liable to harbour monsters which straddle

across its major classes. But such creatures do not necessarily get any attention. If they are noticed, they can be judged very auspicious. Alternatively, they can inspire horror, aversion, disgust. When this is recorded, we have the strong guts reaction. Many are the Old Testament scholars content to explain the abominableness of creeping things in Leviticus 11 by a universal loathing of reptiles and insects, and to accept snakes being lumped together with the uncleanness of leprosy and death as a perfectly self-evident, unnecessary-to-explain collection of same meanings intelligible to all. But some religions pay cult to snakes and others associate them with fertility and the renewal of life. The Christian doctrine of the Incarnation insists that god-man belongs fully to two contrasted sets. For centuries the Israelites were in contact with Egyptian religion which venerated man-gods and god-beasts, and with the Assyrians likewise. But to the Israelites all hybrids and most mixtures were abominable. I have argued and believe that their abomination of creeping things was part of a larger habit of abominating beings which did not tidily conform to their established criteria of air, water and land creatures. And this was part again of a still larger pattern of social behaviour which used very clear, tight defining lines to distinguish two classes of human beings, the Israelites and the rest.

These remarks summarise too briefly the analysis I made of the Mosaic dietary laws in *Purity and Danger* (1966) and the fuller statement of the meanings enclosed in the Rabbinical interpretation of these laws, given in 'Deciphering a meal' (*Daedalus*, winter 1972). It will be easier to understand what follows after reading them, but probably the most important point to clarify if this essay is to stand alone is the status of the pig as a monster in the ancient Israelite classification system. The pig, in Leviticus 11, is put into the class of abominable unclean, creatures, along with the hare, the hyrax and the camel. The grounds alleged are that these creatures either cleave the hoof or chew the cud, but do not do both. In other words, they don't quite make it into the class of ungulates. By itself, seen from the viewpoint of another pattern of classification, having some but not all the criteria of the class of edible animals would not make them automatically unclean, revolting, abominable. But this classification system, throughout, in all its application, picks on the borderline instance and tags it abominable. The meaning of clean and unclean only gets its full resonance when the classification of the whole universe is complete. When the scheme is drawn in its totality, one of the criteria of cleanness is revealed which before was hidden: the clean species must have all the necessary criteria of its class. To the three major habitats, air, land, water, is assigned a mode of locomotion proper to the clean species inhabiting each one. Conversely, each species must have the necessary physiological characteristics for locomotion in its habitat, fins in the water, wings and two legs in the air, four legs on the land. Creeping things have a mode of locomotion which is not distinctive of any one element: their existence confounds the tidy logical scheme of things: this marks them abominable. The pig, with the right mode of locomotion to get into the same class as sheep, goats and cattle, does not chew the cud. It is the only non-cud-chewing hoof-cleaver in the whole of creation, a monster with no other judgment possible of its improper, law-defying existence than outright abomination.

In *Purity and Danger* I supposed that the Hebrew response of

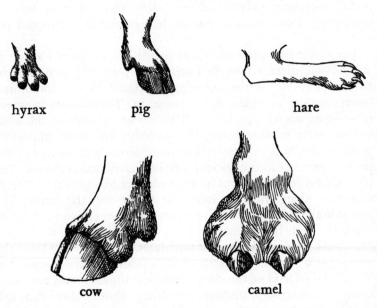

hyrax   pig   hare

cow   camel

Figure 17.1

rejecting anomaly was the normal one. I argued that to classify is a necessary human activity and that there is a universal human tendency to pass adverse judgment on that which eludes classification or refuses to fit into the tidy compartments of the mind. A too facile solution. I failed to exploit the full interest of the contrast between my fieldwork in the Congo and my library research in the Bible. For the Lele, many anomalies are auspicious and they religiously celebrate the most anomalous of all, which carries defining marks of land and water creatures, humans and animals, the pangolin or scaly ant-eater. On the other hand on this showing, every anomaly conceived according to the Biblical classification of nature is a defiling monster (Douglas, 1966). I swept under the carpet, as too difficult for my theorising, the contrast between the abominable pig and the revered pangolin. Bulmer (1967) and Tambiah (1969), who have pointed out these and other shortcomings, have also made such signal advances in their own analyses of animal taxonomy that I am ready, thanks to their work, to have another try. Foul monster or good saviour, the judgment has little to do with the physical attributes of the being in question and much to do with the prevailing social pattern of rules and meanings which creates anomaly. I shall now try to discover the properties of a classification system which will not overlook anomalies, and which, having recognised them, attributes to them efficacy either for evil or for good. Such a response to a mixed category is essentially a gut reaction. It judges the creature at a fundamental level which brooks no question, either to be divinity or to be abominable. The two studies, Tambiah's of north-east Thailand, Bulmer's on the Karam in the New Guinea Highlands, both demonstrate how the classification of animals is imbued with strong social concerns. In each case the taxonomy organises nature so that the categories of animals mirror and reinforce the social rules about marriage and residence. We have known since *Primitive Classification* (Durkheim and Mauss, 1903) and after Lévi-Strauss (1962) we shall never forget that totemic systems of thought stand in this relation to the social system. But it is one thing to know, another to apply. I myself failed to apply this knowledge to my own interpretation of Lele taxonomy. I was able to translate the game-warden's zoological classification into Lele terms and describe the categories which the animals' morphology and behaviour suggested to the Lele. I was able then to relate this native taxonomy to their cult associations. When it came to relating these two levels of realisation (the organising of the world of nature and the organising of cults) to other levels in which meaning is generated, it seemed enough to say there were oppositions and tensions in Lele society which the pangolin cult figuratively transcended as the animal itself transcended the boundaries of animal kinds (Douglas, 1957). Luc de Heusch developed the theme more richly in a re-analysis of my material.

On peut se demander pourquoi cette synthèse socio-religieuse se situe sous le signe du pangolin. Le Pangolin est le médiateur par excellence entre le monde humain et le monde animal. A l'intérieur du monde humain l'écart significatif qui oppose le clan matrilinéaire (univers tendu de la 'fraternité') au groupe d'âge (univers agréable du compagnonnage, assiette du village) reproduit à moindre échelle l'écart primordial qui existe, aux yeux, des Lele, entre la nature et la culture. De ce point de vue, les Hommes-pangolins *au village* et les pangolins *en forêt* occupent des positions homologues. L'une des conditions d'initiation est d'avoir tué un pangolin en forêt; le rituel implique l'absorption de la chair de cet animal. Un rapport de contiguité s'établit donc entre les Hommes-pangolins et les pangolins. Les premiers sont médiaturs entre les deux composantes antagonistes de la société d'une part, entre l'homme et la femme d'autre part; les seconds sont médiateurs, plus généralement, entre la culture et la nature. L'activité rituelle des Hommes-pangolins intéresse à la fois la chasse (activité masculine) et la fécondité des femmes, alors que les sphères socio-économiques propre aux deux sexes sont rigoureusement séparées ... la femme et l'homme, le clan et le village, la diachronie et la synchronie réalisent une synthèse harmonieuse, difficile et rare (de Heusch, 1964:87 – 109).

At the time we were both satisfied with this result. In their social life the Lele achieved a difficult synthesis: the mediating powers of the pangolin celebrated the synthesis and its cult contributed to it. However, there is a kind of smug incuriosity which is content to analyse a symbolic system until it is phrased in terms of a universal contrast between nature and culture without specifying the particularities of the case in hand. There are different kinds of synthesis, yet not all are expressed by cults of mediators: the problem needs to be posed comparatively.

In north-east Thailand and in New Guinea, Bulmer and Tambiah convincingly demonstrate that the interpretation of the natural world is dominated by incest rules and tense relations with in-laws. If the otter in the flooded rice-fields was a foul monster to the Thai villagers it was because it doubly and even trebly imaged disordered sex, the forbidden incestuous partner. The cassowary in the taro plots was tabooed for the Karam, an image of encroaching, untrustworthy affines. The strength of feeling about both animals derived from the strength with which violent passions were contained, passions which flowed in the same pattern which identified these animals with critical phases in human affairs. No need in these two analyses to explain the local attitude to these animals in terms exogenous to the social system under study. By contrast analysis of the pangolin's meaning had little to do with giving and taking in marriage. Yet the Lele were obsessed with the competition for wives; abductions and vengeance were daily preoccupations; they used to fight continually and always for women; their political units were riven by strife. In the light of this other research, the earlier explanations seemed inadequate and some aspects of the later arguments of *Purity and Danger* worse still. There I fell back on the universal human experience of classification and posited a universal human need to recognise its facticity and to transcend it by mediating cults (1966: 159–79). Luc de Heusch (1971) pointed out the difficulties in that argument. On their own showing the Lele categories of spirit animals were not necessarily anomalous or disgusting and their attitude of suspicion towards the anomalous flying squirrel had not made it into a spirit-animal. But even with such detailed criticism, the answer came slowly and was difficult.

The question about the meaning of the Lele pangolin cult had first to be sunk in the wider question about the response to hybrids and anomalous beings. It is rather the question of why Egypt and Mesopotamia should have paid cult to divine animals, man-birds, man-gods, and not Israel. Lévi-Strauss has suggested a natural propensity of mythical thought which postulates mediating existences (1958:227–55). Following this idea in the analysis of the Garden of Eden story, Edmund Leach (1969: 11) remarks:

> Mediation (in this sense) is always achieved by introducing a third category which is 'abnormal' or 'anomalous' in terms of ordinary 'rational' categories. Thus myths are full of fabulous monsters, incarnate gods, virgin mothers. This middle ground is abnormal, non-natural, holy. It is typically the focus of all taboo and ritual observance.

In the first place it is not the case that all taboo and ritual observance are typically focused on the abnormal; I have already argued that cognitive categories are made external and visible by taboos (1966). As part of an entirely rational process by which categories of thought are stabilised, taboo marks off those experiences which defy classification. Any reflection on any ethnography about taboo shows that these latter are not the only focus of taboo. Many taboos take the form of do-not-touch rules which protect the normal social structure and moral code. Critics of *Purity and Danger* were quick to point out that possible confusion between different kinds of taboo situation (Ardener, 1967: 139; de Heusch, 1971: 10–12). If taboo is to be treated simply and only as a reaction to the abnormal, the non-natural, the holy as opposed to ordinary 'rational' categories, we are no nearer understanding it than were the nineteenth-century anthropologists. In the second place, less plausibly, there is the suggestion that the human mind always and everywhere tends to invent mediating existences to reconcile oppositions. If such a tendency is found in the structure of myth, its presence is often the result of analytic procedures which place it there. Between myth-making and taboo, between recitative and practical situations, we find a puzzle of our own making. If the one bias causes us to accept anomaly and the other to reject it, neither can be taken seriously as an account of how the human mind works. More to the point to recognise the monstrous beings discovered in myth as the product of fully rational analytic and synthesising procedures and the monstrosity-rejecting behaviour of taboo as part of the process of constituting meanings in practical daily life. Both are therefore to be understood by rational procedures of enquiry, according to the approach here advocated, whereas the argument which appeals to a tendency to invent mediators closes enquiry.

Since we are interested centrally in how meanings are constituted, we would do well to avoid mythical material. Apart from being notoriously pliant to the interpreter's whim, it is thought in relatively free play. Myth sits above and athwart the exigencies of social life. It is capable of presenting one picture and then its opposite. We are on more solid ground by concentrating on beliefs which are invoked explicitly to justify behaviour. The more inconvenient the rules of behaviour and the more pervasive their alleged effect, the more weight should be attached to the beliefs invoked to uphold them. With this principle of selection we can turn again to the fact that some cultures accept the possibility of good mediation between man and nature and some do not. For it provides a guarantee that the beliefs under study are taken seriously by the people who act upon them. Thus we avoid the charge of subjective interpretation.

My general argument supposes that in each constructed world of nature, the contrast between man and not-man provides an analogy for the contrast between the member of the human community and the outsider. In the last most inclusive set of categories, nature represents the outsider. If the boundaries defining membership of the social group have regulated crossing points where useful exchanges take place, then the contrast of man and nature takes the imprint of this exchange. The number of different exchanges envisaged, their possible good and bad outcomes and the rules which govern them are all projected on to the natural world. If the institutions allow for some much more generous and rewarding exchange with more than normally distant partners, then we have the conditions for a positive mediator. If all exchanges are suspect and every outsider is a threat, then some parts of nature are due to be singled out to represent the abominable intruder who breaches boundaries that should be kept intact. In sum, the argument here advanced is that when boundary-crossing is . forbidden, a theology of mediation is not acceptable, and that every theology of mediation finds its adherents in a society which expects to do well out of regulated exchange.

To demonstrate the imprinting upon nature of the rules and

categories which are dominant in social life, I turn again in single detail to Ralph Bulmer's analysis of Karam animal kinds. When he tries to understand why the Karam count the cassowary as a game animal and not a bird he is led to piece together the rules which set the creature apart. Note that the rules are part of a general causal theory. If they are not obeyed, root crops

Figure 17.2

wither and nut crops rot. One of the rules prevents the cassowary from being domesticated. Though other neighbouring peoples do so, Karam believe that the cassowary is a creature whose eggs they cannot hatch and whose young will not thrive if they try to rear them in the village. So it remains by this rule and belief in the class of wild creatures which are hunted for their meat. When the hunt is successful, the hunter who has killed a cassowary has to observe a period of pollution and undergo long rites of purification as if for killing a man. The rites are only slightly modified for the cassowary. When he slays a man, to purify himself he must eat the heart of a pig. When he slays a cassowary he must eat his victim's heart. Modified rites for homicide pollution are required for killing two kinds of marsupials and the dog. The rule places these three animal kinds inside the set for humans. Killed humans have full rites, killed animals have no rites, killed cassowary, dog and marsupial have modified rites. Thus a bend is made in the line between man and nature to accommodate those beasts on the human side. When it comes to killing the cassowary, the rules require the hunter to club it with the butt of his spear, a risky enterprise. It is forbidden to shed its blood, so no sharp weapon is used. The same rule applies to killing dogs, should this be necessary. Apart from turning the hunt into a well-matched combat, this rule brings the cassowary and the dog further into the set of humans, for it also applies to a very small set of humans: sharp weapons may not be turned against kinsmen. Thus for all other humans and animals there is unrestricted killing. Only the dog, the cassowary and the kinsman constitute the set in which bloodshed is forbidden. Then a further restriction locates the cassowary (without the dog this time) in a still smaller set of humans. When the Karam go to hunt the cassowary they must use a special language which avoids common names. For example, instead of the word for cassowary, it is referred to as 'mother of game mammals'. It is the language they use for speaking to their affines and cross-cousins. For all other humans and all other animals no special language is required: only for the cassowary and those close relatives by marriage, language is restricted. The answer to why the cassowary is identified with these affines and cross-cousins lies in the total system of animal and vegetable classification and the further application of analogous rules. The special language rule also applies when collecting pandanus nuts (see Figure 17.3). To explain this we need Bulmer's notion of 'special taxonomic status', which presupposes a system in which each major class in nature is represented by one species. The cassowary as a species is

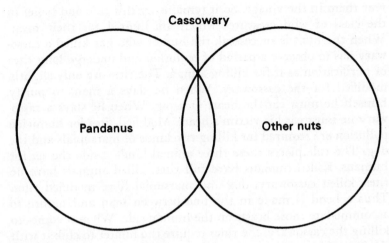

Figure 17.3 Karam: kinship model of wild nuts propagated by cassowary

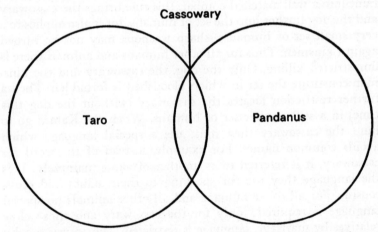

Figure 17.4 Karam: avoidance rules relate wild and cultivated crops to cassowary on model of human society

singled out from all the other game animals. Similarly, in the vegetable kingdom, the pandanus palm is treated as a prime wild crop, counterpoised against the prime cultivated crop, taro (see Figure 17.4). Rules create an avoidance situation between the

game animals and the human food crops in a form that recalls
the avoidance between in-laws. The cassowary must be kept out
of the village when the taro is grown, and it must not be eaten in
the taro planting and growing season. Otherwise (a causal con-
nexion) the taro will not grow. Karam believe that wild palms are
propagated naturally by passing through the digestive system of
wild game animals, including the cassowary. They do not plant
pandanus palms and believe that they would not grow if they
tried to do so. Thus the natural generation of forest species
contrasts (thanks to these rules and beliefs) with the human
planting and tending of crops and feeding of pigs and dogs. The
game animals and wild plants are related by a system of natural
affinity and descent. The cassowary is made to represent the
natural affine, nature's sister and sister's child. It bestrides the
boundary between vegetable and animal. It not only links up the
descent groups of game animals (through being classed as their
mother) with the wild nuts it propagates, but furthermore, it
comes right out across the boundaries between wild and cultivated, animal and human, to be classed, on a kinship model, as
an affinal link between man and nature. For it is made to relate
to the prime cultivated crop by a replication of the avoidance
rules for affines. The same representative of the wild animals
bears the same relation to two contrasted systems of vegetable
propagation, one natural, one cultivated. By these rules the
cassowary becomes a kind of mediator but not unequivocally
good. It is a mediator to be treated warily and honourably. This
becomes clear when the tricky relation between Karam affines is
known. I quote from Bulmer (1967: 18) that they depend on their
sisters' children for help, but always fear that they will try to
grab their land.

> Because of the dense population and the shortage of taro land
> in the mountainous country, the Karam, commuting between
> highland and valleys, depend on their affines for help in taro
> cultivation and the giving of feasts. The cousin relation is one
> which wavers between close dependence, risk that the cousin
> will try to take over the taro garden, and finally at worst, fear
> that he may be practising witchcraft and so become the enemy
> who has to be killed, but killed with a blunt instrument
> because he is a kinsman. Your cross-cousins are the people with

moral claims on you which you are nevertheless sometimes quite reluctant to meet: and whose names you should not say. You cannot keep your real cross-cousins out of your inheritance, or out of your taro gardens, at least not unless and until you are beginning to suspect witchcraft and to consider homicide. How appropriate that you should treat your metaphorical cross-cousins, the cassowaries, with due respect when you kill them, and make entirely sure that they never come anywhere near your taro.

Only by applying the kinship model and so drawing a series of homologies can the various rules yield sense (Figure 17.5). First, the Karam social world pivots between ego's agnates and ego's

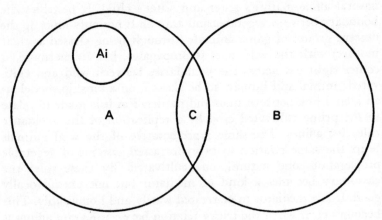

Figure 17.5 Karam social world

A {
A   My kinsmen
Ai My agnates
C   My sister's children,
    affines and cross-cousins
B {
    Non-kinsmen of mine,
    kinsmen of persons
    in C.

Avoidance rules
Restricted weapons apply to A+C
Restricted speech applies to C only
A+C=ego's total range of relations
         by consanguinity and affinity

affines. My affines and sister's children, picked out by the special language avoidance, are related to me and also to other groups of agnates. I suspect them of trying to sequester my land, the basis of my social existence. The same picture applies to the wild vegetable world, represented by the prime wild nut, and its relation to other wild nut species, both propagated by the cassowary and other game animals. Any crossing or blurring of the boundary between cultivated and wild will have effects on the plants equivalent to the loss of its land for an agnatic unit. Both forms of plant life have to avoid the same creature, since the cassowary may not be eaten in their planting and gathering seasons respectively and the in-law avoidance language must be used. The logical picture of the avoidance rule manifests the cassowary and the affine or sister in the same form. Bulmer's rich material has encouraged him to emphasise the role that man-made rules play in setting up the causal system. He has thus thrown light on the force of habit by which causal connexions are imposed on nature. His notion of 'special taxonomic status' could be greatly developed. It has to be a status derived from a social category which it represents. It figures in a logical picture or formal pattern which is replicated over and over again. There must be many kinds of special taxonomic status according to the kinds of social pattern which the taxonomies depict. In this case, the two opposed social categories are agnates and affines. The agnates are seen as vulnerable to the encroaching demands of persons linked to them through females: their labour is very desirable but their greed for land is a menace. With such conflicting and intensely felt goals, Karam understandably would find anomalies in nature to show forth their dilemma. The cassowary is no saviour. Nor is it an abomination. Its status is exactly the honourable but untrustworthy one of the Karam affine. Here the interpretation of nature clearly reflects the dominant system of exchanges. The study of native taxonomic systems can never be the same after this cogent demonstration. But we are still in the stance of Lévy-Bruhl, looking from afar at a primitive mentality.

And what about the Lele pangolin and what about the pig in Judaism? Some big planks in the theoretical bridge are still missing. Bulmer's is a work of translation. He translates from the categories in which nature is thought to the categories in which social life is lived, the one into the other and back again. The next challenge is to go beyond the translation job to examining the properties of classification systems as such. My wish has always been to take seriously Durkheim's idea that the properties of classification systems derive from and are indeed properties of the social systems in which they are used. The questions Durkheim suggested were: how fuzzy are the boundaries of the categories? How well insulated the meanings they enclose? (1903:6–7). How many categories are there? Are the principles relating them to each other systematic? If there is a system of thought, how stable is it? (1903:35–41). These questions can be addressed to our own thought processes.

But the questions about classification systems have to be well-matched by questions about the social systems that generate them. We cannot shirk the problem of finding a relevant classification of human societies.

Recall that the argument depends on a scale of readiness to do exchange. The boundaries of the categories of nature are expected to show a parallel with the inclusions and rejections permitted on social boundaries. Where society is based on the structuring of birth and marriage, the most significant exchanges will concern transfers of women. Ideally the thesis should be capable of being illustrated from those societies which anthropologists traditionally study and from which the puzzles of kinship theory derive. The examples I have to discuss clearly fall into each of the two recognised categories of kinship system. The Lele are in the class of elementary structures, since they enjoin marriage between the children of cross-cousins.[1]

The Karam are in the class of complex forms of kinship, since they only use the negative prohibition of incest to regulate their marriage alliances. Their rules, complicated by the distribution of bridewealth and land in each generation, end by ruling out many second cousins and third cousins.[2]

The Israelites fall also into the class of complex forms, but not in a way which is described or anticipated in alliance theory. For, on my reading of the list of prohibited degrees, they are an instance of those numerous peoples[3] who have no rule to ensure a wide network of alliance.

In all three cases we are interested in the extent to which the operation of the marriage rules allows for the incorporation of strangers into the circle of kinsmen. How the rules are worked is contingent on politics and practice. As I read it, the Lele are the most open to foreign alliance, the Israelites the least, and the Karam come somewhere in between. This interpretation goes beyond the basic rules to their mode of operation.

I have already summarised the case of the Karam. Now for the Lele: everything in the Lele working of their rules turns them to hope for sons-in-law or brides from distant places or along half-forgotten genealogical links going several generations back. Clan exogamy applies to the father's and to the mother's clan. Every village contains some members of four or five clans or more. Since every mother aims to keep her daughter by her side and every girl hopes to marry her first sweetheart in the village of her birth, the rules of exogamy by themselves would not frustrate their wishes. The village would become an endogamous unit. However, positive rules of exchange entitle a man to ask for his daughter's daughter in marriage, for himself or for another member of his clan.

His claim is based on the honour due to a son-in-law. All small populations are demographically vulnerable. The group that is recruited by matrilineal descent is doubly so (as I have argued elsewhere (1969: 121–35)). The Lele have written into their culture an awareness of demographic risk for the local section of the clan. For the Pangolin cult is a privileged membership open only to men who return to live in the village which their own clan founded. Its honours call them back and check the fractioning and disappearance of local clan units. Furthermore each clan honours the man who begets its female children. The affine then is counterpoised to ego's clan in a wholly positive sense, with none of the anxiety and suspicion which the Karam affines arouse. Once he has begotten a daughter, her clan owes him the right to dispose in marriage of his daughter's daughter. A man may make a similar claim on his son's daughter. The status of grandfather then becomes a permanent relation of alliance by marriage between the clans of three men who have a say in the allocation of a girl: her father's father's clan, her own clan, and her mother's father's clan. The tussle between these three and the use of girls for settling blood debts and other debts ensure that the women's preference, which I observed, for local and village endogamy, was overruled. Women were widely exchanged and links of permanent in-lawship established all over the country. So much was the system committed to wide-ranging exchange that no one clan would have been stably associated with any one village were it not for other rules which gave cult and political privileges to members of founding clans and further privileges to offspring of their intermarriage. This widespread exchange of women did not of itself break down the political barriers between enemy villages. Marriage alliance did not make links freely through the entire society. Each small village was autonomous. It had its allies and traditional enemies. The movements of population normally flowed down sharply cut political grooves rather than across them. A girl demanded in payment for an offence against an enemy village would be less likely to be paid over than between friendly villages. Forcible abduction would be the rule in the case of the enemy village. But a girl stolen to settle a debt still had her clansmen. For them the rule of honouring the son-in-law was still valid; moreover, the right of her father to claim one of her daughters was still valid, though enmity between the villages would make it difficult to enforce. The Lele adjusted to this. A political abduction was made into a political marriage. The girl became the wife, not of one man, but of the age-set of her abductors. The whole village took on the legal role of husband and legal father to her children. Anyone who would claim her daughter in marriage would become the son-in-law of the whole village. His courtship and groom-service would be fittingly arduous; his marriage-payments appropriately splendid. The son-in-law of the village had diplomatic immunity, a role of political go-between and great honour, both in the village of his origin and in the village from which he had taken his wife. In due course, when his own daughter had grown up, his in-laws would claim the rights of a grandfather and demand for the village a girl in return. Thus the feud could be turned into an alliance, but not necessarily an effective one. Seen in this light and in the perspective of what has gone before, the Lele system of politics and marriage gave them experience of dangerous exchanges with hostile groups in which the first most precious bargain was to obtain a woman, and the next was the possibility of a continuing supply of daughter's daughters and the last was the chance of a permanent alliance through generalised exchange of women. And all these prospects were mediated through the role of the son in-law, honoured in his own right, doubly honoured as the son-in-law of the sovereign village, trebly honoured as the third generation matrilineal descendant of a former son-in-law become grandfather.

Consistently, one should expect a role of double odium in the social system where double pollution is found in nature – and conversely. The Lele son-in-law of the village enjoyed double and treble honour since in him the system of exchange might profitably transcend all its boundaries. I would not go so far as to say that the son-in-law of the village was represented by the pangolin. But that the pangolin cult explicitly attracted back to the village sons-in-law who had been born in distant parts, and so reconstituted the relation of founding clan to village is an inescapable conclusion that I have put on record (1963). At most I am supposing that these rules of marriage with their political penalties and rewards are to be found imprinted upon the categories of nature. The same Lele set up both the exchanges of women, the fragile patterning of villages and clans, and their own theory of causality. So I argue that their experience of mediation in marriage and political alliance allows them to imagine an effective religious mediator.

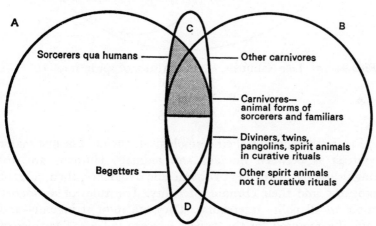

Figure 17.6 Lele:

    A Humans (living)
    B Animals
    C Dead sorcerers   } non-
    D Other dead humans and spirits } corporeal

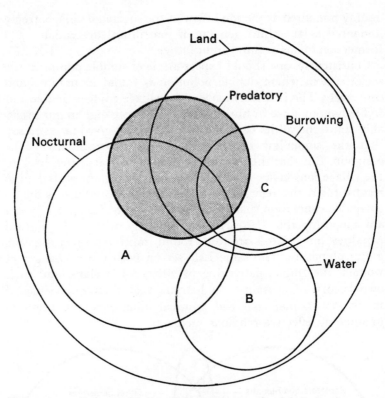

Figure 17.7 Lele: animals. Characteristics of spirit animals:
  A Nocturnal
  B Water
  C Burrowing

Figure 17.6 sums up their cosmological scheme. The first major contrast is between humans and animals. Humans are distinguished by their rules of shame and avoidance, their rules of exogamy and their chronic infertility. The rules of avoidance apply to all polite intercourse. They are most stringently and typically required for the respect between in-laws. The rules of exogamy give the underlying structure to the exchanges of women. The infertility refers partly to the demographic instability of small matrilineal descent groups. Infertility is moreover a dominant concern for their ritual and medical practice. In each of these respects, animals are held in contrast: they are incestuous, shameless and prolific. Certain humans and animals cross these boundaries and appear as members of the other set. Sorcerers take on the form of leopards; diviners do likewise to counteract sorcery. Other carnivorous animals are sorcerers' familiars who come into the village to do their treacherous work for them. Under one aspect the human world is divided between those who are vulnerable (women, babies, sterile men) and those who attack their fertility (sorcerers) and those who defend them against sorcery (the diviners). A neutral group are the men who have proof of their fertility, the initiated begetters. Their status is signalled by the rule that only they can safely eat the young of animals, the chest of animals, and carnivores, meat which would kill anyone else. Outside the class of living humans, the vicious spirits of dead sorcerers are opposed by the spirits of neutral dead humans and benevolent nature spirits (Figure 17.7). Likewise, the rules divide the animal world into three classes, ordinary animals, carnivorous animals and spirit animals. The killing and ritual consumption of specific spirit animals is a central part of their prospering rituals. The category of spirit animals is constituted by two major criteria, non-predatory and water-inhabiting (fish and wild pig are prime examples) and two secondary criteria, burrowing and nocturnal. These classes sometimes overlap: nocturnal habits are a sign of spirit because the spirit world reverses the order of humans; burrowing suggests co-habitation with the dead; water means fertility. Some spirit animals are counted as dangerous food for all except the appropriate group of diviners; others are dangerous to pregnant women or to any-one undergoing treatment for infertility; others are prohibited in other curative rites. I would draw attention to another aspect of this classification. Whenever a species is allocated by its observed behaviour to one habitat or the other, if one of its sub-species by its behaviour strays into the class of spirit animals they pay special and favourable attention to the anomalous sub-class. This applies to cases of land animals who show water-loving habits. Wild pig is a spirit animal because (unlike other land mammals) it loves to wallow in the boggy sources of streams. Other primates avoid the water but the baboon loves to wash so it is counted a spirit animal. Antelopes are land animals, but one kind hides from the hunters by sinking deep into the water. Antelopes are mostly day feeders; one which feeds by night and sleeps by day is therefore a spirit animal. In sum, the Lele are extremely interested in boundary-crossing whenever they observe it. They associate it with good unless it bears the predatory mark of sorcery. Spirit species are specially favourable exceptions to the course of nature. Since squirrels with birds and monkeys are in the class of sky-creatures commonly prescribed for the diet of pregnant women, the flying squirrel does not cross any major classificatory boundary. An amphibian species of flying squirrel would be another matter. The most extraordinary boundary-crosser of their universe is the pangolin. A scaly fish-like tree-dweller, it bows its head like a man avoiding his mother-in-law. As a mammal which brings forth its young singly, it evidently does not share the fecundity which distinguishes animals from mankind. This anomaly mediates between humans and spirits and assures fertility. In human society the sexually potent son-in-law by his begetting is counterpoised against the destructive sorcerer. In nature the pangolin and the leopard have the special taxonomic status which this general vision of social life imposes. Thus Bulmer has helped me to complete my own translation of different levels of reality and to solve questions posed from my material by penetrating critics. I am now able to hear the meanings of Lele animal terms resonate with a more powerful charge through larger ranges of their experience than at first suspected.

For the more general problem of a taxonomy of classification systems I would like to think we now have two demonstration cases. The Lele expect to do well out of their system of exchanges: they have a welcome for the outsider who walks peacefully into their camp. The Karam have reason to be more pessimistic about their exchanges: their attitude to anomalies reflects their general caution. Both tribes allow the line between culture and nature to be crossed; the crossing places are guarded with rules. The rules represent theories of causality: either they ward off dangerous effects or they channel desirable ones.

Before turning to the Israelites, let me complete the accepted scheme of kinship structures by mentioning the Crow-Omaha which are distinguished from the elementary structures by using only the negative rules of incest and exogamy to organise their pattern of alliances, but using them so forcefully to define such a wide range of non-marriageable kin that the circulation of women through the entire system is ensured without setting up prescribed categories of partners (Lévi-Strauss, 1966: 19):

> the generalised definition of a Crow-Omaha system may best be formulated by saying that whenever a descent line is picked up to provide a mate, all individuals belonging to that line are excluded from the range of potential mates from the first lineage, during a period covering several generations. Since this process repeats itself with each marriage, the system is kept in a state of permanent turbulence which is quite the reverse of that regularity of functioning and periodicity of returns which conform with the ideal model of an asymmetric marriage system.

Any such system, where a possibility of close intermarriage is very unlikely, has one result in common with the elementary structures with which it is contrasted in principle. Both structures of kinship allow the outsider to be brought in as a son-in-law to join the intimate circle of kinsmen. For the marriageable kin prescribed in the elementary structures are general categories which include distant classifications as well as close relations. On my argument it will be easier in both these types of structure (if they are worked as the Lele work theirs) to make identifications which go across the boundary separating human and animal. These are the tribes which marry their enemies, in which it makes sense to say that a man is a red parrot or a twin a bird. For it is argued that the greater the social distance between ego and marriageable persons, the stronger the sense of exchange between known and unknown. In such cases we predict a taxonomic system which draws a favourable attention to anomaly, since the offspring of the marriages are by birth half-known and half-unknown.

The Israelites' rules of marriage allowed them to marry their first cousins. Therefore the distinction between cross and parallel kinsmen, the one distinction which Lévi-Strauss takes to be fundamental to kinship (1966: 16) here is bereft of meaning. When the wife's brother is father's brother's son and in the class of husband's brothers, there is not exchange or alliance by marriage, but in-marrying, a denial of the value of exchange. Here again, as always, the rule itself says nothing without an account of how it is interpreted. Of this, more below, but note how different the ancient Israelite view of nature as shown in the final editing and interpreting of the Pentateuch. Here no anomalies are tolerated. Every living being that appears inconsistently across instead of within the lines of their classification is firmly marked anomalous and hustled into a special, excluded, sub-set.[4] In a paper which has to be treated as part of the evidence for the present argument, I have recently analysed the Israelite rules for altar and table as a particular type of classification system (Douglas, 1972). When its processes of inclusion and identification have been worked through, the result is a series of concentric circles, each larger boundary reinforcing the inner one, each inner one enclosing yet another. Everything that seems eligible to stand across any of the boundaries is picked out and put into the set of defilement. Our speculations about the kind of social intention which organises its universe in this way are straightforward. Here is a people who prefer their boundaries to remain intact. They reckon any attempt to cross them a hostile intrusion. They expect no good to come of external exchange and have no rules for facilitating it. When they think of their social organisation in spatial terms they set the holiest place within several concentric boundaries. The tribes of Israel, when they camped, were to group on each side of the holy tent in which God revealed his presence. The closest area round the tent was occupied by Levites (Numbers 2:17), Judah to the east, Ephraim to the west, on the north the camp of Dan, on the south the camp of Reuben (Ackroyd, 1970:160). A similar concern to enclose the temple with triple boundaries shows in the geographical layout of Ezekiel's new land (Ackroyd, 1970:103). The boundaries keep out the profane. The sons of Aaron were to avoid all strong drink, because they were 'to distinguish between the holy and the common, and between the unclean and the clean' (Leviticus 10:10). Being holy means being set apart. The Israelites cherish their boundaries and want nothing better than to keep them strong and high.

Blessed art thou, O Lord our God, King of the Universe, who makes a distinction between holy and profane, between light and darkness, between Israel and other nations, between the seventh day and the six working days. Blessed art thou, O

Lord, who makest a distinction between holy and profane [from the Habdalah Service contemporary to our own day].

Inside the boundaries is a small political unit, a people surrounded by powerful, rapacious enemies. Defections and infiltrations are familar in its history. Its boundaries are never strong enough. There is no rule requiring them to exchange their womenfolk, either with other lineages, or between their own tribes, still less with foreigners. The critical problems arise with the definition of a foreigner, especially of people who claim some of the criteria of common descent, but not all. Leach (1969: 47–9) has argued

> Even the formal rule book (Deuteronomy 23) equivocates about just how foreign is a foreigner. Edomites (and more surprisingly Egyptians) are not to be abhorred . . .
> The children that are begotten of them shall enter into the congregation of the Lord in their third generation. Ammonites and Moabites, on the other hand, are absolutely tainted, 'even to their tenth generation they shall not enter the congregation of the Lord for ever'. Thus, even for the Patriarchs the distinction Israelite/foreigner was not a clear-cut matter of black and white but a tapering off through various shades of grey. The reason for this must be sought in later circumstances. The Jewish sectarians of the late historical Jerusalem were surrounded not only by foreigners, who were unqualified heathen, but also by semi-foreigners, such as the Samaritans who claimed to be Israelites like themselves. How strictly should the rules of endogamy apply in such cases?

If this is correct, it records a deep concern with the element which shows some but not sufficient criteria for membership of a class. The classification which counts abominable the beasts which either chew the cud or cleave the hoof but not both is isomorphic with the other classification of Israelites which does not object to intermarriage with female captives of far distant foes (Deuteronomy, 20: 14–18) but worries about the prospect of intermarriage with half-blooded Israelites. The pig attracts, with the camel, the hare and rock-badger, the odium of half-eligibility for table and sacrifice. Worse, it is the only one of the four which cleaves the hoof. According to my analysis worked out in *Purity and Danger*, mode of locomotion is a major defining criterion.

Edmund Leach (1969: 36) points out that Lévi-Strauss took the same view. By its cloven feet the pig nearly gets into the class of ungulates, hence a double odium. A further association with the undesirable marriage lies in the fact that the people of Israel, whether in exile, or before, or afterwards, were never living apart from foreigners and they must have frequently succumbed to the temptation to marry foreign girls. How else did the resident Canaanites come to be absorbed? In the relevant periods, betrothal to a foreigner was certain to be celebrated with feasting in breach of the Mosaic rules. But far more likely to appear on the table than the camel, the hare and the rock-badger was the domesticated pig. So we move towards understanding its special taxonomic status.

In the Thailand animal system, the double pollution of sexual disorder is opposed to the double blessing of controlled virility. The Thai villagers treat the buffalo as a metaphor of ordered sexual energy. Tethered at night under the sleeping quarters, yoked for work in the day, the buffalo is reserved for the most important sacrifices. Rules which require it to be given for sacrifice in other households than its own echo the rules of marriage exchange. The noble buffalo is opposed in their thoughts to the ignoble dog: chased out of the sleeping quarters, its name used in sexual insults, the symbol of sex out of place and out of control. But more than the dog, the otter when it swims into the fields in flood time, as an invasive dog-like monster from the wild, appears as the full polar opposite of the domestic buffalo. A double anomaly, it incurs double odium. By the same arguments, the pig reared by Gentiles for food would seem to stand in the Hebrew taxonomy as doubly opposed to the perfect sacrificial victim, the beast without bodily blemish, and of equally perfect pedigree. I leave out the Thai villages from what follows. Their Buddhism involves them in importations and transactions with other cultures which place them beyond my limited comparisons.

Three social types, the Israelites, the Karam and the Lele, provide us with three types of classification system. In the first, exchange is not desired; all anomalies are bad and classed in a special sub-set expected to unleash disastrous chains of cause and effect. In the next, exchange is necessary but risky; anomalies are ambivalent, the rules that hedge them prevent dangerous effects. In the third, some exchange is reckoned clearly good, some is bad; anomalies likewise; the rules for approaching and avoiding them are the means for triggering off good effects. In this way the sociological specification for accepting a mediator is elucidated. A people who have nothing to lose by exchange and everything to gain will be predisposed towards the hybrid being, wearing the conflicting signs, man/god or man/beast. A people whose experience of foreigners is disastrous will cherish perfect categories, reject exchange and refuse doctrines of mediation.

This admittedly speculative idea has implications for the history of religion. To justify putting it forth, the interpretation of the Israelite classifications needs to be located in historical time. What is agreed in Biblical scholarship needs to be separated from what is controversial. The only place and time to which I can safely refer is that assigned by the consensus on textual criticism to the editorial work of the so-called Priestly Code, known as P.[5] This starts in the period of Babylonian exile with energetic and scholarly reviewing of Israel's history. It continues to the end of the fifth century BC. P is generally agreed to be the latest source of material in the Pentateuch and later than the histories, Judges, Kings and Samuel. P is identified by its distinctive style, exhortatory and repetitive, and by a concern for the regulations of the cult. The books which show no signs of the detailed provisions of P are by that fact dated before its promulgation and those which take them into account betray their later date. Likewise the distribution of historical information helps to establish the order of the sources that were collected together and established as the Hebrew Canon of the Bible (Rowley, 1950). P is the source to which is attributed the classification of clean and unclean animal kinds in which I am specially interested (Leviticus 11 and Deuteronomy 14). It suits my thesis well that small groups of learned exiles in Babylon, conscious of their unique historic mission, and conscious of the need to separate theirs from the culture of their conquerors, should have elaborated detailed rules of purity. Nowhere else in the world has such logic-chopping consistency been excelled. But alas for my thesis: the list of animals is not attributed to this source. Leviticus 11 and Deuteronomy 14 are believed to be a much older source, incorporated in the Priestly Code along with other obscure passages. The reason offered for their exception is that the list makes no sense. It is common for ancient law books to incorporate blocks of still more archaic rules, much as our own multiplication table included archaic measures, the rod, pole or perch. The block form is itself taken for evidence of separate origin. The argument assumes that the priestly editors, legalistic and rational though they were, occasionally admitted to the corpus old texts which made no sense to them but which piety forbade them to exclude. This might be convincing, had not great importance been attached to these very dietary laws. We are asked to believe that the people of Israel have been saddled with an irrational, undecipherable set of food-rules imposed on them by the most rigorously logical law-givers imaginable. It becomes even more implausible when the list of animals itself is examined. From the anthropologist's point of view the classifications appear admirably consistent with the rest of Leviticus and with the rest of the Priestly Code, and the Holiness Code to boot. It is hard to believe that the final Pentateuchal editors did not know what they were doing when they twice copied out the dietary rules in full. There seems no good reason for supposing that P stayed his editorial hand and left unsystematised little blocks, or 'balks' as the Scandinavian critic calls them, of uniformly formulated, nonsensical laws from ancient times. But this accounts for the paucity of comment on Leviticus 11. Either nothing is said about the animals which have become so important in Jewish life, or there is the crude medical materialism which I criticised in *Purity and Danger*, or there is this theory of unintelligible 'balks' which are not worth trying to decipher as they were probably quite as mystifying to the scholars of the fifth century BC (Noth, 1965).

My general argument requires P to be rehabilitated and cleared of the charge of inconsistency. In my view, he went on calmly applying the analogy of purity to the rules of the camp, the altar, the body and also to animal kinds. P was never one to let piety override logic. In his theology there could be no conflict between logic and holiness. All this I have argued before. It may well be that these blocks are ancient sources, and so may be much else that was incorporated, indeed. But the strong evidence for the continuity and coherence of the interpretative tradition allows to the disparate origins of the text only limited interest. The provisions of P were promulgated by Ezra in the fourth century BC and were being followed by the Jewish-community in the Christian era. By identifying the historical period in which I am concerned as that in which the Priestly source was edited I am committed to the fifth century. As to its early limits, I shall want to include the Deuteronomic source, and the history books which owe so much to it. The period, therefore, runs from the sixth century BC to the fifth, just before, during and after the exile.

The next step is to establish that the people of Israel at that time did not practise lineage exogamy. At least there is no evidence that they did. Leach's arguments contribute to this result. What is at issue is the absence of any rule organising the internal exchange of women. Understandably, biblical scholars are often unaware of the implications of the list of prohibited degrees of kinship (Leviticus 18). The interpretation varies according to whether the list is taken to be illustrative of the category of forbidden kin, or exhaustive. By comparison with many tribal societies, if it is exhaustive, the list is extremely short. Certain close agnatic relations are not named. I would conclude that they are not prohibited for sex and marriage. Not only are these lineage endogamous marriages permitted in Leviticus 18, but they are mandatory for the High Priest (Leviticus 21 : 14–15).[6]

If the case be conceded that the people who abhorred anomalies in the relevant period also did not accept any obligation to exchange their womenfolk beyond the range of a narrowly defined kindred, then I can proceed to speculate further about their attitude to animals in the light of other classification systems.

Comparative religion has often been a jousting-ground between rival beliefs. When social correlates of a religious response are revealed, the rationalists chalk up a point against the devout. The believers usually agree the score, sharing the doubtful assumption that a sacred doctrine must sprout in thin air and never be the product of social experience. In that debate, my particular thesis about mediators, though radically sociological, is neutral. If anything, it puts the thumb upon the other nose. If these connexions hold good and if this is how classification systems are shaped to social ends, how could the extraordinary destiny of the Jewish people have been otherwise achieved? If you were God, could you devise a better plan? If you wanted to choose a people for yourself, reveal to them a monotheistic vision and give them a concept of holiness that they will know in their very bones, what would you do? Promise their descendants a fertile land and beset it with enemy empires. By itself that would almost be enough. A politically escalating chain would ensure the increasing hostility of their neighbours. Their mistrust of outsiders would ever be validated more completely. Faithful to your sanctuary and your law, it would be self-evident to them that no image of an animal, even a calf, even a golden one, could portray their god.

When two champions are in combat it is tempting for bystanders to guide their hands to more ammunition. Paul Ricoeur (1963) once challenged Lévi-Strauss to explain why his technique of structural analysis could be so splendidly demonstrated in exotic totemic tribes, but not for those ancient civilisations of Judah, Greece and Rome on which our own history rests. The answer that a radical difference separates totemic and non-totemic cultures might have been damaging to Lévi-Strauss's claim to reveal a universal feature of the human mind. He himself has tried to avoid that reproach by proving that his myth analysis does apply to any culture whatsoever. And so it does. But in the course of the demonstration the technique became so pliable that it lost its claim to reveal the structures of any mind save its creator's. More effective, in reply to Ricoeur, would be to admit that there could be radically different types of society. Then the structural analysis of forms of kinship could be fitted to the analysis of classification. Curiosity would oblige us to seek out for study the most variant types of classification of nature and the most extreme variations of exchange of women. One notices that the array of marriage systems studied in his *Elementary Structures of Kinship* (1969) and those listed in 'The bear and the barber' (1963) do not include the type where there is no rule demanding exchange. And yet he has foreseen the case: 'A human group that considers itself a distinct species will see the rest of nature as constituted by separate, unrelated species.' Like an uncanny echo, Ecclesiasticus said: 'All living beings associate by species and man clings to one like himself; what fellowship has a wolf with a lamb?' (Ecclesiastes 13: 19–21).[7]

In *La Pensée sauvage* Lévi-Strauss noted that the emphasis of a classification system may shift from the analogy between systems of relationships (which is characteristic of totemic systems) to the analogy between one item and another, for example, the single human group contemplating its likeness to a single animal species (1962:116). This remarkable insight suggests that when the single human group sees itself thus there will be no room for a mediator in its theology. For surely a single group will only tend to see itself when high boundaries separate it from the rest of humanity. Thus isolated, it may understandably divide its constructed world of nature into separate and hostile species.

A group of humans that sees itself as a distinct species will not need to mirror in nature their society seen as a system of regulated transactions with other humans. Ideally they will not be engaged in such transactions. Here it is argued that the concept of wild nature can stand for the archetypal outsider at multiple levels, the outsider to the family, to the local unit, to the clan and the tribe. In the totemic system the outsider is entitled to a defined role in a regulated exchange. But if the priestly books tell the people to have no truck with the outsider, under any guise, then in those books we will expect a different patterning of nature.

Throughout the Bible the close observation of natural life is full of comments on the tenderness of animals to their offspring. 'Even the jackals give the breast and suckle their young' (Lamentations). All creation reveals the glory of God. The Book of Job (4:3) expresses intense awareness of wild nature. So observant, so sensitive to its metaphoric possibilities, these are the people whom Moses enjoined (Deuteronomy 4:16–18):

> Beware lest you act corruptly by making a graven image for yourselves, in the form of any figure, the likeness of male or female, the likeness of any beast that is on the earth, the likeness of any winged bird that flies in the air, the likeness of anything that creeps on the ground, the likeness of any fish that is in the water under the earth.

The prohibition could weigh painfully. But on my argument one compelling reason for animal depiction is missing here in the Hebrew case. For they had no reason to use animals to represent the internal differentiation of their society. Animals represent God in general, humans in general, foreigners in general. As the High Priest and his kindred to the common people of the nation, as the clean to the unclean, as life to death, as humans are to animals, so were the Israelites as a whole to the rest of human kind. Such a situation may make it easier to accept a law against images of living beings and even account for the striking poverty of animal art forms left by the Israelites compared with the wealth of their literature and compared with the art of the expanding empires of their neighbours (Klingender, 1971).

Can we reverse the argument to consider the paintings of paleolithic man who left no other records of this thought? I risk the idea that if he painted animals at all it signifies something positive about his openness to commerce with his fellows. When he painted humans with antlers or animal masks it might say even more about his friendly relations with fellow humans of other groups. To see blasphemy in the idea of a baboon-god or a goat-footed one, or in the deification of bulls or cows, is to reject other people's certainty that gods in animal form are proper objects of adoration. It also rejects an attitude towards foreign human beings. The argument takes logic beyond the universal propensities of the human mind to the devious ways in which humans use logic to deal with one another. This is what Durkheim indicated when he argued against Hume and Kant that the origin of classification is not either in nature nor in the subjective constraints of the mind, but in society.

I started by considering the *a priori* in nature. My intention was to show how a guts reaction is founded. I argued that knowledge in the bones, a gut response, answers to a characteristic in the total pattern of classification. Something learnt for the first time can be judged instantly and self-evidently true or false. This flash of recognition would correspond to the split-second scanning of animal knowledge. The essence of my argument is that the stable points of reference for this kind of knowing are not particular external events, but the characteristics of the classification system itself. We are talking about the way the system has been set. It may be a setting that welcomes some anomalies and rejects others or one that rejects all anomalies. Using such a classification system there is no need to work out by slow deductive processes how to respond to a new anomaly that turns up. This argument is not developed in order to serve as an aid for interpreting the bizarre classifications of exotic civilisations. It relates to arguments between logicians about how relations of identity are constituted, not by primitives, but by ourselves.

The relation of the Karam cassowary to wild plants and animals has the same patterning of logical forms as the relation of the cassowary to human and non-human beings and this is of the same pattern as the relation between a woman's brothers and her children. For the Karam, all these instances are true in the same unchallengeable way. For the Israelites the meaning of purity for table, bed and altar is given in a single pattern of logically formed statements. But it is they themselves who have created the order of their universe so that the statements they make about it in this form are self-evidently true.

Religious doctrines of mediation have only afforded a field in which to develop an argument concerning self-evident statements about the world. The anthropologist does not hope to lead the logician out of the circle which the definition of synonymity encloses. Enough head-butting against that wall has proved its strength. Anthropology suggests, not a solution to a problem, but new problems with more hope of solution. Each category of thought has its place in a larger system. Its constituent elements are there because of rules which distinguish, bound and fill the other categories. The rules and categories are generated in the processes of social intercourse. The drive of the fore-going argument is away from considering isolated categories and their application to particular series of events. Instead, consider the total universe in which the categories are used. Remembering that categories are for use, and remembering that each usage has implications for the rest of the system, and invoking some principle of economy or consistency within a system of classification, the problem of the *a priori* in nature can be probed in different terms. This essay has compared three classification systems with regard to their treatment of anomalous beings: one abhors, one respects and one venerates them. Each happens to be remarkably homogeneous in its response to the anomalies it defines. Classification systems could similarly be compared along a dimension of homogeneity of principles for assigning events to classes. They could be compared along other dimensions.

Quine (1960: 78) has said:

our theories and beliefs in general are under-determined by the totality of possible sensory evidence time without end . . . when two systems of analytical hypotheses fit the totality of verbal dispositions to perfection and yet conflict in their translations of certain sentences, the conflict is precisely a conflict of parts seen without wholes.

I have tried here to provide some clues about how our schemes of the world are determined by pointing to the logical patterning deployed in social behaviour. There are fewer possible varieties of social system than possible varieties of worlds to be known, but all possible universes do not have equal credibility for any one society. There is scope for semantic ascent by comparing the various social conditions for credibility. The comparative project shows how the structure of nature comes so satisfyingly to match the structure of mind, without blurring the fact that it is a different structure each time. Intuitional philosophies come to grief upon their failure to discover a list of intuitions or innate ideas common to the human race. Once beyond the simplest propositions of logic they are plunged deep into the artificial conventions of mathematics or paddling in trivial examples. A sociology of the uses of logic can do something to explain both the sense of certain knowledge and its erratically distributed content.

Notes

This lecture was given in a shorter version as the Henry Myers Lecture, on 4 May 1972, in University College, London. On 19 September in the same year I delivered it in an amended form at Barnard College, New York, as a lecture in honour of the late Virginia C. Gildersleeve. It still needs amendment but it has been a long time brewing already.

At least ten years ago Professor Cyril Barrett and Professor Ernest Gellner pointed out the relevance of Hume's philosophy to the arguments in *Purity and Danger*. Since then I owe further debts, apart from those acknowledged in the text, to colleagues in the Department of Anthropology of University College, London for criticism of parts of this paper as it took shape, and to Dr Martin Hollis and Dr I. Zaretsky who went through the whole argument. I am particularly grateful to Anne Akeroyd, Adam Kuper, Michael Thompson and James Urry, and Arthur Nead. For allowing me to try parts of the argument in other places, I thank Mr Richard Parry,

Dr Bryan Wilson, Dr R. Werbner, Professor C. Haimendorf, Professor Paul Stirling, Professor Roland Robertson and Dr James Woodburn and Professor T. Luckmann. For advice on biblical sources I record my gratitude to Professor Jacob Milgrom and Professor J. Neusner.

1 I owe a debt of gratitude to Luc de Heusch for clarifying the pattern of generalised exchange of women that the Lele followed (1964).

2 Lévi-Strauss expects the complex structures of kinship to parallel the elementary structures at the minimum point at which they are distinguished. 'All systems of kinship and marriage contain an "elementary" core which manifests itself in the incest prohibition . . . all systems have a "complex" aspect deriving from the fact that more than one individual can usually meet the requirements of even the most prescriptive systems, thus allowing for a certain freedom of choice . . .' and he goes on to characterise the complex structures, such as our own, as ones in which 'the incest prohibition that we deem sufficient to ensure a probability distribution of alliance links co-extensive with society itself still persists among us as a mechanical device . . . but a much lighter mechanical model, including only a few prohibited degrees' (1965: 1–19).

3 Rather the contrary: they supplement the rule of incest avoidance with a positive preference for marriage with the father's brother's daughter. Such a system, instead of achieving anything like a circulation of women through the entire society, encourages men to regard their womenfolk as part of their patrimony, to be held and shared exclusively within the narrow group of agnates. This is how the same rule is interpreted by the Marshdwellers of the Euphrates Delta (Salim, 1962) and by Fulani herdsmen (Stenning, 1954). If the case for interpreting the Israelites' custom in the same way may be admitted, then the contrast of Lele, Karam and Israel is even better suited to demonstrate my thesis.

4 Living beings, not mythic beings are at issue. It is true that the cosmogony of the Israelites included hybrid beings such as the Cherubim and the extraordinary being of Ezekiel's dream, and that these were not judged adversely. But it was not expected that everyday life would bring a face-to-face encounter with such beings, and the rules of Leviticus 11 are concerned only with physical encounters. The arguments I have advanced against using myth material applies to rule out the relevance of Ezekiel's dream monster. In any case, no cult was paid to it.

5 In general it would suit my thesis to follow the minority view that takes P to be a very early source, since the unity and

315

coherence of the Pentateuch in regard to purity laws supports this view, but obviously in such a technical matter I have no option but to follow the consensus.

6 The sense of marrying into a narrowly defined circle is not kept in the RSV translation, nor does it make clear that Numbers 36 is a requirement to marry within the tribe. Moses arranged for five girls with no brothers to marry their father's brother's sons and so to keep their inheritance intact. In the Westminster Version he also said: 'For all men shall marry wives of their own tribe and kindred. And all women shall take husbands of the same tribe, that the inheritance may remain in the same families and that the tribes be not mingled with one another, but remain so as they were separated by the Lord' (Numbers, 36:7–9). Close textual criticism would be necessary to judge between these versions.

7 Textual criticism would be interesting here too. Compare the Westminster Version of Ecclesiasticus: 'Every beast loveth its like: so also every man him that is nearest to himself. All flesh shall consort with like to itself: and every man shall associate himself to his like. If the wolf shall at any time have fellowship with the lamb, so the sinner with the just.'

Bibliography

ACKROYD, P. R. (1970), 'Israel under Babylon and Persia' in *New Clarendon Bible: Old Testament*, vol. 4, London, Oxford University Press.

ARDENER, E. (1967), Review of M. Douglas: *Purity and Danger. Man* (N.S.) 2, 139.

BULMER, RALPH (1967), 'Why is the cassowary not a bird? A problem of zoological taxonomy among the Karam of the New Guinea Highlands', *Man* (N.S.) 2, 5–25.

CAZENEUVE, J. (1972), *Lucien Lévy-Bruhl* (trans.) P. Rivière, Oxford, Blackwell.

DOUGLAS, MARY (1957), 'Animals in Lele religious symbolism', *Africa*, 27, 46–58.

DOUGLAS, MARY (1963), *The Lele of the Kasai*, Oxford University Press for the International African Institute.

DOUGLAS, MARY (1966), *Purity and Danger: an Analysis of Concepts of Pollution and Taboo*, London, Routledge & Kegan Paul.

DOUGLAS, MARY (1969), 'Is matriliny doomed in Africa?', in *Man in Africa* (eds) M. Douglas and P. Kaberry, London, Tavistock.

DOUGLAS, MARY (1972), 'Deciphering a meal', *Daedalus, J. Am. Acad. Arts Sci.*, Winter 1972, *Myth, Symbol and Culture*, 68–81.

DURKHEIM, ÉMILE and MAUSS, M. (1903), 'De quelques formes primitives de classification' (*Année sociologique*, 1901–2).Translated: *Primitive classification*, R. Needham, London, Cohen & West, 1963.

EVANS-PRITCHARD, E. E. (1956), *Nuer Religion*, Oxford, Clarendon Press.

GRICE, H. P. and STRAWSON, P. F. (1956), 'In defence of a dogma', *Phil. Rev.*, *65*, 141–58.

HEUSCH, LUC DE (1964), 'Structure et praxis sociales chez les Lele du Kasai', *Homme*, *4*, 3, 87–109. Reprinted in *Pourquoi l'épouser? et autres essais*, Paris, Gallimard, 1971.

KLINGENDER, FRANCIS (1971), *Animals in Art and Thought to the End of the Middle Ages* (eds) E. Antal and J. Harthan, London, Routledge & Kegan Paul.

LEACH, E. R. (1958), 'Trobriand clans and the kinship category *tabu*', in *The Development Cycle in Domestic Groups* (ed.) J. Goody (Camb. Pap. Social Anthrop., *1*), Cambridge University Press.

LEACH, E. R. (1969), *Genesis as myth and other essays*, London, Cape.

LÉVI-STRAUSS, CLAUDE (1958), 'La structure des mythes', in *Anthropologie structurale*, Paris, Plon. Originally: 'The structural study of myth', in *Myth, a Symposium* (*J. Am. Folkl.*, *78*, 270. 428–44: 1955).

LÉVI-STRAUSS, C. (1962), *La Pensée sauvage*, Paris, Plon.

LÉVI-STRAUSS, C. (1963), 'The bear and the barber', *J. R. Anthrop. Inst.*, *93*, 1–11.

LÉVI-STRAUSS, C. (1966), 'The future of kinship studies', *Proc. R. Anthrop. Inst. 1965*, 13–22.

LÉVI-STRAUSS, C. (1969), *The Elementary Structures of Kinship*, London, Eyre & Spottiswoode.

LÉVY-BRUHL, LUCIEN (1910), *Les Fonctions mentales*, Paris, Alcan.

MALINOWSKI, B. (1935), *Coral gardens and their magic*, vol. 2, London, Allen & Unwin.

NOTH, M. (1965), *Leviticus: a Commentary*, London, SCM Press.

QUINE, W. V. O. (1943), 'Notes on existence and necessity', *J. Phil.*, *40*, 5, 113–27.

QUINE, W. V. O. (1960), *Word and Object*, Cambridge, Mass., MIT Press.

RICOEUR, PAUL (1963), 'Structure et herméneutique', *Ésprit*, *598–625*.

ROWLEY, H. H. (1950), *The Growth of the Old Testament*, London, Hutchinson.

SALIM, S. M. (1962), *Marshdwellers of the Euphrates Delta*, London, Athlone Press.

STENNING, D. (1954), *Savannah Nomads: a Study of the Wodaabe Pastoral Fulani of Western Bornu Province, Northern Region, Nigeria*, London, Oxford University Press for the International African Institute.

TAMBIAH, S. J. (1969), 'Animals are good to think and good to prohibit', *Ethnology*, 7, 423–59.

Index